The Resourceful Writing Teacher

A Handbook of Essential Skills and Strategies

Jenny Mechem Bender

Foreword by Lucy Calkins

HEINEMANN
Portsmouth, NH

Heinemann
361 Hanover Street
Portsmouth, NH 03801–3912
www.heinemann.com

Offices and agents throughout the world

Library of Congress Cataloging-in-Publication Data
Bender, Jenny Mechem.
The resourceful writing teacher : a handbook of essential skills and strategies / Jenny Mechem Bender ; foreword by Lucy Calkins.
p. cm.
Includes bibliographical references.
ISBN-13: 978-0-325-00947-6
ISBN-10: 0-325-00947-3
1. English language—Composition and exercises—Study and teaching—Handbooks, manuals, etc. 2. Report writing—Study and teaching—Handbooks, manuals, etc. 3. Learning strategies—Handbooks, manuals, etc. I. Title.
LB1576.B436 2007
808'.042071—dc22 2007027584

Editor: Kate Montgomery
Developmental editor: Kerry Herlihy
Production editor: Sonja S. Chapman
Cover design: Joni Doherty
Author Photograph: Josh Mechem
Compositor: Reuben Kantor
Manufacturing: Jamie Carter

Printed in the United States of America on acid-free paper
12 11 10 09 08 EB 2 3 4 5 6

For my boys:
To you, Harrison, for being my inspiration.
And to you, Josh, for being my hero.

CONTENTS

FOREWORD

There are so many books now about the teaching of writing! We browse through catalogs and websites, bookstores and conference displays, looking for that special book that can change our teaching lives. Which book will be so important that it keeps us reading past midnight on a school night because it shows us how to transform our teaching? This is such a book.

In the pages of this book, Jenny synthesizes the lessons of hundreds of teachers, staff developers, and writers. Into this rich mixture, she brings new insight. Jenny has a gift for revealing, with elegant simplicity, ways that the skills writers need and the effects writers yearn for can be achieved through a handful of practical, doable strategies.

Jenny offers here a collection of significant teaching points, and she shows how to incorporate these points into established structures such as minilessons, small group strategy lessons, and conferences. These teaching points will help students as they write in many different genres and in many different modes.

Jenny sees herself as a student of writing and of teaching. She is always striving to outgrow herself, making her that restless learner who is never finished learning. That eagerness leads Jenny to investigate classroom practices, to study student performance, and to try everything herself. The result of this passion and hard work is that Jenny breaks trails—and, in her writing, she invites others to follow.

One of the gifts of this book is that Jenny Bender has been part of many writing communities. She has been a teacher and a colleague in two of New York City's finest schools—PS 126 and IS 89—both places where writing workshops have flourished. She's also been part of a university where she creates curriculum alongside other literacy leaders. Then, too, she's been part of coaching and leadership groups where she and other educators pilot pedagogy. And so, she brings a richness of experience to every lesson. Jenny can help teachers envision the classroom environment, the preparation, the lesson, and the follow-up, because she knows from her work in these communities of practice that good teaching doesn't appear out of the air. Good teaching is born of forethought and of planning; it's born of balancing response and adaptation with curriculum and ongoing support structures.

In this book, Jenny takes all that she has learned about the teaching of writing over many years, and she synthesizes it into manageable, practical lessons for teachers to use as starter lessons for their own writing workshop plans. This book will be a cherished teaching companion for every teacher lucky enough to hold it.

—Lucy Calkins
2007

ACKNOWLEDGMENTS

Every time I sat down to work on this book, there was someone new to be grateful for, or even more often, someone to be grateful for yet again. People like Carl Anderson, who for years, whenever I saw him, said with the utmost faith and encouragement, "How's your book coming along?" He asked me this long before there was any inkling of a book, until finally, I began to think that maybe I really could write one after all. At which point Carl helped with my proposal and, later, with my life as a writer.

There are people like Maggie Bittel, whom above all I thank for a friendship that gives me courage and strength, both of which I drew from as I worked on this project. Maggie graciously read a chapter here, a chapter there as I wrote, and then the entire draft in the final hour. Her wise suggestions helped me clarify key parts of the manuscript as well as improve the overall structure. Just as valuable was her continued enthusiasm about the book, which encouraged me to the very end.

I want to thank Jen Seravallo, friend, colleague, writing partner, for making me and the state of this book feel in such good hands; Jen has been a cherished source of comfort and knowledge. I want to thank Kirsten Widmer for reading a draft from beginning to end with a keen eye and answering so many of my questions along the way. I also want to thank Dina Redman for decades of support, but more specifically, for so eagerly reading parts of my draft with the eyes of a writer outside of education.

There are so many people to thank at The Teachers College Reading and Writing Project, the community in which I do the most learning and growing as an educator. If I could, I would fill these pages with everyone's names because surely they have all, in one way or another, contributed to my knowledge and hence to the writing of this book. There are some to whom I am especially indebted: I am beholden to Mary Ehrenworth for being overly generous with her insight and support in all the years before and since we came to the project. I am similarly beholden to Kathleen Tolan, who at every single one of our Thursday think tanks seems to bring to the table something new and worthwhile and wonderful to consider and who has in turn impacted my teaching more than most. I am indebted to Mary Chiarella, Colleen Cruz, Amanda Hartman, and Audra Robb for the specific ways in which they pushed my thinking as a writer and as an educator. I am indebted to Stephanie Parsons for her unduly generous spirit. I thank Cory Gillette for being the kind of friend who is forever available to ponder my queries about work and for being the kind of colleague who does so with such thought. I thank Shanna Frazin and Melanie Woods for getting me unstuck that day at Joyce Café; Laurie Pessah for her calming presence; Timothy Lopez for days of technical support; Beth Neville, Kathy Neville, and Maurie Brooks for helping things run so smoothly, and with such patience to boot; and Rob Amell, Karen MacArthur and Julia Mooney for so willingly being my go to people.

Thank you to Nancy Needle for helping me find my first teaching job at P.S. 126 and to Daria Rigney for taking a chance on me and helping me soar. Thank you to Ellen Foote for making a place for me at I.S. 89. Thank you to Donna Santman for letting me live in her classroom and learn from some of the most extraordinary teaching I have seen. Thank you to Isoke Nia and Katherine Bomer for impacting me first from afar and then up close with their brilliant teaching and their fierce commitment to children.

To my parents, Sula Harris and Harvey Bender, I extend a deep, endless gratitude, first and foremost, for spending a lifetime (mine) helping me believe I could accomplish the unthinkable; and then, for all they do to help me bring my dreams to fruition. I thank Rachel Simmons for her support as a writer and, along with my dear friend Megan Lardner, for the hours of company while I wrote. I thank Leslie Richmond, Christine Holley, Karen Cardinali and Sarah Picard for being the best "teacher friends," and resources of such great teaching, all these long years. I am forever grateful to Tosha Silver and Tom Jackson for guiding me through hard parts. Thank you to Alisha Camioni and Francesca Romo, babysitters extraordinaire; the way they cared for my son with such genuine love meant I almost didn't feel guilty leaving him to write all those long hours. Thank you to Harrison, who is too young to know it yet, but who motivated me to write and to use my writing time well, so I could have more time with him; I also want to thank him for blowing me kisses when I left and gleefully pulling me by the hand when I came through the door, never seeming to hold my absence against me.

Of course, this book would not be a book at all were it not for the students and educators with whom I work. Thank you to my own students at P.S. 126 and I.S. 89 in Manhattan for inspiring me and helping me find my voice as a teacher. I thank Katie Evan and her students at P.S. 29 in Brooklyn for welcoming me into their classroom. I thank everyone at P.S. 154 in Brooklyn, especially Kandace Blumberg, Mark Greller, and Emily Sosland, for letting me work with their writers at all times of the day and year. I thank everyone at John Jay Middle and High School, also in Brooklyn, especially Principal Jill Bloomberg, Literacy Coach Leah Grossman, and teachers Jill Sandusky and Jen Schoen. I thank everyone at P.S. 38 in Queens, especially Principal Lenon Murray, Assistant Principal Cassandra Hundley, and teachers Stephanie Camillone and Cheryl Ruland. Thank you to everyone at P.S. 122 in Queens. A special thanks to the principal, Mary Kojes, and to the assistant principals, Anna Aprea and Pam Sabel, for always supporting my work and helping to make their school feel like my home; to the literacy coach, Tina Garanes, for helping me in two million and one ways over the years; and again, to the teachers who so willingly let me work with their writers: Vicki Anzoulis, Adele Dinstein, Stacy Econopoulis, Aliki Giakas, Maria Maliagros, Kathy Racynsky, and Rebecca Victoros.

Thank you to my editors at Heinemann. I want to thank Kerry Herlihy for treating each page with such care. Kate Montgomery I thank first for spending months helping me find the right topic and later for helping me outgrow my vision so this book could become more than I first imagined. I thank both for so gracefully navigating me through the bumps along the way. I also want to thank my production editor, Sonja Chapman, for helping me to the finish line.

Most of all, I want to thank my mentor, Lucy Calkins, and my husband, Josh Mechem. Though it seems endless, the list of people who have in ways big and small impacted this book, it never would have been written at all were it not for Lucy and Josh.

That Lucy read parts of my manuscript and talked with me for hours about what I was doing well and what I could do better is the least of her contributions. The fact is, I know what I know about teaching writing because of Lucy, either because she taught it to me herself or because I learned it in a community into which she invited me. But more than teaching me about writing, Lucy has helped me *be* a writer. For years, she encouraged me to publish, and ultimately said, "Jenny, you should be writing a book.

Contact my editor." It is from that conversation—and from all of Lucy's teaching and encouragement in the years prior—that this book is born.

And then there is Josh. When I think about what it means to be or to have a partner, I think of him. Friend, spouse, coparent, soul mate, life-love. Above all, I thank Josh for being each of those things with me. Then I thank him for the ways in which he made this book possible by doing what he does in those roles: I thank him for cooking and cleaning and spending long, loving hours with our son so I could write; for saying, "Do whatever you need to do, love, take all the time you need," when that's exactly what I needed to hear; for saying, "One more hour and then we're doing something fun," when that's what I needed to hear. I thank Josh for saying night after day after week, "I'm so proud of you, baby," in a voice that made me proud, too, and that kept me writing and rethinking and reworking until I was finally ready to let this book out into the world.

INTRODUCTION

Whether working with teachers brand-new to or more experienced than I am with writers' workshop, the same issue emerges again and again: they want to know *how* to teach the writing skills their students need to learn. Regardless of grade level, school, state, I continually hear different variations of the same question: Is there a book or something that lists the strategies writers use to write well?

I recently sat around a table with several teachers who were getting ready to launch writers' workshops for the very first time. I started our day together by sharing some of the fundamental beliefs behind writers' workshop, one of which is that we give students choice: choice of topic, choice of what to put into a piece, choice of how to revise and how to get their drafts ready to share.

"Half my kids don't write even when I *do* tell them what to do," one teacher chimed in. "Won't it be even worse if they suddenly have all this 'choice' on their hands?"

"Yeah, I can't quite imagine it," another teacher said. "How do they figure out what to write about? How do they figure out how to make their stories better and fix their mistakes if I'm not telling them what to do?"

I smiled because I remembered the week before, sitting around a different table, this time with teachers who were in their second and third and even tenth years of running writers' workshops; this time, instead of introducing them to workshop teaching, I was helping them plan and revise their writing curriculum.

"The last stories my kids wrote were so bad because they all solved the problem in about two sentences," one teacher said. "So I know they need help building tension, but I really don't know how to teach that."

"A lot of my students also need help developing their setting," another one said. "I keep teaching the same thing over and over, and I have no idea what else to do because they still don't include any details about where their stories take place."

And then one of the teachers said, "Isn't there a list somewhere of ways to do these kinds of things?"

It is from this question—this *pleading*, really—that this book is born. I have drawn from the knowledge of Lucy Calkins and my colleagues at The Teachers College Reading and Writing Project where I have spent four years working as a staff developer in kindergarten through eighth grade classrooms; I have drawn from my experience as an elementary and middle school classroom teacher, from the knowledge of the teachers with whom I now work, and from the writers and educators who have written and taught before me to gather and organize what so many elementary and middle school teachers have requested of me: concrete tools for teaching your students how to write, and how to continually lift the quality of their writing over the course of a school year.

How This Book Can Help

In my experience as a teacher and as a staff developer, teaching writing becomes exponentially easier when we have at our disposal a repertoire of things to teach and easy-to-access, easy-to-use texts with which to teach them. I have spent years helping teachers gather lists of strategies and collections of writing to exemplify those strategies, and so in a sense, I have spent years on this book—on creating a resource that fits the needs of almost any writing teacher in almost any situation.

Clearly, this book can help plan curricula. It can also help supplement curricula; whether following plans you have written in the past or someone has written for you, you will inevitably find places where students need extra support. You can use this book to look up additional strategies for acquiring those needed writing skills.

This book can also help when you know what you want to teach, but you do not have at your fingertips a way to model your teaching. You can easily use the table of contents to find the desired skill and then use the student samples under each strategy to exemplify your point.

Understanding Skill and Strategy

One thing my teaching structures have in common is a teaching point: a clear and concise statement of *what* is being taught and *how* students might try this as writers, as well as an explanation of when and why they might try this. Based on what I have learned at The Teachers College Reading and Writing Project, I refer to the "what" as a skill or a goal and the "how" as a strategy; I know that for every skill, there are multiple strategies for acquiring and applying the skill.

I think of *skills* or *goals* as that which we ultimately want our students to be able to do; they are the end result. For example, we ultimately want our students to develop the setting in their stories. But this does not happen over night. Nor does this happen for most of our students when we simply say, "Develop your setting." Instead, we need to tell and show them how to develop their setting, and we need to show them different ways they might do this.

Strategies are the ways to work toward a particular skill or goal. If we want our students to develop setting, for example, we might teach them to use their senses, to include details about the weather, or to show their characters interacting with their surroundings. Writers have a repertoire of strategies they draw upon when working to achieve a particular goal; no one strategy can consistently accomplish a goal. Furthermore, different strategies work, and don't work, for different writers. It is therefore important for teachers of writing to understand and have at our disposal a range of strategies for teaching toward the goals we set for our writers and that they set for themselves.

It is similarly important that whenever we teach or revisit a strategy, we remind students of all the other strategies they know for applying the skill at hand and that we emphasize for students that they can draw from any or all of those strategies when they write. In other words, no one strategy should be taught as a directive but rather should be taught as yet another option for acquiring a skill.

No matter what the situation, we turn to strategies when the skill we need to utilize does not yet come naturally; this means that once students internalize a skill, strategies become habits of mind that they draw upon without even knowing they are doing so. When I was first learning to throw a football, my husband taught me to align my fingers with the stitching that runs down the side of the ball; he taught me to point my shoulder in the same direction I wanted the ball to go; he taught me to hold my wrist in line with my arm and snap it back as I let the ball go into the air. Without those strategies for throwing a football, I might never have learned to make it spin across a field. But now that I *can* throw a football, I do not think twice about the placement of wrist or shoulder. I simply toss the ball. I have outgrown the need for strategies because I have internalized the skill.

Similarly, once your students are, for example, developing the setting in their stories, it matters very little whether they are using their senses or the weather or their characters' interactions with their surroundings to do so; what matters is that they know how to ground their stories in time and place.

Teaching Purposeful Writing

When I first started teaching writing, I gathered skills and strategies and presented them to my students like gems. "Can I tell you something really good writers do? They develop setting by including sensory information in their stories!" I had my skill (developing setting) and my strategy (including sensory information), and so I assumed I was doing great teaching. When my students would begin to clutter their pieces with insignificant details (writing things like "I saw brown square wooden boxes that felt hard and splintery and were filled with long, thin green stems with bright, sweet-smelling purple petals on the top" instead of, "I saw flower boxes filled with sweet-smelling, purple flowers"), I wanted to say yes, you should use sensory detail, but no, *not like that.*

I now understand that while I was teaching my students the qualities of good writing, I was not teaching them how to use those qualities in purposeful ways. I was not teaching my students *when* and/or *why* writers use a given skill. Now, instead of teaching students that they can use sensory information to develop the setting, I might teach them that they can use sensory detail to show the *important* things a character sees, smells, hears, feels, or tastes so that readers can feel more inside the story and experience what the characters experience. In this case, considering what is important to their story and what, exactly, they want their readers to experience helps students to avoid or eliminate unnecessary details so their writing is not cluttered like the example I give in the previous paragraph.

No matter what skills and strategies you pull from this book, it is imperative that you make explicit to students how to use a skill purposefully; in addition to teaching students what writers do and how we do it, teach them when and why we do these things. You can find all this information beneath the "Tell" subheading in Sections 2 through 4.

An Overview of Writers' Workshop

In most classrooms that have writers' workshops, the curriculum consists of units of study across the year, each unit ranging from about two to five weeks. Units focus either on a particular genre, such as realistic fiction or editorials; on a writing habit, such as building stamina or mentoring oneself to another author; or on a writing process, such as using a notebook to collect ideas or revising drafts in purposeful and effective ways. In elementary classrooms, where you spend every day with your students, writers' workshop is generally a daily occurrence that spans from fifty to sixty minutes. In middle school classrooms, where you usually meet with your students between six and ten periods a week, half of these periods are generally devoted to a writers' workshop and the other half to a readers' workshop.

Fundamental to writers' workshop are a few beliefs about what writers need. Perhaps foremost, we need regular and extended time to write. We also need explicit instruction around how to write, the ability to make our own choices about what to write, exposure to models of good writing, and a writing community in which we can share and learn from one another's writing.

Writers' workshop contains four major teaching structures: whole class minilessons, whole class teaching shares, individual conferences, and small group strategy lessons. Each of these structures contains predictable components that allow for explicit teaching, the kind of teaching demonstrated in Sections 2 through 4 of this book. Coupling explicit teaching with extended time for your students to write independently will provide the key ingredients in a writer's life and in a writers' workshop.

Writers' Notebooks and the Writing Process

Though certainly none of us move through the writing process in the exact same way, we all do some fundamental things when we write. We all collect ideas. Some may collect them on scraps of paper, others in notebooks, still others on computers; some may collect them more in the form of lists, others mostly as paragraphs. But whatever the particulars, we all gather possible ideas for our writing. We all hone in on the ideas we want to somehow make public, and we explore and develop those ideas to figure out exactly what it is we want to say. We draft, revise, edit. We make our work "pretty," ready to share. Again, there are differences along the way. For example, I draft and revise as I go, reading and rereading every couple sentences so that it can take me hours to write a single page; others draft quickly, pour their thoughts onto the page and only then, once everything is out, do they labor through the revision process. But despite the nuances, the big steps are more or less the same.

I encourage my students to find for themselves the particulars of their writing process. But before they can discover the nuances, they need a general framework, a general process, to help them write. And so I teach them to use what I have discovered in my learning community are fundamental stages for all writers: collecting ideas, picking an idea, developing the idea, drafting, revising, editing, and publishing.

I teach my students to use a writer's notebook. Again, I recognize that not every writer uses a notebook, but as classroom teachers, asking our students to work in some consistent ways can help us set clear expectations and assess their work. Among my expectations is that students take care of their notebooks and value them as a place to hold their writing—not their math or science or reading notes. I expect them to write in their notebooks at school and at home. I expect them to be intentional and thoughtful in their notebooks, which means I expect them to use conventions and the qualities of good writing to the best of their abilities and to write what matters to them. But I also expect them to take risks in their notebooks; I expect them to explore and try on different writing ideas as well as different ways to write these ideas.

As my students use the writing process to help them explore and craft and share their ideas, I teach them to collect and develop those ideas in their writers' notebooks and to draft their ideas on loose-leaf paper. Revision usually happens on loose-leaf paper, as well, though some students also return to their notebooks to reenvision certain parts of their pieces.

Because what I teach the class and individual students depends on my ongoing assessment of the writers in my class, I collect and grade each student's notebook every week in elementary school classrooms where there are about thirty students to a teacher, and every two weeks in middle school classrooms where there are about one hundred students to a teacher. I do not spend hours poring over every entry, but instead, a few minutes with each notebook, quickly skimming the collection of entries and reading a couple more closely to get a general idea of what the writer, and the class, is doing well and what help I still need to provide.

How This Book Is Organized

My aim in Section 1 is to help you write and teach minilessons, conferences, strategy lessons, and teaching shares that contain components which have proven effective for my colleagues and me and the students with whom we work. All of these teaching structures share two fundamental components, which Lucy Calkins, in *Units of Studies for Teaching Writing* (2006), names *teaching* and *active involvement.* I explain these components in Section 1 and use them to convey the teaching in Sections 2 through 4. You can use Section 1 to figure out which components to add to the teaching and active involvement, depending on whether you want to do a minilesson, conference, strategy lesson, or teaching share.

I have organized Sections 2 through 4 according to writing skills. Section 2 focuses on narrative skills (skills used to write any genre of story), Section 3 on nonnarrative skills (skills used to write procedural, expository, and informational texts), and Section 4 on convention skills (skills used to edit, spell, use correct punctuation). You can use the table of contents to easily reference what you want to teach your writers to do. Each chapter in Sections 2 through 4 begins with an explanation of an essential writing skill, followed by a series of subheadings, each of which is a strategy for teaching that skill. Under each subheading, I look closely at the strategy by giving an example of how to teach it, marking each step as *teaching* and *active engagement.* Following the teaching, I include student writing that exemplifies the strategy. Regardless of how you structure your teaching of writing, you can use the content in Sections 2 through 4 to support the needs of your students.

* * *

As teachers, we have to find our own voices and our own ways. Even when someone else is telling us what and how to teach, it is up to us to take risks with our students, to fail as well as succeed, to try again. It is up to us to do everything we can to give our students what they need to succeed in school and, more importantly, in life. My hope is that whoever you are, that wherever and however you may teach, you will find in this book tools to make that teaching and your students' learning stronger, smarter, deeper.

CHAPTER 1

Minilessons, Conferences, Strategy Lessons, and Teaching Shares

Writing has always been important to me. Because of this, even as the newest of teachers, I always made time for it in the day. Unfortunately, I had no idea how to actually teach writing. I had heard of this thing called "writers' workshop," so every morning, I would announce "Writers' workshop!" and all the students in my class would take out their marble notebooks and sit down to work. Every once and awhile, I would notice something my students were or were not doing and get an idea (perhaps that the writers in my class could use more detail or end their pieces in more interesting ways), and I would either gather the class together or sidle next to an individual to discuss my thinking.

Since then, I have learned some things. I have read books and attended conferences, and most of all, I have worked with Lucy Calkins and a community of learners through The Teachers College Reading and Writing Project. I have learned that although the most important thing is to give students time to write, the next most important thing is to teach them what they might do with that time. I have also learned what to teach and structures in which to teach.

Now, when I announce "Writers' workshop!" the students with whom I work expect to learn strategies for writing through predictable structures: whole class minilessons and teaching shares, individual conferences, and small group strategy lessons. As we know, there are many ways to teach and teach well; there are even many ways to lead an effective lesson, share, conference, or small group. In this book, I show how one can teach strategies within each of these structures through explicit instruction. I rely on what Calkins names *teaching* and *active engagement.* In order to highlight the steps involved, I break the teaching into "tell" and "show" and the active engagement into "tell" and "coach." Though there are differences between my minilessons, conferences, strategy lessons, and teaching shares (which I discuss later in the chapter), they all aim to lift the level of student writing through these fundamental components: teaching and active engagement (or tell, show, and coach).

Teaching

Tell

I cannot learn to do something if I do not know what it is I am trying to learn. And even when I know, I cannot do it unless someone tells me how in little increments. For example, I will never learn to swim with someone telling me, "Swim"; I am much more likely to internalize the skill if someone first says, "Swimmers often lie on their bellies," and eventually, "They often kick their legs" and "They usually use their arms."

Furthermore, I am much more likely to learn something if I know why it would benefit me. Learning to swim for the sake of swimming is hard, especially for someone like me who is somewhat fearful of water and hates having her head submerged. On the other hand, learning to swim in order to join my friends on the beach in summer, or tone my body, or rescue myself or my child were we ever caught in a body of water gives me a purpose for learning; it gives me a sense of when and why I might want to draw upon this critical skill.

Knowing that learners need direction and purpose, I begin my teaching in a minilesson, conference, strategy lesson, or teaching share by telling the student or students before me what I want them to know and why I want them to know it. This *telling* always takes the form of what my community of learners calls a *teaching point:* a writing skill, one or sometimes more strategies for internalizing that skill depending on how much the writers can access at one time, and a brief explanation of when and why a writer might use the skill. Again, the skill is what I ultimately want students to learn and the strategy is a tool they can use to get there. Because I want to keep my teaching as specific and clear as possible, I try to name my teaching point in one to three sentences.

Show

I know from experience as a learner as well as from experience as an educator that telling is not teaching. If you tell me to swim by kicking my legs in water, I am easily confused about what to do: Should I stand upright and kick my legs as if on a chorus line? Should I lie on my belly and kick in violent thrusts? Or perhaps on my back and kick with short, rapid movement? The possibilities, and the potential for error, seem endless.

In turn, once I tell students the skill and strategy I want them to learn and when or why they might use the skill, I show them. There are two major considerations when showing students what it looks like to use a skill. One, we need to decide whether we will write in front of students to highlight the process of applying a certain strategy or group of strategies or whether we will use text that either a student, a published author, or we already wrote, again highlighting for students how the writer used the strategy at hand and how this impacts text and reader.

We also need to decide whether we are going to teach a strategy as students are composing or as they are revising. To teach something as a revision strategy, we need to prepare an imperfect text beforehand and show how we make the writing better by using the strategy we are teaching.

Across a unit of study, and throughout this book, I vary my methods so students have the opportunity to learn in a variety of ways and from a range of authors. Know that whatever I teach, you, too, can vary the method. To do so, reenvision the show; teach or reteach the same strategy using a different method as explained above.

Active Engagement

Tell

I begin the active engagement in a minilesson, conference, strategy lesson, and teaching share by repeating my teaching point to get students ready for what they are about to practice.

Coach

Telling and showing is just the beginning of teaching and learning. Once my swim teacher tells me to move my legs and shows me how she does it, I still need to do it myself before I can begin to perfect and eventually internalize the action. Furthermore, I most likely need help; simply hearing and seeing what I am supposed to do is rarely enough for me to immediately do it myself without mishap or error. Most likely, I need someone to watch me move my legs and then help me adjust their position slightly; I need someone to watch me again, and this time, help me adjust the breadth of movement or the speed. Hence, once I tell students what strategy I want them to try and how, I coach them; while students work, I assess their use of the strategy and provide additional support when necessary.

Like the teaching, the active engagement is brief, somewhere between two and five minutes. Sometimes, and most often in conferences and strategy lessons, I ask the student or students to practice the strategy in their own writing. Other times, especially during whole class teaching, I provide a brief activity for trying a strategy. For example, if I am teaching a strategy for leads, I may ask students to write, either independently or orally with a partner, the first couple sentences for a story about something that recently happened in class, or perhaps I'll ask them to help me revise a lead I wrote for one of my stories. However, as soon as students return to their independent writing, they always choose their own topics and strategies with which to work.

* * *

Though the teaching and active engagement are the fundamental components to all my teaching structures, there are some differences depending on whether I am doing a minilesson, conference, strategy lesson, or teaching share. For each of these teaching structures, which I explain below, I rely on additional components also characterized and named by Calkins.

Minilessons

Those of us who teach within a writing workshop begin each workshop with a minilesson. Because I want everyone's full attention for this teaching, I create space in the classroom large enough for the entire class to gather. My minilessons are usually five to ten minutes, and whatever I teach is based on the needs of the majority of writers in the class and the current curriculum goals.

I begin my minilessons with the connection: In about one minute or less, I introduce my teaching point by connecting it to something else with which my students can relate. Sometimes, I lure students into my minilessons with a metaphor or a story that relates to my teaching point; sometimes, I remind students of other things they have learned that connect with the day's lesson. Either way, my aim is to provide my students with a context in which to better understand what I teach. Once I introduce my teaching point, I transition into the teaching and active engagement, as described earlier in the chapter.

I end with the link: Before I send students back to their seats, I take a quick moment to remind them of what they just practiced and how it fits into their repertoire of strategies for working toward a particular skill. What I do not do, except for on very rare occasions when I think my teaching is immediately relevant and critical for all my students, is ask the entire class to return to their seats and apply what I have taught to their day's work. For one, there will almost always be students for whom the day's minilesson is not immediately relevant. Consider, for example, if I were doing a lesson on endings and I asked the entire class to return to their seats and apply this teaching. What about those students who are just beginning their pieces and far from ready to write an ending at all?

Moreover, what's important is that writers begin to internalize the skill I teach, and to do so, almost any strategy will do, whether or not it is the strategy in the day's minilesson. Consider what it would mean if I were doing a lesson on how writers sometimes end their stories with reflection to convey the meaning of their pieces, and I told everyone to go back to their seats and try this, even those students who wanted to use dialogue to convey meaning at the end of their pieces—another perfectly appropriate way to conclude a story.

Instead of making my minilessons directives, I let the class know that the skill is something I expect everyone to work on when relevant to their writing at hand. I also let them know that some might use the strategy I just taught when they return to their seats if doing so would be appropriate for the writing work before them.

Tips for a Successful Minilesson

- Keep your minilessons from five to ten minutes.
- Lift the level of student engagement by beginning your minilesson with a story or metaphor that connects with your teaching point.
- Make explicit the connection between what you are teaching and anything else the class has learned in writing or other parts of the curriculum.
- Ensure that the content you plan to teach meets the needs of a majority of your students and that you do not teach more than they can access in a single lesson.
- Make sure your teaching point includes a skill and a strategy, as well as an explanation of when and/or why to draw upon this knowledge. State

your teaching point in one to three sentences and repeat it throughout the lesson.

- Show students what it looks like to successfully use the strategy. Highlight the process, especially points of difficulty, as well as the end result.
- Give the entire class an opportunity to practice the strategy and coach students while they work.
- Send students off to write with the *option* of trying during workshop what you just taught, reminding them, when applicable, how your teaching fits into a repertoire of strategies they know for the skill at hand.

Conferences

In *How's It Going? A Practical Guide to Conferring with Writers,* Carl Anderson (2000) explains conferring as conversations. He writes:

> *If you make a picture in your mind of a conversation you've had with someone you care about, you probably see a colleague, a friend, a relative. Connected to that person you probably see a certain kind of place—a table in a restaurant, a path in the woods, the stoop of your apartment building. And you probably hear a certain kind of talk—it's intimate, personal, shared. This is the kind of feeling I want to create as I talk with students about their writing.* (7)

Like Carl, I want to get to know my students intimately as writers when I confer with them, and I want to do this so that I can better support them as writers.

Every day after the minilesson, students spend thirty-five to fifty minutes engaged in their own writing on topics of their own choosing. During this time, I circulate the room and meet with writers. One thing I do is confer, taking about five to seven minutes each time I work with an individual.

I aim to meet with all my writers at least once over the course of a week, either in a conference or in a small group tailored to their individual needs (which I address in the next section); furthermore, I aim to meet with my struggling writers at least twice a week. (For middle school teachers who have writers' workshop only three or four days a week, you will probably meet with your students a little less often.)

I begin with the research component of a conference; during these couple minutes, I assess what the writer is beginning to do well and what I want to teach him or her to do better. I assess through observing, reading student work, and asking open-ended questions.

Learning from Carl Anderson (2005), I try to set goals for each writer and follow lines of thinking inside and across my conferences. Inside of each conference, when I start asking questions to assess one skill, I do not jump to questions about a different skill unless I've determined the writer does not need to learn something more about the former. Across confrences, I repeatedly teach into one to three skills—sometimes with a strategy I have already taught, sometimes with a new strategy for the same skill—until a writer is ready to move on to a new goal. This may take anywhere from days to months, depending on the writer and the skill.

After the research, I move into the compliment. Based on my assessment, I compliment the writer's use of one, specific skill and strategy she is beginning to use well, followed by an example from the writer's work and an explanation of how this makes her writing stronger; my compliment feels and sounds very much like a teaching point. Often, a student may not realize what she has done that is so important; the compliment is meant to boost confidence, but also to encourage a writer to keep doing something she may not yet have internalized.

From my compliment, I move into the teaching and active engagement, which follow the same guidelines as with my other teaching structures. Whenever possible, I link my teaching point to my compliment so I can build on students' strengths. This usually means I compliment and teach different strategies for the same skill, or that I compliment something the writer is just beginning to do and teach him to do it more consistently and purposefully.

I end each conference with the link by reminding the writer what I just complimented and taught. Because my teaching is tailored to the individual needs of the student (which is not the case for everyone before me in a minilesson), I also let the writer know it is his job to practice the strategies discussed so they become part of his repertoire and help him to internalize the skill at hand.

I record my teaching point—or more specifically, the skill plus the strategy I taught—as well as any other information I think will be helpful in the future, such as other work I might do with a writer or things the writer is doing particularly well, on a record sheet with the student's name and date. (See Figures 1–1 and 1–2 for two possibilities for conference notes.) This way, I know with whom I have and have not conferred; furthermore, I have a system for following up with each student during future conferences

Writing Conference/Strategy Lesson Notes, Week of: Febuary 10, Class 701

Dean 2/10 periods – say complete thought in head	Lana 2/10 (SL) Focus – connect through cause and effect	Rachel 2/11 (SL) Get ideas – recall comments	Ella 2/10 Tension – contrast words + thoughts
Nawar 2/11 (SL) Tension – leave clues	Adrian	Barry 2/11 (SL) Tension – leave clues	Julia 2/11 (SL) Show character – break apart important actions
Unique 2/11 Focus – connect parts through cause and effect	José	Harvey 2/11 (SL) Focus – connect through cause + effect	Harrison 2/10 (SL) Show character – weave together action, thought, dialogue
Angelica 2/11 (SL) Show character – break apart actions	Steven 2/11 (SL) Show character – break apart actions	Sophie 2/11 (SL) Find topics – recall comments	Josh
Maggie 2/13 Tension – leave clues	Annie 2/13 (SL) Focus – most emotional part	Ryan 2/13 (SL) Paragraphs – scene change	Megan 2/13 Show character – weave action, dialogue, thought
Allyson	Sula 2/13 Tension – show character waffling around choice	Dina 2/13 (SL) Paragraphs – scene change	Louise
Lucia 2/10 Ending – reflection	Jake 2/13 Get ~~topics~~ moments of success	Jordan	Alex 2/11 (SL) Tension – leave clues
Jacqueline 2/11 (SL) Find topics – recall comments	Eddy 2/13 (SL) Focus – most emotional part	Leo 2/11 2/13 Tension – repetition	Isabella

Figure 1–1 *Conference notes, class at a glance*

so I can hold everyone accountable to trying what I taught over the course of the week. (I also use my conference notes to look for patterns across the class so I can tailor my minilessons to the specific needs of my students.)

Tips for a Successful Conference

- Keep your conferences between five and seven minutes.
- Before you begin a conference, consider what you already know about the writer, especially her current goals and what strategy you taught in

Writing Conference/Strategy Lesson Notes

Student: Harrison

Date	
1/30	Develop setting – show characters interacting with their surroundings
2/5	Show don't tell about character – break important actions into a series of smaller actions
2/11 (SL)	Show don't tell – weave together action, dialogue, inner thinking

Figure 1–2 *Conference notes, student at a glance*

your last conference. (You should be able to find all this information in your conference notes.)

- Stay with a line of thinking by researching the same skill until you determine the writer successfully and independently uses that skill.
- Make sure your compliment includes a skill and a strategy and that you clearly name both in one to three sentences. Follow this with an example of the strategy from the writer's work and an explanation of why it is important to keep doing what he is doing.

- Make sure your teaching point includes a skill and a strategy, as well as an explanation of when and/or why to draw upon this knowledge. State your teaching point in one to three sentences.
- Show the student what it looks like to successfully use the strategy.
- Coach the writer as she practices the strategy in her own writing.
- When applicable, conclude by reminding the writer how your teaching fits into a repertoire of strategies he knows for the skill at hand.
- Record the date, teaching point, and anything else you want to remember in your conference notes.

Strategy Lessons

Instead of teaching the same strategy in three or four or ten different conferences, I can pull together a group of two to five students with similar needs and teach the strategy to multiple writers at one time. This means that in addition to conferring one-on-one with students during the thirty-five to fifty minutes following my minilesson, I also assemble small groups of writers for strategy lessons that span five to twelve minutes depending on the number of writers.

Strategy groups are *not* ability based, but rather, are based on my assessment of a common need regardless of level. If, for example, I notice a less proficient and a more proficient writer both struggling to come up with their own writing topics, I can gather them together and teach them a strategy to help them overcome this difficulty. Strategy groups are flexible, meaning the following day or week, if a writer is ready to move on to a new skill, I may pull her into a different group with different writers. I am careful not to meet with a student more than once on any given day unless it is to follow up on something I just taught; I do not want to teach more than a writer can absorb at one time, and I want to leave students time to actually write.

Group configurations occur in a few ways. Many of my strategy lessons are impromptu. For example, often I will have a conference and realize there are other writers in the room who would benefit from the same teaching, and so I pull them together for a strategy lesson. Or perhaps during my minilesson I noticed a handful of students struggling to grasp my teaching; I may give them extra support by holding them in the meeting area to reteach my minilesson as a strategy lesson.

Many of my strategy lessons are planned. When I read my conference notes and my students' writing and when I observe students during workshop, I look for evidence of the skills I have taught thus far. When students lack a given skill, I then consider what strategies would best support them and group them with other writers who need similar help.

Many students, of course, fall into multiple groups. Although the temptation may be to pull these writers into various groups across the week, this often means pulling them in very different directions from one day or week to the next. The result can be overwhelming, and instead of learning a range of skills, many students end up learning no skills. I therefore make sure each writer is focused on learning between one and three skills at a time depending on the writer and the skills. Just as when I confer, I consistently teach into those skill(s), assessing how the writer grows as a result of using a new strategy and then challenging him to take the same line of work further by expanding his repertoire of strategies. For example, in my strategy lesson grouping sheet (Figure 1–3), you will notice that Dean needs additional help developing setting, tension, and using periods; however, for now, he is focused on setting and periods. When I meet with Dean to teach him how to develop setting, I can do so by pulling him into a strategy lesson with Harrison and Allyson as they all share that focus. When I meet with Dean to teach him to use periods, I will do so in a conference because he is the only one currently focused on that skill. Once Dean gets a better hold on one or both of his individualized learning goals, his focus will shift to learning how to develop tension. As always, I know the goal is not learning and checking off individual strategies but learning to draw from a range of strategies in order to achieve a critical skill.

My strategy lessons follow the same structure as my minilessons. I begin with the connection, during which I very briefly compliment something I have noticed about them as writers that leads me to believe they are ready to learn something new. From here, I move into the teaching and active engagement. One of the main differences between a minilesson and a strategy lesson is that in strategy lessons, my teaching point *is* a directive because it is tailored to students' individual needs. I end my strategy lessons with the link by reminding students what I have taught and how it fits with their repertoire of strategies for using a skill. Before I move on, I record the date and teaching point in my conference notes; I also write *SL* so I know which teaching occurred in a small group versus during one-to-one instruction. As with my conferences, keeping track of my teaching allows me to hold students accountable for practicing that individually tailored teaching.

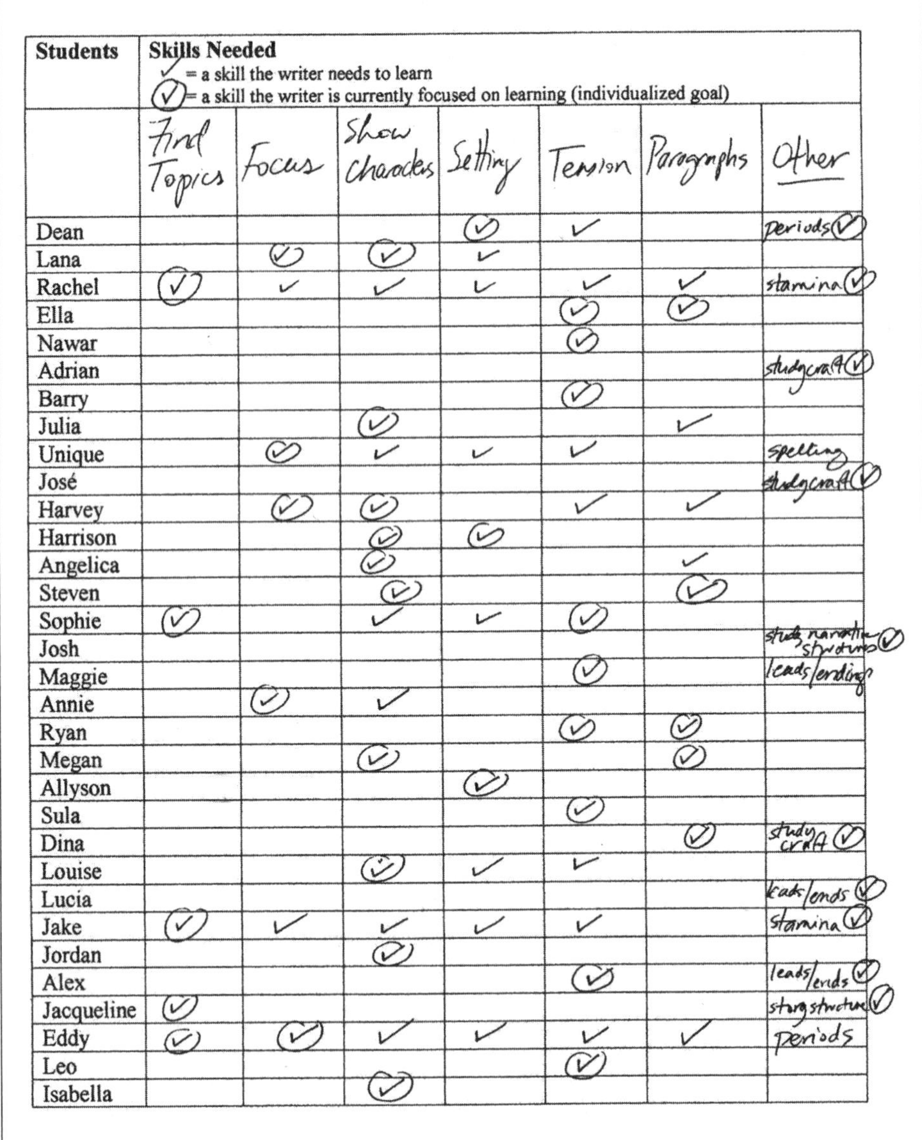

Students	Skills Needed ✓ = a skill the writer needs to learn (✓) = a skill the writer is currently focused on learning (individualized goal)						
	Find Topics	Focus	Show Characters	Setting	Tension	Paragraphs	Other
Dean				(✓)	✓		periods (✓)
Lana		(✓)	(✓)	✓			
Rachel	(✓)	✓	✓	✓	✓	✓	stamina (✓)
Ella					(✓)	(✓)	
Nawar					(✓)		
Adrian							study craft (✓)
Barry					(✓)		
Julia			(✓)			✓	
Unique		(✓)	✓	✓	✓		spelling
José							study craft (✓)
Harvey		(✓)	(✓)		✓	✓	
Harrison			(✓)	(✓)			
Angelica			(✓)			✓	
Steven			(✓)			(✓)	
Sophie	(✓)		✓	✓	(✓)		
Josh							study narrative structures (✓)
Maggie					(✓)		leads/endings
Annie		(✓)	✓				
Ryan					(✓)	(✓)	
Megan			(✓)			(✓)	
Allyson				(✓)			
Sula					(✓)		
Dina						(✓)	study craft (✓)
Louise			(✓)	✓	✓		
Lucia							leads/ends (✓)
Jake	(✓)	✓	✓	✓	✓		stamina (✓)
Jordan			(✓)				
Alex					(✓)		leads/ends (✓)
Jacqueline	(✓)						story structure (✓)
Eddy	(✓)	(✓)	✓	✓	✓	✓	periods
Leo					(✓)		
Isabella			(✓)				

Figure 1–3 *Strategy lesson grouping sheet*

Tips for a Successful Strategy Lesson

- Keep strategy lessons from five to fifteen minutes.
- Group two to five students who need support with the same strategy and briefly let them know what you have noticed that makes you think they are ready for what you are going to teach them.
- Make sure your teaching point includes a skill and a strategy, as well as an explanation of when and/or why to draw upon this knowledge. State

your teaching point in one to three sentences and repeat it throughout the strategy lesson.

- Show students what it looks like to successfully use the strategy. Highlight the process, especially points of difficulty, as well as the end result.
- Coach each student as she practices the strategy in her own writing.
- When applicable, conclude by reminding students that your teaching fits into a repertoire of strategies they know for the skill at hand.
- For every student in the group, record the date and teaching point in your conference notes.

Teaching Shares

When I was a new teacher, I used shares as an end-of-the-workshop opportunity for students to read to the class what they had just written. Since then, I have learned to reenvision these student shares as *teaching* shares; in other words, they are another opportunity for the teacher to share something that good writers do. (An important exception to this is when I give students the opportunity to share with a partner something with which they have been working in order to receive feedback or simply to celebrate their use of a given skill.) I almost always wrap up writers' workshop with a teaching share and often do one in the middle of workshop, as well, if the need arises.

Again, during workshop, I travel the room to confer with individual writers and pull together small groups based on common needs. As I meet with students, I am not only teaching, I am also assessing. My teaching shares, like my minilessons, emerge from what I see a majority of my students need to learn as writers. If the class needs more support with the day's minilesson, that usually takes precedence for a share. Otherwise, I might revisit something I taught earlier in the week or year, or I might introduce a new concept—again, whatever feels most urgent for the majority of writers in the class.

Whenever possible, I use student work to exemplify my teaching point; oftentimes, this happens because I have taught in a conference or a strategy lesson what I want to teach to the entire class, and so I can ask one or more of the students with whom I worked to share what they just did as writers. Unlike my early days in the classroom, I almost never ask someone to read his entire piece; instead he reads just the part that exemplifies my teaching point. When I have not found a student example of what I want to teach during workshop, I use my own writing or a piece of published writing to illustrate my point.

The share always includes the teaching. Sometimes, when I teach something that is immediately relevant to the entire class, I also include an active engagement. In cases of the former, the share should not take more than two minutes. In cases of the latter, it may take up to five minutes.

Tips for a Successful Teaching Share

- Keep teaching shares from two to five minutes.
- Revisit the minilesson when a majority of students need additional support with what you taught; otherwise, teach into another common, pressing need.
- Make sure your teaching point includes a skill and a strategy, as well as an explanation of when and/or why to draw upon this knowledge. State your teaching point in one to three sentences.
- Show what it looks like to successfully use the strategy, using an example from a student in class when possible.
- When you teach something immediately relevant for the majority of your students, you might ask them to practice the strategy in their writing before returning to their own agendas (or before putting away their writing if it is the end of workshop).
- When applicable, conclude by reminding students how your teaching fits into a repertoire of strategies they know for the skill at hand.

INTRODUCTION: TEACHING NARRATIVE WRITING

Everyone loves a good story. I know I love losing myself in and learning from someone else's life. But for this to happen, the writer must have tools for making the people and events on the page come alive. Only then can the writer successfully reflect life and impact the life of the reader. (Which, I believe, is the whole reason for reading and writing stories in the first place.)

In the following section, I include skills and strategies for teaching students how to write powerful stories, or narrative. Narrative writing includes fictional genres like mysteries and fairy tales, but also nonfiction genres like biographies and autobiographies. What classifies these genres as narrative is that they all have a plot with characters who move through time, reside in a given setting, and experience some kind of change between the beginning and the end of the piece.

The first thing to consider when teaching narrative is the genre in which you want students to write. In my community of practice, we teach students to write true stories before fictional pieces. Though students are often eager to write fiction, they usually do so more successfully when they have had practice taking events that have actually occurred and shaping them into well-told stories; starting with true stories means the writer need not worry about how to make up the parts and can therefore focus more on how to craft and convey the parts.

Once you know the genre in which your students will write, the next thing you and your students need to know are the defining features of that genre because they will guide your teaching and their writing. For example, if your students are writing realistic fiction, you will need to teach them how to create realistic characters who move through realistic events in realistic ways, whereas if your students are writing mystery, you will need to teach them about detectives and red herrings and how to leave their readers clues.

Though you will approach every genre in a slightly different way, you will find the fundamental elements to any narrative the same. Whether realistic fiction or mystery, personal narrative or fantasy, a well-crafted story rests on the author's ability to show events unfolding on the page and to create dynamic characters, a developed setting, tension; regardless of the genre, story writers must create focus for their readers; they must lure their readers into a web of events and release them back into the world with passion and intrigue and meaning. In order to craft the kinds of stories that will mean something to the writer and reader alike, writers rely on skills and strategies included in this section.

CHAPTER 2

Finding Narrative Topics That Matter

I think the single most important thing we can teach our student writers is how to generate meaningful topics for themselves. This is not to say it is not also critical for our students to learn about craft and conventions and process. But one can be a writer without knowing how to write well. I was a writer for years before I gained any skills as such, generating through adolescence terrible poem after terrible story.

Until our students learn to find their own ideas for their writing, they are either utterly dependent on someone else to tell them what to do or totally incapable of writing at all. Either way, they are not yet writers. They do not yet know what it means to use writing to fill the time, to change people's thinking, to explore the world, to explore themselves.

If we do nothing else as writing teachers, let us show our students how they can find the kinds of ideas that will inspire them to be writers and that will inspire their readers to be readers. If your students do not know what to write, or if they simply write to fill up pages but not to impact an audience, it is probably because they do not yet know how to find or make meaningful topics. To help, you might teach any of the following strategies. Students who are writing true stories can use them to uncover moments from their own lives, whereas students who are writing fiction can use the same strategies to create events in a made-up character's life; when teaching your students to write fiction, you might add to any of the following strategies in this chapter the phrase: *When we write fiction, we make up a story about a make-believe character who experiences something similar.*

Recall Unforgettable Moments: *One way writers find meaningful story topics is by recalling unforgettable moments—the moments that linger with us year after year.*

All of us carry memories from the past for reasons we cannot immediately explain. I often wonder, for example, why I can remember lying on a cot one day in kindergarten waiting for nap time to end, but I cannot remember where my first love and I shared our initial kiss. Surely the latter moment feels much more significant, the kind of thing I want and would expect to remember. And yet, some part of me has decided to instead hold onto those moments of lying in the half-dark at school. I can only assume there is a reason; I assume that if I dug deep enough into that moment, I would find something worth writing about.

For some students, learning to consider their unforgettable memories will help them generate topics whose meaning is more inherent: the day their parents divorced; when they had their first kiss. Other students can use the strategy to begin to make meaning when they write; they can begin to write those stories about lying awake during nap time in order to uncover hidden significance.

Teaching

Tell

When I worked with a small group of fifth graders, I said, "One way writers find story topics that really matter is by recalling those moments that we never forget. Often, we don't even know why we remember the things we do, but when a memory stays with us year after year after year, it is usually a sign that it is worth writing about; often, we write about it to figure out why the memory stays with us."

Show

"Watch me as I try using this strategy. Let me think, what are moments that stay with me year after year? I certainly will always remember things like the day my parents separated or the time I broke my ankle. I could definitely write those stories, so I'll jot them on my list of possible topics. Still, there are other moments that don't immediately seem as significant but that stay with me year after year, so they must be important somehow. I want to think about some of those moments, too.

"As I do that, different images are popping into my head. For example, there's this one image from my childhood that I've always carried with me even though I'm not sure why. I'm sitting on the kitchen floor with my knees to my chest crying, and my mom is scooping me up so that my knees are still to my chest. She just reaches down and wraps one arm around my back and the other around my knees so I'm folded into myself, but also folded into her. I'm going to write, *mom scooping me off kitchen floor* on my list of topics. I know that by writing this story, I might uncover more of its meaning. Maybe it's about how I spent much of my childhood feeling scared and alone. Or maybe it's about how I longed to be in my mother's arms. Or maybe it's about how I was always trying to disappear and that's why I was folded into myself and into my mom. Even as I think a little more about this moment, I imagine it could be about all of those things.

"Other images are running through my mind that I carry with me year after year. Like jumping on my dad's bed with a T-shirt pulled around my forehead and hanging down my back. I was pretending that the shirt was really long hair and I was flinging it from side to side while my dad cooked us dinner down the hall. I have no idea why I remember this moment, but it is like permanent marker on my brain; no matter how old I get, it still seems to be there, so it must be important somehow. I'm adding *jumping on my dad's bed* to my list of unforgettable memories. Maybe by writing it I'll figure out why this moment matters so much. Perhaps it's because I always wanted to spend time with my dad and this was a happy afternoon just hanging out together in his apartment.

"Do you see how I'm finding possible story topics by thinking about the memories that linger in my mind? Do you see how these moments can be the more obviously significant events, like divorces and broken bones, but they can also be moments whose significance isn't immediately obvious? Do you also see how these memories often stay with me in the form of images, so it helps me to think about the pictures that are seared in my brain?"

Active Engagement

Tell

"Will you all try this now? Think of some memories that you carry around with you year after year, even though you might not know why you remember those moments. You can begin with a list, or you can just start writing the story of one of those times."

Coach

I support students with this strategy by saying things like:

- "Close your eyes for a moment and just let your mind get quiet. When you think back over your life so far, what images pop into your head?"
- "Think back to when you were much younger, maybe in [first or second] grade. When you remember that time in your life, what are some of the first memories that come into your head?"
- "Mentally scan the places in your life where you've spent a lot of time and see what unforgettable moments occurred there."

Once Eyanna told me a couple of her unforgettable moments, I reminded her that she could always return to this strategy when she wanted help finding stories that matter to her. After I left her, she wrote the list seen in Figure 2–1.

Whether or not Eyanna knows why she remembers these moments, she will write the stories of those to which she feels especially drawn; this might mean using writing to discover *why* she is so drawn to these memories. In cases where she already knows why a moment matters to her, Eyanna is still uncovering stories that have impacted her in some way and are thus more likely to impact her readers, as well.

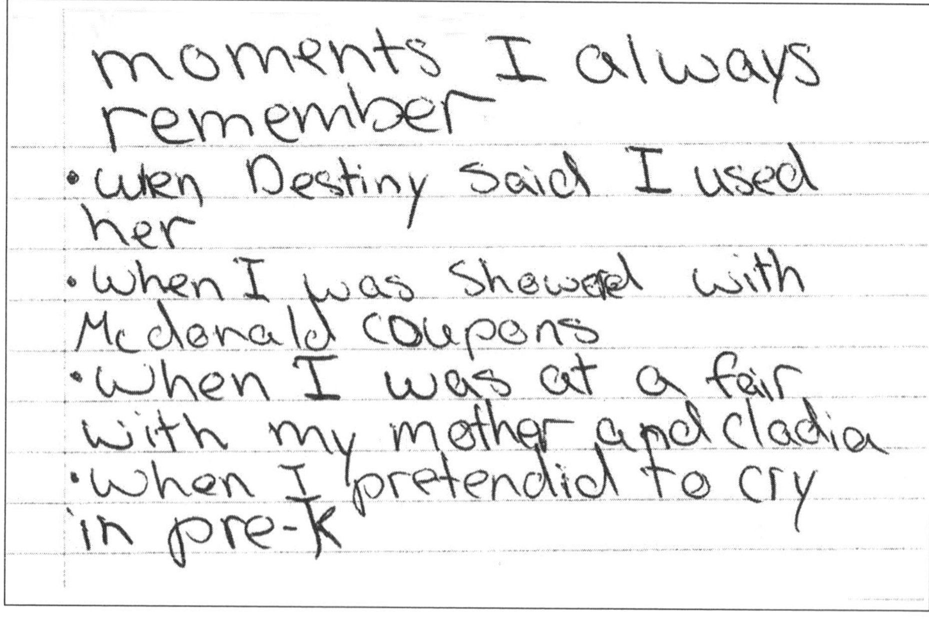
moments I always remember
- wen Destiny said I used her
- when I was showerd with Mcdonald coupons
- when I was at a fair with my mother and cladia
- when I pretendid to cry in pre-K

Figure 2–1 *Eyanna's notebook entry of possible topics: listing unforgettable moments*

Were Eyanna writing fiction, she might take something like, "When Destiny said I used her" and use it as a springboard for make-believe plot-lines. Perhaps this memory would yield a list of topics like *Two friends fight on the playground and don't know how to make up* or *A brother gets mad at his sister because she uses him to get out of trouble with their parents.*

Recall Moments of Success: *One way writers find meaningful story topics is by recalling moments of success.*

Not all stories end with triumph, of course. But teaching students to consider moments of success is an excellent strategy for teaching them to uncover moments of strong, positive emotion. It is also an excellent way to uncover moments in which the character takes a journey of some kind because we usually experience success when we attain desires or overcome difficulty. In both cases, students are likely to find story topics that matter to them and to their readers.

When I conferred with fifth grader Jenya, I decided I wanted to help her generate story entries in which she felt and conveyed to her readers a sense of meaning; I wanted to teach her how to move away from writing to fill up the page and toward writing to explore and share moments that matter.

Teaching

Tell

"One way writers find stories that really matter is by thinking about moments in which we felt successful. We usually feel successful when we take risks or when we really want something and get it. As we know, over-coming obstacles and reaching desires are both ingredients for a great story, which is why recalling moments of success can help us find such meaningful topics."

Show

"Let me show you how I think about moments of success to come up with meaningful story topics. Right now I'm thinking about times when I really wanted something and then got it because again, those are times when I usually feel successful. My whole life, I've wanted my dad to be proud of me. I know he's proud, but sometimes I don't *feel* it. I remember one time, though, I was eight or nine years old and gave a speech in front of hundreds of people. It wasn't so much that I felt successful because of the speech. What I remember was afterward, seeing my dad. He was standing with some other people when I came over, and he said, 'Wasn't my little girl just amazing up there?' And then he looked at me with this face, I can feel it in my heart even now when I think about it. He was smiling such a genuine smile and his eyes were all lit up with pride. In that moment, I felt incredibly successful. I'm going to write, *seeing my dad after my speech* on my list of topics.

"I can also think about times when I was nervous or afraid to do something but did it anyway because I know that when I take risks, I often feel good about myself; I often feel successful. Something that comes to mind is one of the first times I rode my bike all by myself without anyone around. I was older than most kids when I learned to ride a bike, probably nine or ten, and I was pretty afraid of being on one. This one day, all I did was ride up and down the sidewalk in front of my house, but still, I felt like I was accomplishing something really huge because I didn't give in to my fear. I'm adding, *riding my bike on Precita Avenue* to my list.

"Do you see how, by recalling moments of success, I'm coming up with story topics that matter to me—moments that impacted me and that carry a lot of emotion? Do you see how my moments of success don't have to be huge events in the outside world, like winning a championship game? They can be moments like that, but they certainly don't have to be; they can be smaller moments, like seeing the look in my father's eyes or riding up and down my block. Do you also see how I uncover moments of success by thinking about when I really wanted something and got it (like my father's pride) and when I was afraid to do something but did it anyway (like riding my bike alone)?"

Active Engagement

Tell

"Would you try this now? Find some story ideas that really matter to you by thinking of moments of success. Once you have a couple things on your list that you would like to share with readers, pick one to write as a story."

Coach

To support writers, I might say:

- "Think of times in your life when you really struggled. Was there a time when you overcame that struggle and felt successful?"
- "Think of times when you felt proud or joyful because that's often a sign of success."

- "Think of times when you wanted something. Now think about the moments when you got what you wanted. Did you feel successful in any of those moments?"

After our conference, Jenya added to the list she started with me and then wrote the story of one of the moments on her list (see Figures 2–2 and 2–3). By thinking about times of success, she unearthed important memories of moments in which she experienced strong emotion. What she writes clearly matters to her, and by sharing the journey she took from anxiety to triumph and pride, Jenya makes the story matter to her readers, as well.

Were Jenya writing fiction, she could have used this strategy to invent a scene in which a made-up character feels successful. She could have started by considering her own moments of success, or perhaps even those of someone else she knows. But then she would have fictionalized the unfolding of events by taking into consideration things like her characters, the message she wanted to send to readers and her own desires about how things go in life.

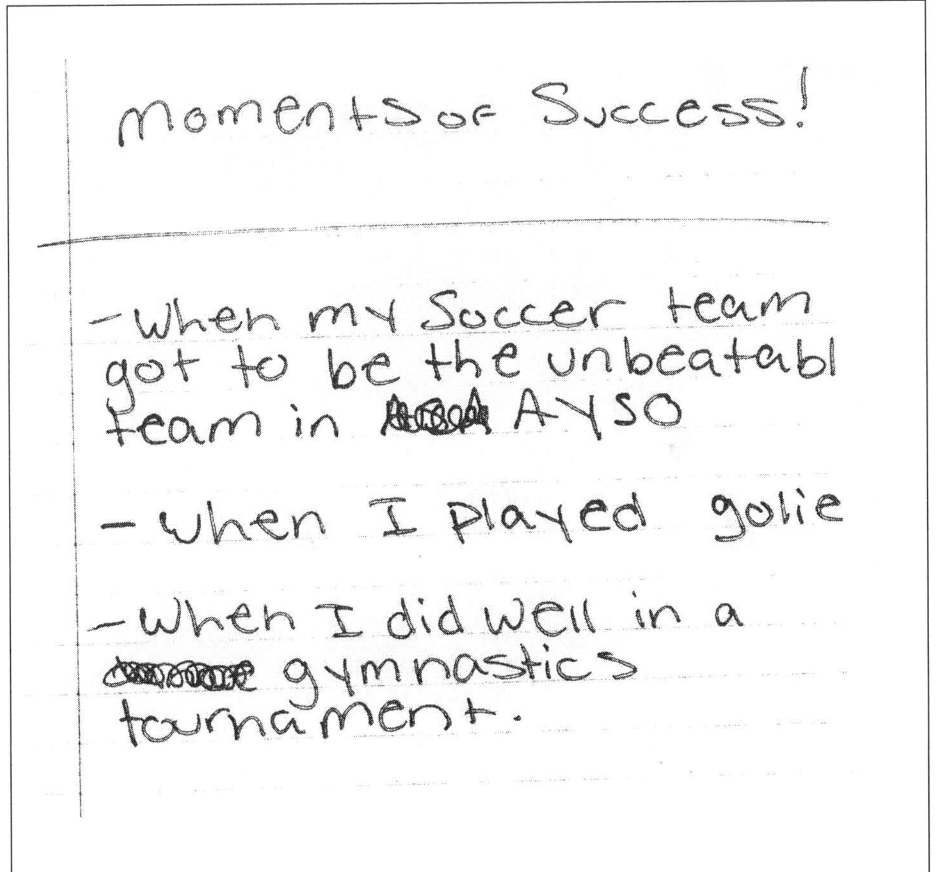
moments of Success!

-when my Soccer team got to be the unbeatabl team in AYSO

-when I played golie

-when I did well in a gymnastics tournament.

Figure 2–2 *Jenya's notebook entry of possible topics: listing moments of success*

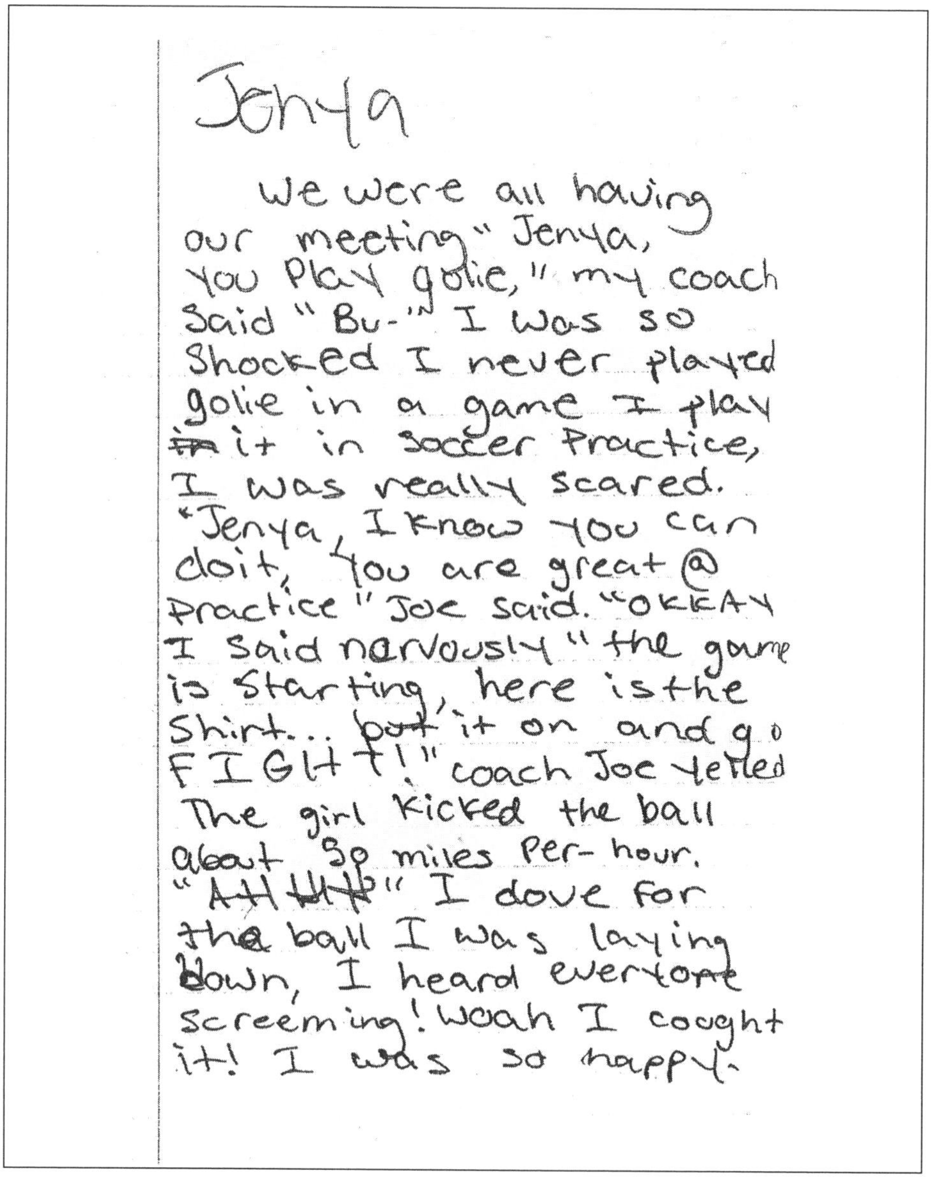

Jenya

We were all having
our meeting "Jenya,
you play golie," my coach
said "Bu-" I was so
Shocked I never played
golie in a game I play
it in soccer practice,
I was really scared.
"Jenya, I know you can
do it, you are great @
practice" Joe said. "OKKAY
I said narvously "the game
is starting, here is the
shirt... put it on and go
FIGHTT!" coach Joe yelled
The girl kicked the ball
about 50 miles per-hour.
"AHHH" I dove for
the ball I was laying
down, I heard everyone
screeming! Woah I caught
it! I was so happy.

Figure 2–3 *Jenya's notebook entry: a moment of success*

Recall Comments: *One way writers find meaningful story topics is by recalling a comment we have said or heard and the emotions surrounding the comment.*

Mary Ehrenworth taught me this strategy as a way to help students bring to light moments that matter—moments that, for some significant reason, linger in their minds and hearts. As writers, we know that words have power; the way someone crafts an argument or the line of a poem or a story can impact readers for a lifetime. Perhaps this is why story writers so often rely on dialogue not simply to move along the plot but to convey emotion and complexity and tension; what people say, when and where and how they say it, often carries more weight than anything else we may think or do. It makes sense, then, that recalling comments from our lives is a powerful tool for generating story ideas.

Teaching

Tell

When I worked with a group of fourth graders who were just beginning to gather ideas for a realistic fiction piece, I said, "Writers sometimes get ideas for stories by recalling a comment we said or heard; when writing fiction like you're doing now, we can create a make-believe scenario in which someone says or hears the same comment. As we know, what people say often has a huge impact, so telling the stories of these moments usually means writing stories that are full of emotion and meaning."

Show

"Let me show you what I mean. When I think about comments that linger in my mind, I remember when I was seven or eight and standing on the playground with Hera. She turned to me and said, 'Your arms are so hairy, you're going to grow up to be a boy.' Even now, when I remember that moment, my stomach tenses; I feel hurt and embarrassed all over again. I know I could use this comment to write a great story, so I'm going to jot it down: *Your arms are so hairy, you're going to be a boy when you grow up!*

"Now I'm thinking, What's a make-believe story in which someone would say the same thing? I know siblings tease each other a lot, so maybe I could write a story about a brother and sister who get into a fight and the boy says that to his younger sister. That's one idea.

"I could also write a totally different story about a little boy who has a crush on a girl at school. You know how sometimes when young kids have crushes they tease each other? The boy could say that to the girl one day because he doesn't know how else to get her attention.

"You know, my story doesn't have to be about someone saying the comment; it could be about someone overhearing the comment. Maybe I could write a story about someone who hears her friend saying those words to someone, and because it is so mean, she realizes she doesn't want to be friends with someone like that.

"I can also think of other comments I remember from my life, like when my grandmother said, 'I love watching you move.' I felt so special in that moment. I could write a story about a girl who says that to someone she has a crush on. There are so many possibilities!

"Do you see how one way I get ideas for fiction is by recalling comments that really impacted me and then imagining make-believe events around the same comment? Do you see that my story ideas are meaningful because they come from an emotional experience? Do you also see how, because I'm writing fiction, I can come up with a lot of different story ideas from the same comment?"

Active Engagement

Tell

"Now it's your turn to try this strategy. Take a moment to remember something you said or heard and jot down the comment or comments in your notebook." When students are writing true stories, I stop here. However, because these students were writing fiction, I also said, "Then, jot down some make-believe story ideas in which a character says or hears the same thing."

Coach

To help students recall comments, I say things like:

- "Think of times when you felt strong emotion and whether you or someone else said something that caused the emotion."
- "First think of people in your life, and then think of things they've said that you've never forgotten."
- "Think of people in your life and the things you've said to them that you've never forgotten."

To help students use their comments to generate make-believe stories, I say:

- "How did you feel when you said or heard that comment? What's a different situation in which someone might feel those same things and therefore say the same thing?"
- "What caused you or the person to say that? What might cause a make-believe character to say the same thing?"

Fatin started generating ideas during the strategy lesson and continued with the strategy once I sent her back to her seat. By the end of workshop, she had a list in her notebook of comments from her own life. Though Fatin could have also collected her ideas for fiction in the form of a list, as soon as she had an idea in her head, she wrote a fictional scene (see Figure 2–4).

Though this scene between Aya and his sister is fictional, it is both believable and powerful. By drawing upon the unforgettable things she has said and heard, Fatin gets ideas for unforgettable fiction. Were Fatin collecting ideas for true stories, she would have simply written the story of what happened when she said or heard one of the comments on her list.

* * *

Many writing teachers are used to giving their students prompts: *Write about something you did this summer. Write about a time you did something special with your family.* The problem with prompts is that we teach

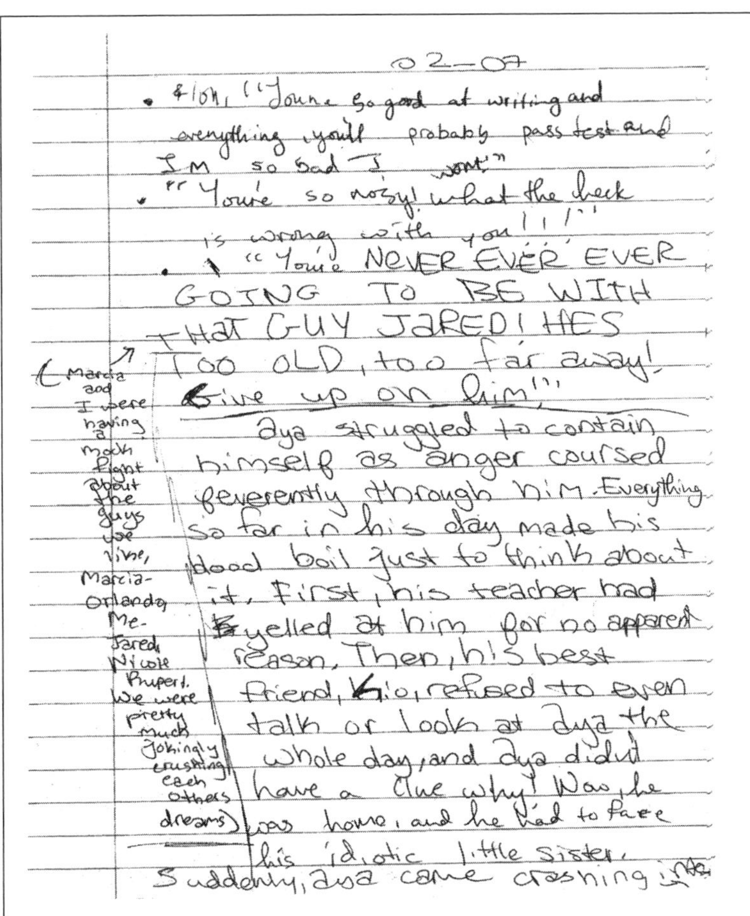

Figure 2–4 *Fatin's notebook entry: listing recalled comments and writing a scene unfolding around a comment*

- "You're so good at writing and everything you'll probably pass [the] test and I'm so bad I won't."
- "You're so nosy! What the heck is wrong with you!!!"
- "You're NEVER EVER EVER GOING TO BE WITH THAT GUY JARED! HE'S TOO OLD, too far away! Give up on him!"

Aya struggled to contain himself as anger coursed fervently through him. Everything so far in his day made his blood boil just to think about it. First, his teacher had yelled at him for no apparent reason. Then, his best friend, Kio, refused to even talk or look at Aya the whole day, and Aya didn't have a clue why! Now, he was home, and he had to face his idiotic little sister.

Suddenly, Aya came crashing into her as he was walking.

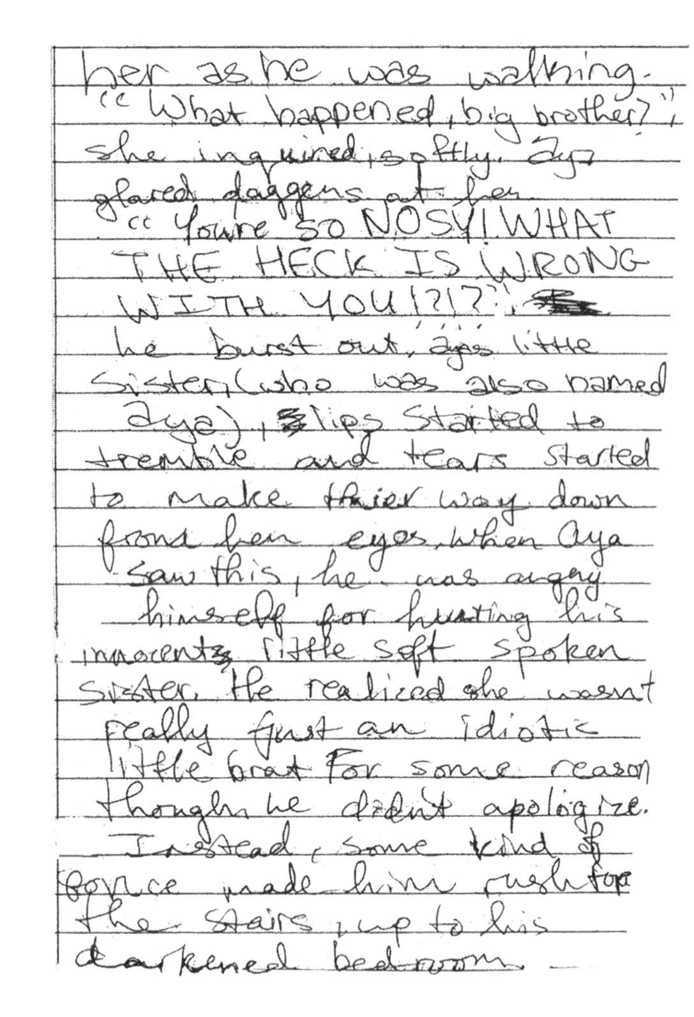
her as he was walking.
"What happened, big brother?",
she inquired, softly. Aya
glared daggers at her.
"You're so NOSY! WHAT
THE HECK IS WRONG
WITH YOU!?!?",
he burst out. Aya's little
sister (who was also named
Aya), lips started to
tremble and tears started
to make thier way down
from her eyes. When Aya
saw this, he was angry
himself for hurting his
innocent little soft spoken
sister. He realized she wasn't
really just an idiotic
little brat For some reason
though he didn't apologize.
Instead, some kind of
force made him rush for
the stairs, up to his
darkened bedroom.

"What happened, big brother?" she inquired softly. Aya glared daggers at her.

"You're so NOSY! WHAT THE HECK IS WRONG WITH YOU!?!?" he burst out. Aya's little sister (who was also named Aya), lips started to tremble and tears started to make their way down from her eyes. When Aya saw this, he was angry at himself for hurting his innocent little soft spoken sister. He realized she wasn't really an idiotic little brat. For some reason though he didn't apologize. Instead, some kind of force made him rush for the stairs, up to his darkened bedroom.

Figure 2–4 *(continued)*

our students to be utterly dependent on us. And just as detrimental, we teach them to write what does not matter to them. If we want our students to be writers in the world rather than students who write in school because they have to, we need to give them tools for generating their own, significant topics.

I believe our job as writing teachers is to help our students understand that we write to find, but also to make meaning; our job is to teach them where to look for meaningful stories and to teach them how to take a story and make it meaningful. Doing so will not only help us nurture lifelong writers, but lifelong learners—the kind of people who look under every stone and under every thought, expecting, and hence finding, significance.

CHAPTER 3

Creating a Focus

Sometimes, I walk into classrooms and am overwhelmed. When charts hang from every wall and corner, when student work is plastered from floor to ceiling, and books, folders, pencil cases, and backpacks line floors and desks and shelves all across the room, I have to stop and catch my breath. Charts and books and student work are wonderful, and, I believe, essential in most classrooms. But too much in too many places makes it difficult to impossible to really see any of it. What I like is a room with focus: the essential charts only, labeled and grouped by content area; the most recent student work, also labeled, also grouped; backpacks in closets, pencil cases in desks, no clutter to distract eyes or minds from the day's work.

When I read stories, I appreciate a similar sense of focus. I appreciate having places to settle. Stories that quickly move from one event to the next to the next, covering huge spans of time in very few words, leave me feeling dizzy. Similarly, stories that jump from one idea to the next or from feeling to feeling without any sense of reason blur my vision.

When you read your students' draft plans or written stories, if you do not know where to rest your attention, it is probably because they are not letting anything go; they are probably holding onto every scene and every detail, even when they do not really belong. To help, you can draw from the following strategies to teach your students at different stages of the writing process how to focus their pieces. If your students are getting ready to draft, you can use the strategies to teach them how to plan a focused piece; you might teach students to use a time line, story map, or other graphic organizer to do so. If your students are composing narratives, they can use the same strategies to help them stay focused while writing. If your students are revising, they can again use the same strategies to help them take out information that detracts from, and add information that will enhance, their focus.

Focus in Time: *One way writers focus our stories is in time, by writing only the most important or emotional part of a larger event.*

Once students learn how to focus, they can better learn how to elaborate; so often, when students are trying to write about a large span of time (their summer vacation; their entire birthday party), they rush through each event so as to get to the next one and thereby summarize the entire account. On the other hand, when they are instead trying to write the story of a small span of time (the day a sibling pushed them into the pool; the moment everyone sang happy birthday and they blew out the candles), they are suddenly free to linger and bring to the page all the details of the moment. If your students are writing summaries of events that occurred over large spans of time, I recommend teaching this strategy first as a way for them to write with focus.

Teaching

Tell

In a minilesson for her third graders, Emily Sosland said, "Writers often focus our pieces on one, small event so we can write that event with as much detail as possible and allow our readers to experience the moment fully. One way to find a focus is to think about the most important or most emotional part—something that may have happened in just a few minutes—of a bigger event. Once you find the part that's most important to you, you can help yourself stay focused on just that part by making a story map of the beginning, middle, and end of that smaller part."

Show

"Let me show you what I mean. I had such an amazing Saturday, I want to write about what happened. In the beginning of the day, my friend came over for brunch and we had a little food fight with the vegetables! Then, in the middle of my day, she and I went for a walk together, but really, we skipped all around the neighborhood, which was silly and fun, we sure laughed a lot! Last, we got hungry again and. . . . Now wait a minute. I'm doing that thing where I write about a lot of different things that happened instead of just one moment. With so many events to cover, I won't be able to write about every single one with lots of details, but then my readers

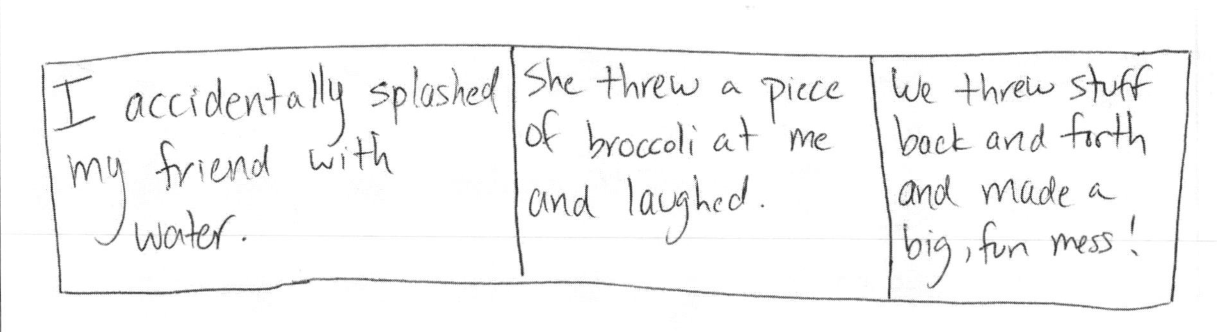

Figure 3–1 *Emily's teaching text*

won't be able to experience what I experienced. I need to focus my attention. I'm going to think about my favorite or most emotional part of the day. . . . Well, it was all really great, but the food fight was definitely my favorite; that was the most fun of all, which makes it the most important and the most emotional part of the day for me.

"OK, now I'm going to try planning my story again, this time writing about the beginning, middle, and end of just the most important part. I'm going to make a story map to help me stay focused." (See Figure 3–1.)

"Did you notice how I started to write about a lot of different events—how I made each big event a different part of my story (like the food fight was the beginning, the walk was the middle, dinner was the end)? But then I caught myself and made my piece more focused by choosing to write only about the most emotional, important part. Do you see how now I'm stretching out that one part across the beginning, middle, and end? This means I'll be able to write my story with lots of details so my readers can experience what I experienced."

Active Engagement

Tell

"I want you to try this before you go back to your seats. Let's say we all want to write a story about our field trip last week. That happened over a long time—our field trip was several hours! So we obviously aren't going to write about everything that happened. Right now, I want you and your partner to each pick a focus for your stories by choosing what you think was the most important or emotional part of that day. I expect several of you will choose different parts than your partners, and that's just fine. I'm going to give you one minute.

"OK, writers," Emily said after calling everyone's attention back to her. "Now I want you to plan how your story would go, making sure to stick with your focus. Can you use your three middle fingers to say what the beginning, middle, and end of your story would be, making sure that every part connects with your focus?"

Coach

When her students encountered difficulty, Emily said things like:

- "Did that happen in three to thirty minutes? What is the most important or emotional part of that experience that did happen in about thirty minutes or less?"
- "Make sure all the parts connect with your one small moment: Is your beginning part of your favorite thing that happened? Is the middle? Is the end?"
- "What was the very first thing that happened inside this small moment?"
- "What was the very last thing that happened in connection with this one moment?"

After Emily's students tried the strategy, she sent them back to their seats, reminding them that, as always, they could choose their own topics; they did not have to write the story of something that happened on their field trip.

Nicole decided to draw from the day's minilesson by making a plan in her notebook before she wrote her story (see Figure 3–2).

Nicole considered the most important part of her day at the mall to narrow her topic from *when I went shopping* to *when I bought a new purse.* By creating a focus for her writing, it is much more likely that she will write her story well; because she has less terrain to cover, she can cover it better, with more attention to detail.

Focus Around Plot: *One way writers focus our stories is around plot, by considering the beginning, middle, and end and making sure each of these parts connects through cause and effect.*

As readers, we know that most writers do not compose and publish single-moment pieces focused in time; novels and short stories in any genre

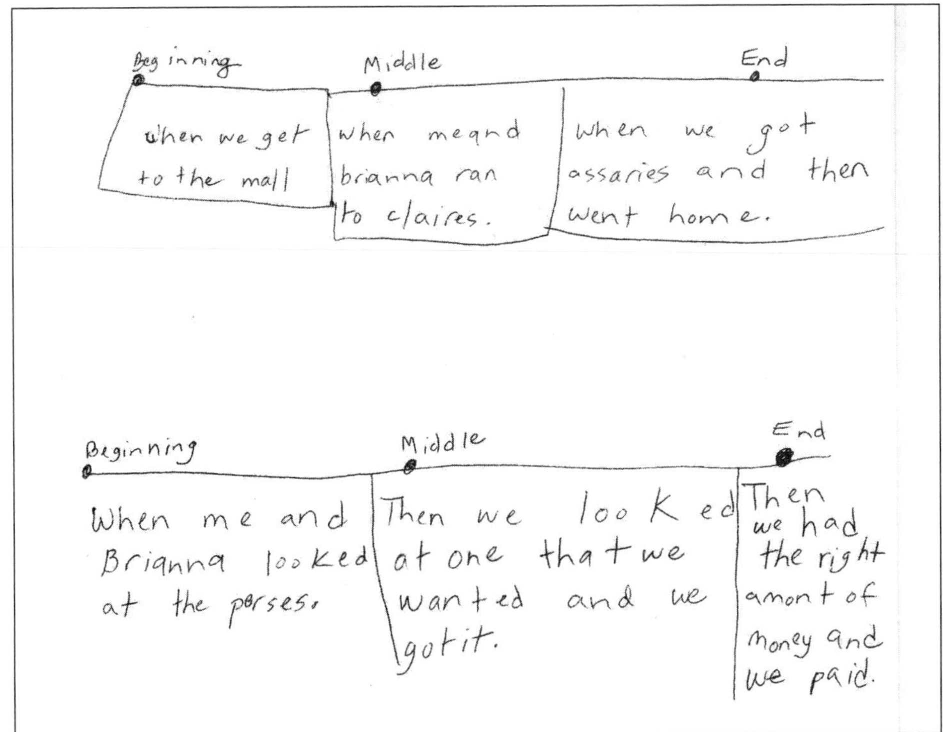

Figure 3–2 *Nicole's plan for a story focused in time*

tend to cover more than three to thirty minutes, just as they tend to contain more than one scene. But what these story writers usually do is string together a series of moments focused in time. Once your students have learned or at least gotten better at showing instead of telling their stories, they can begin to write pieces focused around plot instead of solely writing pieces focused in time.

Teaching

Tell

"Writers always focus our pieces," I said to a class of fifth graders. "This way, our readers can settle into what we have to say without any distraction, and they can understand how the important events fit together. One way to write a focused piece is to think about what happens in the beginning, middle, and end, and make sure that each of these parts is connected through cause and effect. Because you are revising, this might mean taking out information that doesn't connect, and adding in new information to make your parts connect."

Show

"Let me show you what that looks like. I'm writing a story about a girl who is teased at school. In the main part of my story, she's on the playground and a group of girls torment her and tell her she can't play with them. Here's the last part of my piece. As I read it to you, I'm going to look for places that don't feel focused."

> *Kassy fled across the yard, tears streaming down her cheeks. "I hate being a kid," she thought. "I can't wait to grow up and have real friends."*
>
> *That night, after Kassy finished her homework, she went upstairs and brushed her teeth. "Good night, mom," she called down the hall. Then she climbed into bed and went to sleep.*

"I realize this ending doesn't really work because it isn't a cause or an effect of Kassy being bullied; even though I'm sure she brushed her teeth and went to bed sometime after being teased, the two events really have nothing to do with one another, right?

"Let me think how I'm going to revise my piece. . . . I could take out that last scene where she goes to bed and end my story when she runs off the playground. Then my end would connect with the rest of my story.

"Or, I could add in that while she is brushing her teeth, Kassy's crying so hard she can't even get the toothbrush in her mouth. I could add in that she gives up, just goes to bed and cries into her pillow. By including more information, that same end scene would connect through cause and effect, and my readers would be better able to make sense of how the events in my story fit together. I like my second idea so let me try adding in some of that information.

"*That night, after Kassy finished her homework*—You know, I'm thinking that even doing her homework should be a struggle. Let me see, let me add in: *That night, Kassy could barely do her homework because every few minutes, she would start crying again. When she finally finished, she went upstairs to brush her teeth.* Now I'm thinking again about how I have to make everything connect, and just brushing her teeth isn't a cause or an effect of what's happening in my story. I could cross it out, but I'm actually thinking about what Kassy might do in the bathroom that would be a cause or effect of her being teased; I'm thinking she could talk to herself in the mirror or something. Let me add that in: *She stood in front of the mirror and stared into her own eyes. For a second, looking at herself, she felt a little better. 'It's going to be okay,' she said to the face looking back at her. 'It won't always be like this.' Somehow, Kassy believed it. She still didn't want to go to school. She still felt sad.* I like that; I like how it shows a change. Now I have those last lines about her calling good night to her mom and going to sleep; how can I connect that? I think I'm just going to cross out that line about her mom. I could add in stuff about her talking with her mom about the day, but instead, I think I'll add in that she goes to sleep without crying because she feels a little better. Let me try that: *She still felt sad. But when she climbed into bed, she actually fell asleep without crying.*

"Now my piece is focused because all the parts and details connect through cause and effect. Did you see how when something doesn't connect, I think about whether I want to take it out, or whether I want to add in more information to make it connect?"

Active Engagement

Tell

"I want you all to practice this now with your own pieces. Reread your stories thinking about every part from beginning to end, and decide whether you need to add in or take out parts to make everything connect through cause and effect. If you find a place where you need to make these kinds of revisions, put a check in the margins so you remember to go back to it after the minilesson."

Coach

To support writers with this strategy, I say things like:

- "Tell me again what your story is mostly about. Now, what is this part about? How do the two connect?"
- "Make it clear to your readers how the parts connect by adding in what you just told me." "Or, What do you do when a part doesn't connect?"

Lily intended to write a piece about a girl who realizes her neighborhood and her brother aren't so bad after all. Her revised piece is shown in Figure 3–3. (Underlined text in the transcription indicates additions Lily made to her piece and striked text indicates deletions.) In her first draft, I could certainly make sense of the events in her piece, and in the end could recognize a change in the narrator's feelings. Still, certain parts did not quite connect. For example, before she revised the opening scene by cutting most of her first three paragraphs, her piece included details that detracted from her focus; information about the brother's whereabouts and the conversation with the mother about breakfast have nothing to do with what Lily's piece is really about.

Furthermore, in her initial draft, Lily never showed what causes the change for the narrator. In the sentence just after the narrator falls to the ground, her brother "Anthony wasn't in sight." Just a couple sentences later, she walks home thinking about how nothing is wrong with her neighborhood and that people care for one another. The shift is sudden and unexplainable.

Lily's revised piece reflects an understanding on her part about how to write with focus. She doesn't only delete the extraneous opening scene. Even more sophisticated, she realizes that she did not show what caused the change in the narrator. By adding in toward the end of her story the extended interaction between the narrator and her brother, Lily now connects every part of her story through cause and effect, and consequently conveys the meaning of her piece much more effectively.

Focus Around Meaning: *One way writers focus our stories is around meaning by considering what we want our readers to think and feel, and including just those scenes and details that will convey this.*

Again, once students have learned the art of focusing and elaborating their stories, they can learn how to write many-moment as well as single-moment pieces. But they can also learn how to focus their pieces, whether one scene or multiple scenes, in a more sophisticated way: through meaning—through what they want their readers to think and feel as and after they read.

Teaching

Tell

When I conferred with fifth-grader Tahiya, I said, "In addition to writing with details, writers write with focus so our readers can better concentrate on and understand what our pieces are about. One way we write with focus is by considering what we want our readers to think and feel as they read, and then including only those details that will help accomplish this goal; similarly, we often add new details that we think will help get across the meaning of a story."

Lily 1/11

It was Saturday, school yard day! ~~I always wanted to walk alone and be independent. Saturday's are when Anthony (my brother) did chores. I do them on Sunday's. Anthony get's up early and does chores so then he has time to play football. I woke up at 11:00 so Anthony is already at the schoolyard. And I walk alone. "Lisa time for breakfast" My mom hollard from the kitchen to my room. "It's fine Ill have some fruit on the way out," I yelled as I ran through the blue hall.~~

I left my house no one said hi, people just walked by with no answer or statement I always wanted to like the neighborhood. Some people are so rude and I couldn't change that. I walked down the steps and headed for the schoolyard. It was quiet. You saw groups of people hanging out. Not really gangs, but people that like cars, sports, doubledutch. Weird huh? I moved here when I was 5 1/2 years here. I never

Figure 3–3 *Lily's revised draft focused around plot*

It was Saturday, school yard day! ~~I always wanted to walk alone and be independent. Saturday's are when Anthony (my brother) did choirs. I do them on Sunday's. Anthony get's up early and does chores so then he has time to play football. I woke up at 11:00 so Anthony is already at the schoolyard. And I walk alone.~~

~~"Lisa time for breakfast," my mom hollered from the kitchen to my room.~~

~~"It's fine I'll have some fruit on the way out," I yelled as I ran through the blue hall.~~

I left my house no one said hi, people just walked by with no answer or statement. I always wanted to like the neighborhood. Some people are so rude and I couldn't change that. I walked down the steps and headed for the schoolyard. It was quiet. You saw groups of people hanging out. Not really gangs, but people that like cars, sports, double-dutch. Weird, huh? I moved here when I was 5½ years old. I never liked it here. My parents say it's because I didn't get to know people like my brother Anthony. I don't care about him. He's mean to me, and he's kind of like a bully in my house. I can't deal with him. Someday I hope he will be nice to me.

I walked down the street. Motorcycles mumbleing. Sauce was cooking, and pasta was too. I've lived here for 6 years. I hate it. My brothers a bully in my house.

"Lisa wait up!" Jen exclaimed running up to me.

I quickly turned.

"Hi how are you feeling," I asked.

"None of your business," Jen said with an attitude.

"What a snob," I mumbled.

Jen's parents are going through a divorce. So when she talks about her feelings she cries. I found that out from her brother that follows her!

I walked into the schoolyard. There was my brother. Anthony, captain and wide receiver of the Middle school and highschool football team. Anthony was 16 years old. John, Mike, Jore, and Chris were sitting on the red stair case. Chris looked, then got the football in front of the team. He pegged it hard

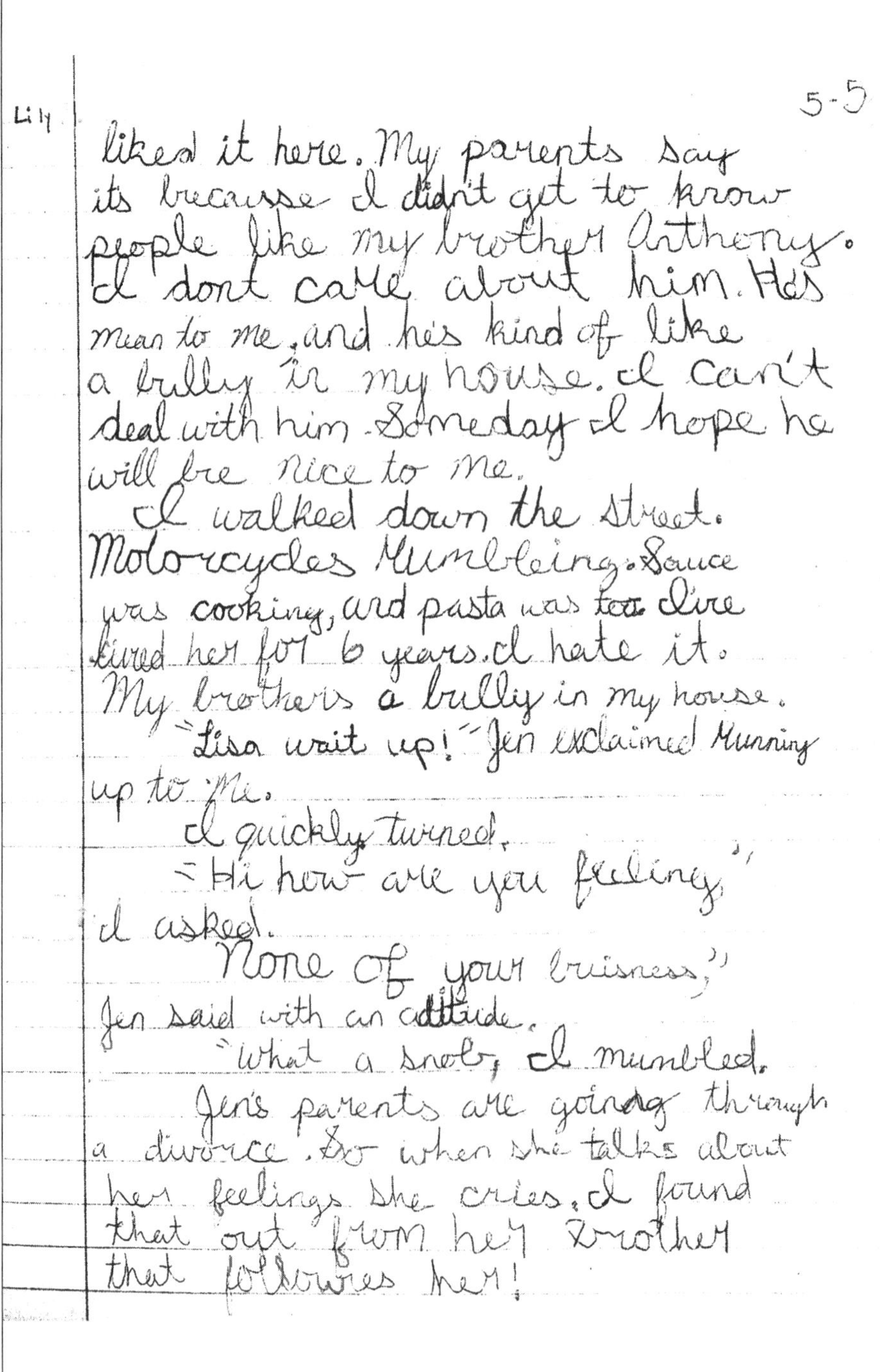

Lily

5-5

liked it here. My parents say
its becausse I didnt get to know
people like my brother Anthony.
I dont care about him. He's
mean to me, and he's kind of like
a bully in my house. I can't
deal with him. Someday I hope he
will be nice to me.
I walked down the street.
Motorcycles Mumbleing. Sauce
was cooking, and pasta was too. I've
lived her for 6 years. I hate it.
My brothers a bully in my house.
"Lisa wait up!" Jen exclaimed running
up to me.
I quickly turned.
"Hi how are you feeling,"
I asked.
None of your buisness,"
Jen said with an attitude.
"What a snob, I mumbled.
Jen's parents are goindg through
a divorce. So when she talks about
her feelings she cries. I found
that out from her brother
that followes her!

Figure 3–3 *(continued)*

I walked into the schoolyard. There was my brother, Anthony, captain and wide reciver of the middle school and highschool football team. Anthony was 16 years old. John, Mike, Jose, and Chirs were sitting on the red stair case. Chris looked then got the football infront of the team. He pegged it hard at me to show he should be quarterback of the team. K-plonk, the ball hit me in the head. I fell to the floor like a baseball bat hitting the dirt.

Tony ran up to me.

"Are you okay?" Tony asked gasping for air.

"Yes thanks," I responded.

More people came over. Anthony wasn't in sight. (1)

"Lisa are you okay?" Anthony asked. (2)

~~"Yes thank you," I responded.~~

"Lisa go home and get ice on your head," Anthony stated.

"Okay," I responded. Woah where is Chris, my brother will squash him. I thought as I walked at home.

Figure 3–3 *(continued)*

at me to show he should be quarterback of the team. K-plonk, the ball hit me in the head. I fell to the floor like a baseball bat hitting the dirt.

Tony ran up to me.

"Are you okay?" Tony asked gasping for air.

"Yes thanks," I responded.

More people came over. Anthony wasn't in sight. Then I heard his voice getting closer.

"Lisa are you okay?" Anthony asked.

~~"Yes thank you," I responded.~~

Is that my brother speaking? I thought. I wasn't used to him being so nice.

He grasped my hand and lifted me. Then he picked me up and sat me down on the red staircase. He gave me his sweater.

"Thanks Anthony," I said, then I gave him a hug. He was a little shocked, we haven't gave each other hugs since we were both 5 and 6.

"Anything for my sister," he responded. I was in aw.

Right then and there I knew my brother was going

to look out for me and care for me like what I've always wanted him to do.

"Lisa go home and get ice on your head," Anthony stated.

"Okay," I resonded. Woah where is Chris, my brother will squash him. I thought as I walked at home.

As I walked home I realized nothing wrong with my neighborhood. People care for you. Also Anthony started to care more. I started to enjoy the neighborhood. But there is always room for changes.

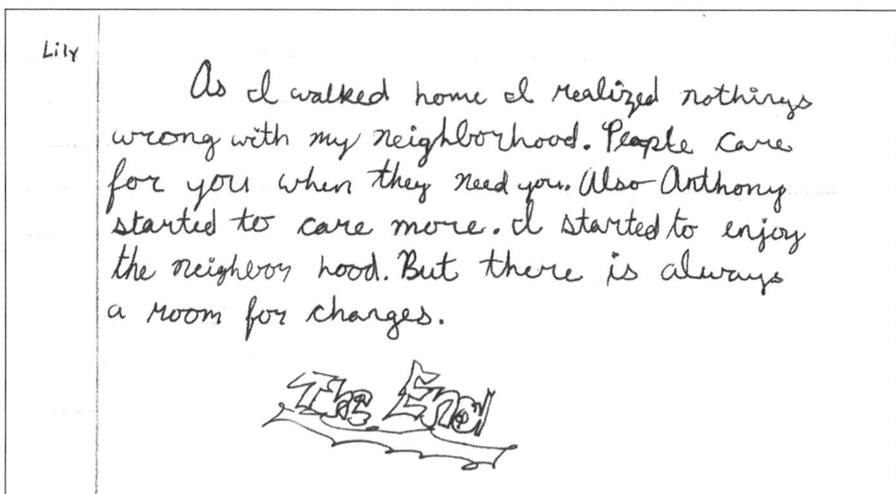

Lily

As I walked home I realized nothings wrong with my neighborhood. People care for you when they need you. Also Anthony started to care more. I started to enjoy the neighboor hood. But there is always a room for changes.

The End

Figure 3–3 *(continued)*

"Do you see how he reread his draft, holding in mind what he wants his readers to think and feel? Do you see how he crossed out details that do not connect with his intentions and sometimes added details to make his intentions even clearer to his readers?"

Active Engagement

Tell

"I want you to use your piece to practice this: Hold in mind what you told me you want your readers to think and feel, and then reread, making sure each and every detail connects with that."

Coach

To support writers with this strategy, I make sure to question parts that do as well as parts that do not connect; this way, they learn to reflect and make decisions for themselves, rather than rely on me to notice parts that do not hold together. I say things like:

- "Does that connect with your reason for writing, and if so, how?"
- "What does this detail make you think or feel? What do you want your readers to think or feel when they read this piece? Are those things similar?"

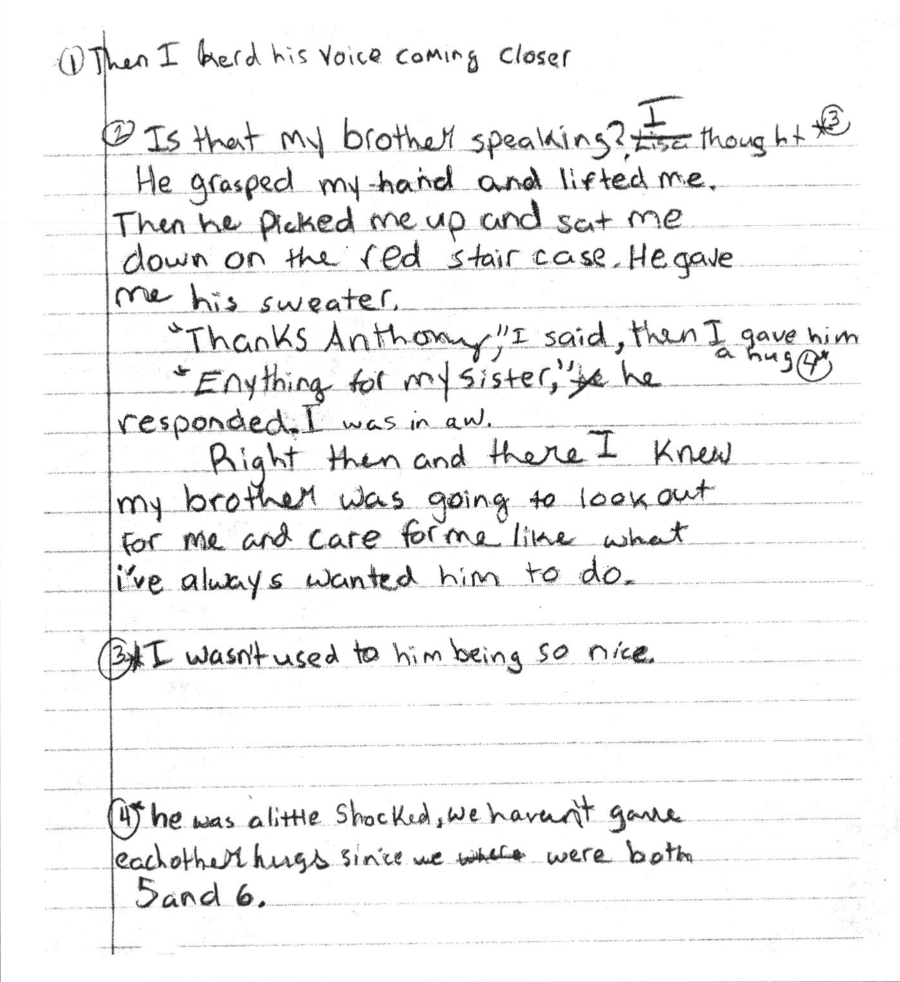

(1) Then I herd his voice coming closer

(2) Is that my brother speaking? I ~~Lisa~~ thought *(3)
He grasped my hand and lifted me.
Then he picked me up and sat me
down on the red stair case. He gave
me his sweater.
"Thanks Anthony," I said, then I gave him a hug (4)*
"Enything for my sister," ~~sa~~ he
responded. I was in aw.
Right then and there I knew
my brother was going to look out
for me and care for me like what
i've always wanted him to do.

(3)* I wasn't used to him being so nice.

(4)* he was alittle shocked, we haven't gave
eachother hugs since we ~~where~~ were both
5 and 6.

Figure 3–3 *(continued)*

Show

"Let me show you what I mean," I said before showing Tahiya another student's draft and revisions. "This writer told me that one thing he wants his readers to know is that the narrator is really nervous in the beginning of the story. When he reread his draft, he decided to cross out things like *Birds chirped outside my window* because birds chirping doesn't really create a nervous feeling, right? And look, a little later he crossed out, *I smiled when I saw all the snow was finally gone,* because again, he thought that if his readers saw the narrator was smiling, they wouldn't know he was nervous. Over here, he actually added in some details; he added, *Right then, I had to remind myself to breathe,* because he thought that would help show that the narrator is nervous.

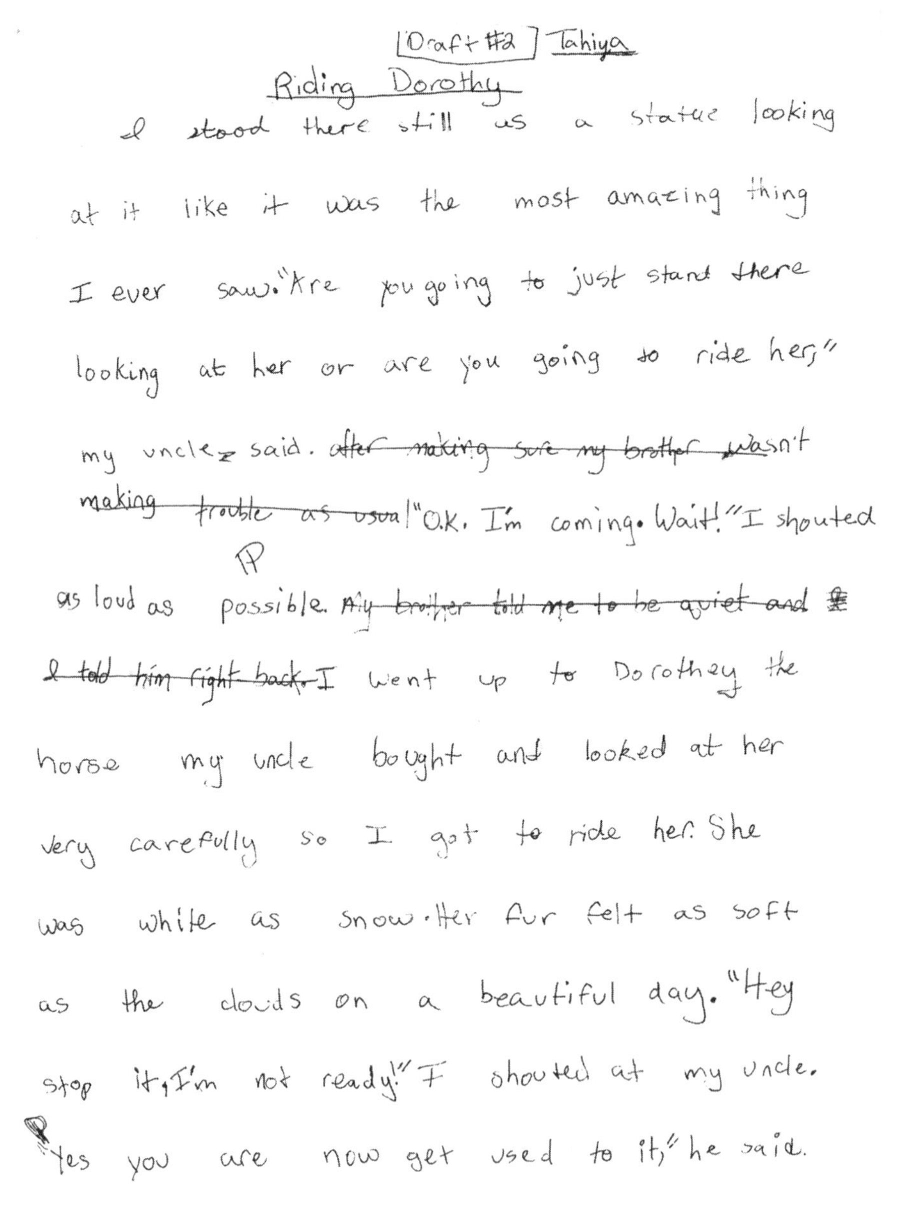

[Draft #2] Tahiya

Riding Dorothy

I stood there still us a statue looking at it like it was the most amazing thing I ever saw. "Are you going to just stand there looking at her or are you going to ride her," my uncle said. ~~after making sure my brother wasn't making trouble as usual~~ "O.K. I'm coming. Wait!" I shouted as loud as possible. ~~My brother told me to be quiet and I told him fight back.~~ I went up to Dorothey the horse my uncle bought and looked at her very carefully so I got to ride her. She was white as snow. Her fur felt as soft as the clouds on a beautiful day. "Hey stop it, I'm not ready!" I shouted at my uncle. "Yes you are now get used to it," he said.

Figure 3–4 *Tahiya's revised draft focused around meaning*

After our conference, I left Tahiya to continue revising her draft. When I returned at the end of workshop, she had crossed out several details and added to her ending. (See Figure 3–4.)

Though for the most part Tahiya's first draft was a focused piece, the handful of details that did not connect with the overall meaning of the story definitely acted as distractions; when I read her initial draft, the experience was one of walking along a path and occasionally tripping over a rock or losing my balance in a pothole. Each time I read something like, "'Yuck! It

He lifted me up and put me on Dorothy
When I got on her I felt like I was on top of
the world. My uncle softley patted her. She moved
slowley at first then she began moving faster
and faster. She moved liked the wind. ¶"Don't be scared,
don't be scared, don't be scared," I repeated to myself.
When I was a little girl I alway's wanted to
ride a horse but ~~a~~I didn't have the guts.
"Hey Dorothey, want to go that way?" I asked as I pointed
to the big space at the right. It had flower's
and apple's trees and lot's of grasses. I opened
my mouth to taste the air, as she moved to where I told her ~~Yuck! It tastes like~~
~~salty and gingery kind of air.~~ I felt so happy and
proud of myself. "I'm never going to get of you,"
I said to Dorothy. ¶"Neigh, Neigh, Neigh," she neighed.

Figure 3–4 *(continued)*

tastes like salty and gingery kind of air," or "I made my little sister sit in the middle seat," I was pulled out of the central ideas of the story; each time I continued reading, I had to regain my focus. Now that Tahiya has recognized and omitted extraneous details, there is nothing to distract her readers from what she wants us to know: that this was the day she got over her fear of horseback riding and fell in love with Dorothy. By rewriting her ending with new details, she further emphasizes this meaning for her readers.

"Ok. I will get off you" I said. "Let's go back to the farm" I told her. As we were walking to where my uncle puts Dorothey, she kept licking me. "I wish I had a horse that's just like you," I told her. ~~The adults were talking and my brother and sister's were playing tag.~~ "Let's go guy's. We need to go," my dad said. "Owww," we cried. "I'll come back next weak. Don't forget," I wispered to Dorothy. I went back in the car and looked back at Dorothy. "Bye," I said. "Tahiya if you want to keep her and take care of her, you could," My uncle said. I felt so happy. "I'll be glad to," I said happily. "Thanks

Figure 3–4 *(continued)*

* * *

When I first wake up mornings, before I put on my glasses or put in my contact lenses, the world is a blur. The edges of my son's nose blend in with the contours of his cheeks; the corners of open doors blend in with the empty space around them. Even though I can still recognize my son or successfully walk through doorways without bumping into walls, I find it unsettling to navigate myself in a world that is so out of focus.

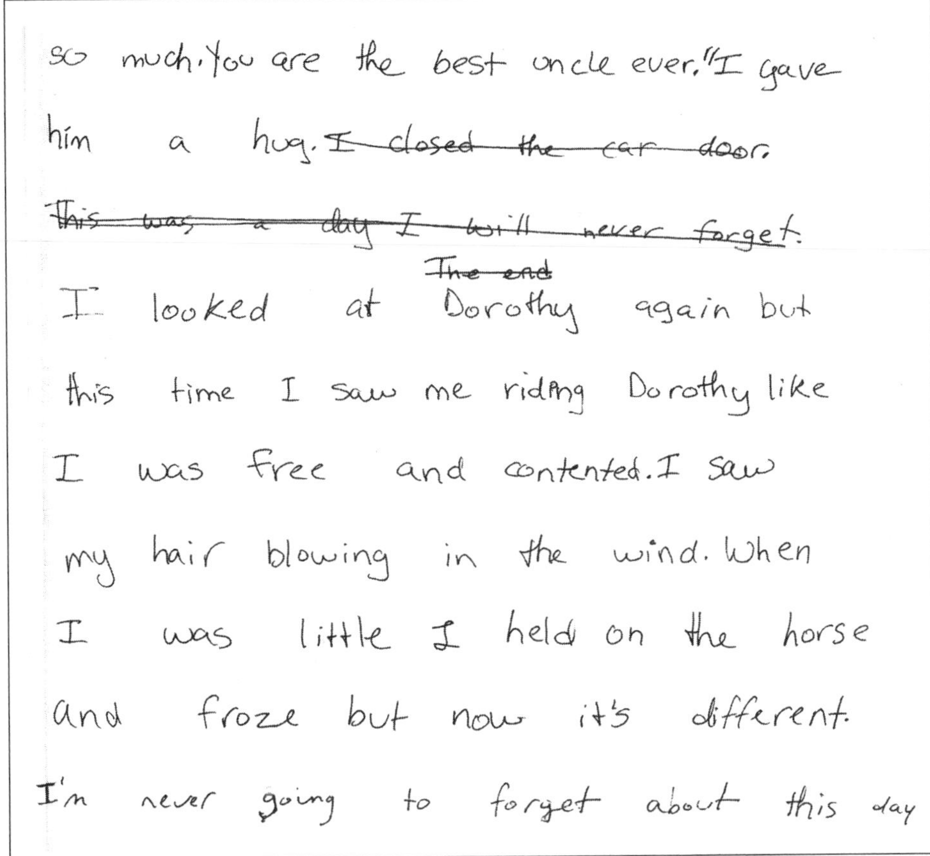
so much. You are the best uncle ever." I gave him a hug. ~~I closed the car door.~~

~~This was a day I will never forget.~~

~~The end~~

I looked at Dorothy again but this time I saw me riding Dorothy like I was free and contented. I saw my hair blowing in the wind. When I was little I held on the horse and froze but now it's different. I'm never going to forget about this day

Figure 3–4 *(continued)*

As soon as I slip on my glasses and my world comes into focus, I breathe more easily. Suddenly, I feel grounded again. Suddenly, there are places where I can rest my eyes: now when I look at Harrison, because I am no longer struggling to make sense of blurred features, I can gaze at his ever-growing lashes, lose myself in the dimple in the middle of his chin or the hair just starting to curl around his ears.

When our students write stories, their readers should enjoy a similar sense of grounding. It is not enough for readers to simply make sense of what is happening, just as it is not enough for me to simply recognize my son. Instead, we need to teach our students to focus on whatever it is they really want to share—a moment in time, certain ideas or feelings—so their readers know where to rest their attention and can bring into view what really matters in a story.

CHAPTER 4

Showing Not Telling About Characters

"Do you want to join them?" Josh teases.

I turn my head to look at him across the table. "Huh?" I ask.

"Do you want to join them?" he asks again.

I smile. Cover my face with my hands. "Sorry," I giggle. My husband and I joke that I have a disease: incessant eavesdropping and blatant staring. "I feel so embarrassed for her," I might say. "She keeps touching that man's shoulder and leaning into him, but look, if he moved any farther away on his chair he'd land on the floor." Or, "They must be on a first date. They keep asking each other those getting-to-know-you questions, like what their work is like and how they ended up here. I don't think she's interested, though; she keeps looking at her nails and at other tables." I weave whole stories in my head about who strangers are and what their relationships and lives are like based on my study of their words and reactions, their clothes and body language and tone of voice.

When I read narrative, I want to enter the characters' lives much the same way I like to enter from across the room the lives of strangers; I want to see for myself what kind of people characters are, how they feel, how events impact them. In *A Writer Teaches Writing* (1968), Donald M. Murray writes, "The most effective writer is the one who can make you see the facts so that they become your own facts, and knowing them, make you come to your own conclusion"(43). When story writers only tell what happens to characters (he fell off his bike; she fought with her mother) or only tell what kind of people they are (he is kind; she is competitive), I cannot experience for myself what is happening in their hearts and in their days; I cannot draw my own conclusions, and so I lose interest.

If you feel locked outside the world of your students' stories, unable to see and experience for yourself the people and events on the page, you might use the following strategies to teach them how to show instead of tell what happens to and around and inside of their characters.

Show Physical Contact Between Characters: *One way writers show instead of tell about our characters and their relationships is by revealing moments of physical contact between characters.*

For most of us, it is very different to tell friends about, let's say, a fight with our partner than it is to actually fight with a partner *in front of* friends. This is because showing is a much more vulnerable experience than simply telling. Accordingly, one way to teach students to show instead of tell is to teach them to include intimate details about characters. Intimate details either can be the kinds of things we only reveal in private, or the kinds of things that are not immediately obvious but that, when noticed, provide insight, such as subtle, physical interactions with other people.

Teaching

Tell

In a minilesson for a fifth-grade class, I said, "The kind of physical contact we have with other people is very specific depending on who we are and with whom we are interacting. Knowing this, one way to show your readers who your characters are and what kind of relationships they have with other people is to include details about their physical contact with one another."

Show

"For example, in my story about the girl who is teased at school, there's a scene where her mom drops her off at school and the girl doesn't want to leave. I think I can show more about my characters by adding in details about the ways they touch one another. Here's that part of my story."

> *"Angel, I'm going to see you in just a few hours," Kassy's mom said.*
>
> *"I can't do it," Kassy said. "I can't."*
>
> *"Yes you can, sweetheart. You need to. And I need to go to work. But remember, I'm always with you." She leaned over and gave Kassy a hug. Then Kassy turned, pushed open the passenger door, and pulled herself out of the car.*

"Before I add in details about the physical contact between Kassy and her mom, I need to think about what kind of people they are and what their relationship is like. I know Kassy is pretty timid and shy; she's also very kind. So is her mom; her mom is really nurturing and loving. They have a good relationship; Kassy relies on her mom a lot and her mom does what she can to protect her and help her feel better. Her mom feels terrible when she can't help Kassy.

"So now I want to think about how I can show some of those things through the physical contact between Kassy and her mom. Let me reread this scene, noticing when they interact and thinking about how people like them, in a relationship like theirs, might touch one another: *'Angel, I'm going to see you in just a few hours,' Kassy's mom said. 'I can't do it,' Kassy said.* OK, so right there my characters are interacting, but only with their words, so far. If Kassy is timid and the mom is loving, and Kassy really depends on her mother, how might they touch each other in this moment? I'm thinking about times when I feel timid but I'm with someone I really trust, and usually I reach for their hand, or lean into them. Also, when I'm nurturing someone who is sad, like Kassy's mom is doing, I do things like rub their back or hair with my palm or brush away their tears with my hand. Let me see whether I can have Kassy and her mom do some of those things. . . . Yes, I think that when the mom says, 'I'll see you in a few hours,' she could reach across to Kassy and stroke her hair with her palm. Then maybe Kassy could respond by leaning into her mom, maybe even squeezing her mom's arm. So let me add those details in.

> *"Angel, I'm going to see you in just a few hours," Kassy's mom said, reaching out to brush Kassy's hair with her palm.*
>
> *Kassy leaned in and rested her head on her mother's chest. "I can't do it," Kassy said. "I can't." She wrapped her fingers around her mom's arm, never wanting to let go.*

"Let me reread that and see whether it shows more about my characters and their relationship. . . . I really think those details about their physical contact make my story better because without ever telling my readers about my characters, they can see what they and their relationship is like. When Kassy's mom brushes Kassy's hair and Kassy leans into her mom, can't you tell right away that they have a loving relationship? Doesn't it also show that they are kind and affectionate?

"Did you notice how I imagined what kind of contact my characters might have by thinking about how I, or people I know with a similar personality as my characters, would act in a similar situation—like when I thought about how I touch people when I feel timid like Kassy, or when I'm taking care of someone who is sad?"

Active Engagement

Tell

"I want you to try this now before you go back to your seats. I'm going to show you another scene in my story where Kassy is on the playground and the other girls are being mean to her. I want you and your partner to figure out what I could add about the characters' physical interactions."

Coach

"Remember, the first thing we need to think about when we do this work is what kind of people the characters are and what their relationship is like. You already know about Kassy; you also know that Wendy is bossy and often very mean to Kassy, so they don't have a very steady or kind relationship. I'm going to read my scene, and then I'm going to give you two minutes to revise it with your partner."

> *Wendy got in line behind Kassy and followed her outside to the playground. "Should I turn around and say something to her?" Kassy wondered. "Maybe if I act like we're friends and everything is fine, she'll be nice to me today."*
>
> *But as soon as Kassy thought this, she heard Wendy say, "You walk funny!" Kassy held her breath and bit the inside of her cheek. "Hey Laura, doesn't Kassy walk funny?!" Wendy continued. Out of the corner of her eye, Kassy could see Laura in the line next to her; she could see Laura turning towards her and laughing.*
>
> *"She does walk funny! And look how her hair bounces up and down like an elephant with every step!"*

"Talk to your partners now and decide what details I can add; I can add information about the physical contact between Wendy and Kassy, Laura and Kassy, and/or Wendy and Laura."

As students worked, I knelt beside them to listen to their conversations and lift the level of their writing. Some students said things like, "When Laura says, 'And look how her hair bounces like an elephant,' we could add in, *Wendy reached her palm to Laura and slapped her five.*" And, when

Wendy says, 'You walk funny,' we could add, *she said, while poking Kassy in the back with her finger.*"

When students struggled, I said things like:

- "Point to a place where the characters are interacting, either with their words or their actions, and tell me how they feel in that moment. How do people touch one another when they feel like that?"
- "Imagine being in a situation like this; imagine a time [when you were mean to someone, or were watching someone be mean]. How did, or how might you or the other person physically interact with others in that situation?"

After the minilesson, Rebecca returned to her story about a boy who plays baseball, but not very well, and so is tormented by some of his team members. When he asks his brother to help him practice, his brother is not very supportive, either. Luckily, someone new joins the team and the two boys become friends.

One way that Rebecca revised her story was by finding places where she could reveal more about the characters through their physical interactions. Figure 4–1 shows excerpts from her original draft. Figure 4–2 shows her revisions, the additions she made using the strategy from the lesson.

Rebecca does more than simply reveal physical contact between characters; she reveals character's thoughts about that contact. Doing so gives us additional insight into the characters and how they are impacted by their interactions. But even if Rebecca did nothing more than add details about their physical contact, she would paint a fuller picture for readers of who these people are and what their relationships are like. Take the instance when, "for a split second [John and the narrator's] shoulders touched." Rebecca invites her readers into a deeply intimate moment that reveals a longing on the part of the narrator, as well as a flicker of hope for all of us who know what it is like to gently brush someone's fingers or arm and hope that they are making as much of the moment as we are. Similarly, when Mike nudges the narrator in his "lower back, right where it hurts the most," and then at the end of the story, brushes his brother's "cheek with 3 fingers [and] a sorry look in his eyes," we learn a lot: that Mike can be a typical bully of an older sibling, but that he also loves his brother and has the capacity to show it with tenderness; that the narrator is a sensitive young man who is hurt by his brother's cruelty but also accepting of his kindness and willing to forgive.

"Hey Mike, will you play catch with me?", I started to say, "becau-"
"NO! Now stop it! Stop interuptinig me! I am trying to read!", Mike yelled and (4) turned back to his book.

"Hello coach! Can I pl-" I started to say. (1) "Hello Tony. Why don't you play catch on the wall until somebody else comes", said the coach.

"John, why don't you try first base, MAX you go to shortstop, and Tony, you go to left field," the coach said. I ran over to get my (2) glove and started off to left field.

"Can I go over to John's house?", I asked Mike when I got there, "please? Can I?"
"Um, ah, O.K. Fine. But remember to call before you leave," Mike said. (3)
"wait, where do you live?", asked Mike, and he turned to John.

Figure 4–1 *Excerpts from Rebecca's original draft*

"Hey Mike, will you play catch with me?" I started to say, "becau—"

"No! Now stop it! Stop interrupting me! I am trying to read!" Mike yelled and waved his hands in the air. Then he took his hand and nudged my lower back, right where it hurts the most. He nudged me again and I realized he was trying to shoo and push me away. . . .

"Hello coach! Can I pl—" I started to say.

"Hello Tony, why don't you go play catch on the wall until somebody else comes?" said the coach as he slowly reached out his hand. It looked as if it had froze in that position, but then it started to move again. He landed gently and lightly on my shoulder and I felt like it didn't matter that I was bad at baseball because my coach trusted me and believed in me. . . .

"John, why don't you try first base, Max you go to shortstop, and Tony, you go to left field," the coach said. I ran over to get my mitt. As I left, John walked by. For a split second our shoulders touched, but it seemed like hours. I looked into his eyes and thought I saw a flicker of friendship in his eyes but then he moved, and I moved, and it was done, gone. I was in left field and he was at first base, but that moment was still with me, and maybe him too. . . .

"Can I go over to John's house?" I asked Mike when I got there. "Please? Can I?"

"Um, ah, O.K. Fine. But remember to call before you leave," Mike said and then brushed my cheek with 3 fingers. He had a sorry look in his eyes. . . .

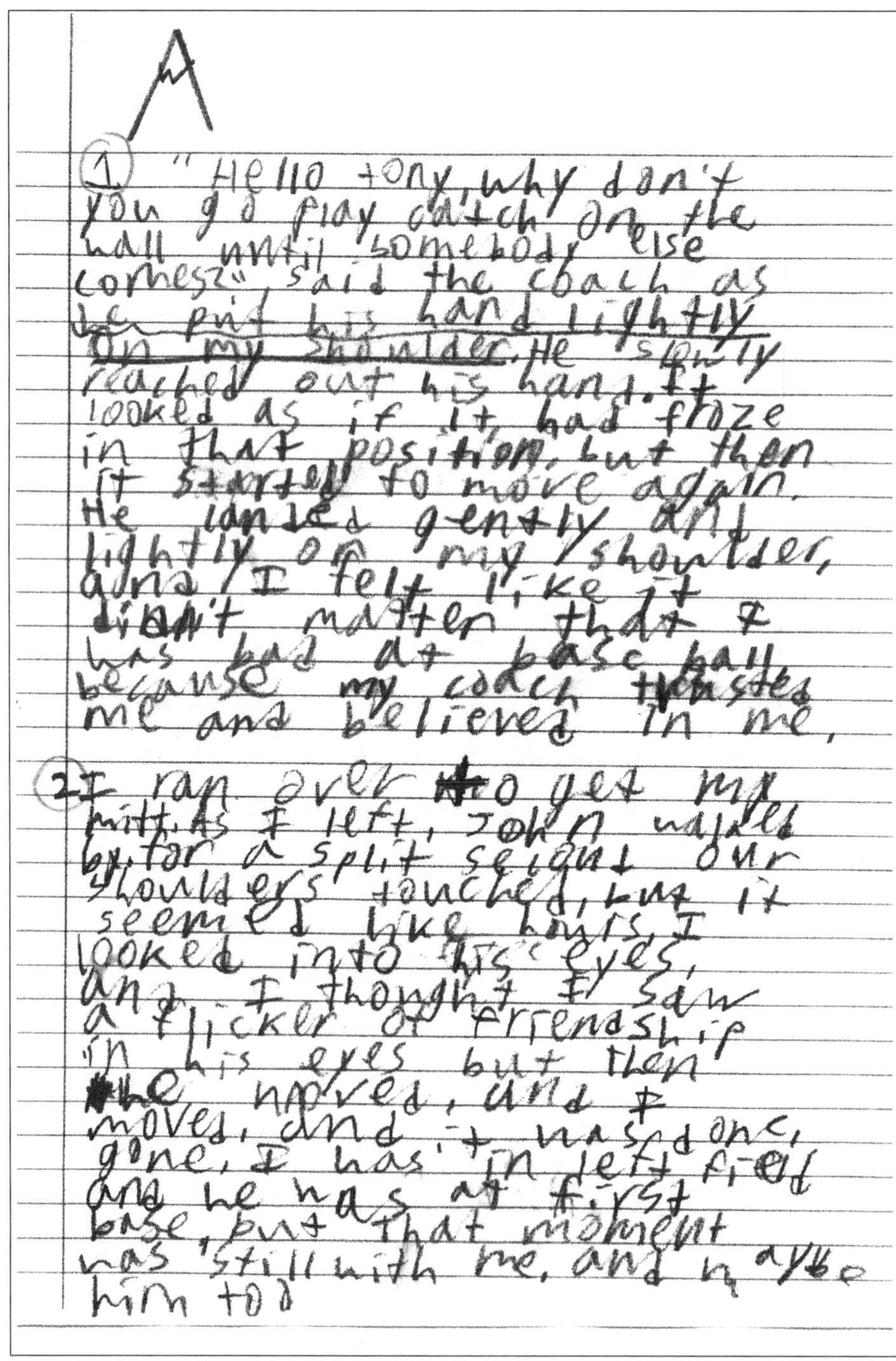

A

1 "Hello tony, why don't you go play catch on the wall until somebody else comes?" said the coach as he put his hand lightly on my shoulder. He slowly reached out his hand. It looked as if it had froze in that position, but then it started to move again. He landed gently and lightly on my shoulder, and I felt like it didn't matter that I was bad at base ball because my coach trusts me and believes in me.

2 I ran over to get my mitt. As I left, John walked by. For a split second our shoulders touched, but it seemed like hours. I looked into his eyes and I thought I saw a flicker of friendship in his eyes but then he moved, and I moved, and it was done, gone. I was in left field and he was at first base, but that moment was still with me, and maybe him too

Figure 4–2 *Rebecca's revisions: adding in physical contact between characters to show personalities and relationships*

Show Facial Expressions and Body Movements: *One way writers show instead of tell about our characters is by describing their facial expressions and body movements.*

The narrator should not always have to tell us how the characters in our stories feel. Continually writing *she was sad* or *he was frustrated* is similar

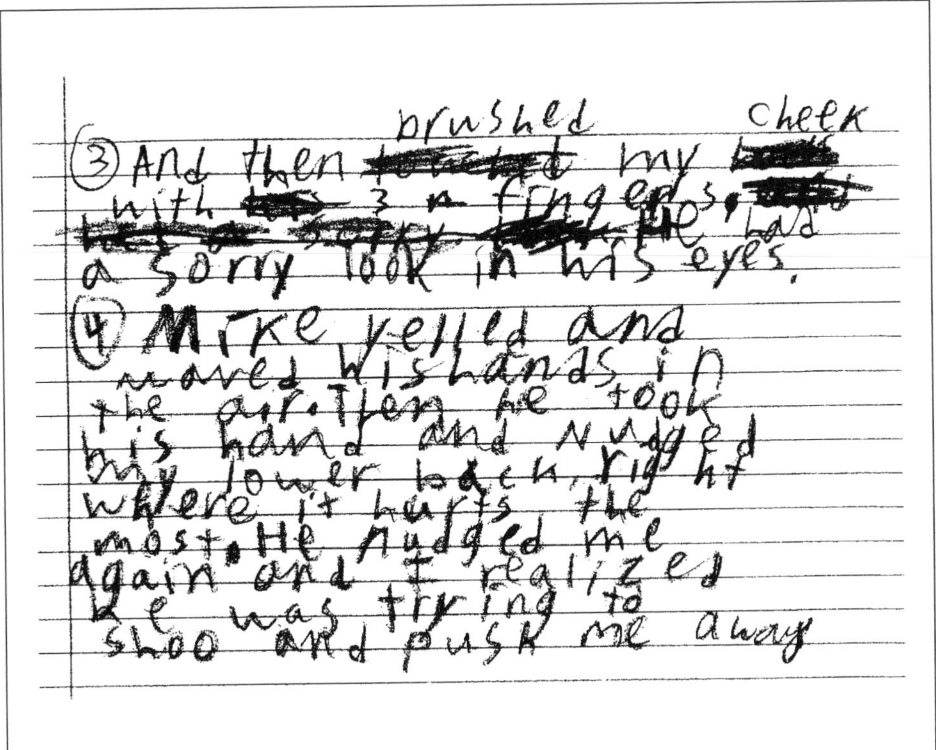

③ And then brushed my cheek with 3 fingers, he had a sorry look in his eyes.

④ Mike yelled and waved wis hands in the air. Then he took his hand and Nugged my lower back, right where it hurts the most. He nudged me again and I realizes he was trying to shoo and push me away

Figure 4–2 *(continued)*

to writing a literal retelling of events. Just as we react to events in different ways, we experience, express, and respond to emotions in different ways. For example, I rent bad romantic comedies and curl up on the couch when I am sad, even when the sun is shining; someone else responds to sadness by going to the gym or getting her hair done. Knowing a character is sad or frustrated does not necessarily give us much insight into who he or she is.

When I read, I want to see my characters, so I can know who they are, and so I can experience what they experience. When authors show me how their characters feel, characters come off the page, or I enter the page, allowing my world to temporarily merge with the world of the story.

Teaching

Tell

When I conferred with fifth-grader Sala, I said, "Writers often show instead of tell how characters feel so readers can experience them as living, breathing people. One way to do this is to show characters' facial expressions and body movements, making sure, of course, that they reflect how the characters are feeling."

Show

"For example, I want to show you what another student, Shawn, did. He wrote a story about this boy Caleb who gets into a big fight with his dad and feels really angry. Shawn could have written something like, *Caleb was really angry at his dad,* and nothing more. But if he wrote that and only that, you probably wouldn't really be able to see Caleb or experience for yourself how he feels in the story. You might see a boy yelling or you might see someone stomping around, but you wouldn't really know what a mad Caleb looks like or does. If Shawn simply told his readers how Caleb feels, his character wouldn't come off the page and feel like a real person.

"Look what Shawn does instead; he writes, *Caleb's eyes popped open and his nostrils flared. He clenched his teeth until his jaw tensed and felt his face turn red.* And a little later, he writes, *He stomped the ground with his right foot and got ready to explode.* Can't you really see Caleb now? Because Shawn includes facial expressions and body expressions to show how his character feels, it's almost like he's right here in the room with us, isn't it?

Active Engagement

Tell

"Can you try that now with your writing? Think about how your characters feel, and instead of writing, *she was mad* or *she is upset,* show it by showing the character's facial expressions and body movements. That way your readers can experience your characters as living, breathing people."

Coach

I coached Sala by saying things like:

- "How is your character feeling in this part? Jump up and show me what you look like when you feel that way?"
- "Think of a time when you felt what your character feels. Close your eyes and really be in that moment. Nod your head when you feel and see yourself there. Now describe what you're doing with your face and body."
- "Look at your character's face and describe what it does when he feels like this. Now scan the rest of his body from head to toe, look from his chest to his hands and fingers to his stomach and legs and feet, and describe every little thing you see."

Once Sala described her character's facial expressions and body movements, I asked her to point to where in her story she would add some of those details. Following our conference, she revised one part of her piece (see Figure 4–3).

Sala now shows her readers that the character in the story is devastated by her friend's move. She also shows that while some people may suppress their feelings, or look on the bright side of hard situations, this character, though somewhat reluctantly (*I tried to hold my tears back*) lets out her sadness. This character cries and trembles. By showing us her characters' facial expressions and body movements, Sala brings her character to life so we can experience her as a real person with real feelings.

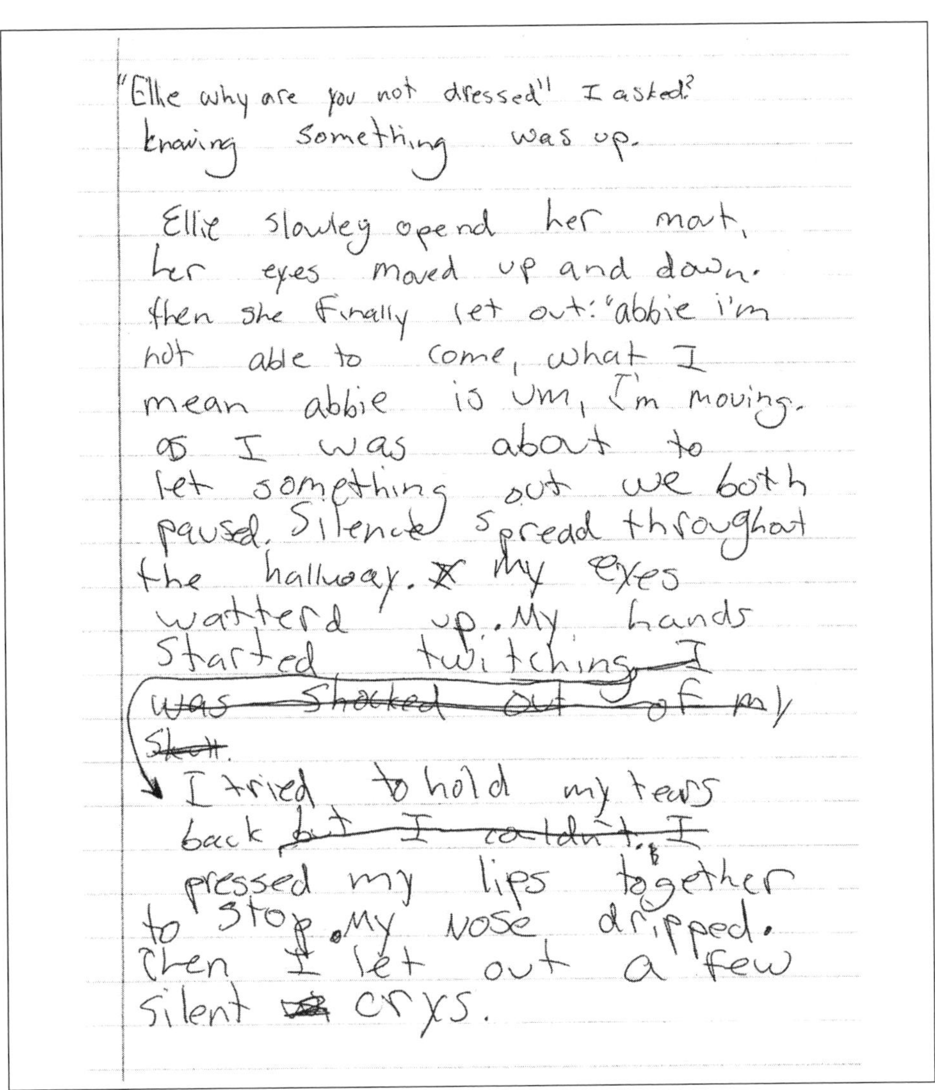

"Ellie why are you not dressed" I asked? knowing something was up.

Ellie slowley opend her mouth, her eyes moved up and down. then she finally let out: "abbie i'm not able to come, what I mean abbie is um, I'm moving. as I was about to let something out we both paused. Silence spredd throughout the hallway. My eyes watterd up. My hands started twitching, ~~I was shocked out of my skin.~~ I tried to hold my tears back ~~but I couldn't.~~ I pressed my lips together to stop. My nose dripped. Then I let out a few silent crys.

Figure 4–3 *Sala's revisions: using facial expressions and body movements to show character emotion*

Show Broken-Apart Actions: *One way writers show instead of tell about our characters is by breaking apart their most important actions into a series of smaller actions.*

Kathleen Tolan often teaches students to act out important scenes in the books they read; when she knows students are struggling to make sense of what they are reading, she teaches them that readers enter the world of the story by envisioning. "Let's try it," she'll say, after modeling how she envisions when she reads. "Stand up! I'm going to reread this part, and as I do, you are going to act out exactly what your characters are doing. Ready?" As Kathleen reads, she watches as the students before her take on the actions of the characters in a scene. "Can you see this part now?" she asks. "Can you see what the characters are doing and how they're talking? Now do you understand what's happening and why this moment is so important?"

From teachers like Kathleen, I have learned that when readers cannot envision the critical things characters do, we cannot truly know who those characters are or why their actions matter. Accordingly, when our students write, we need to teach them how to show the important events unfolding in their characters' lives. Breaking apart significant actions into a series of smaller actions is one way to do this.

Teaching

Tell

When I gathered a small group of fifth graders who were rushing through major events by telling their readers what happened, I said, "One way you can show how your characters are impacted by the events in their lives is by taking the really important things they do and breaking these big actions into a series of smaller actions. Because this will allow your readers to experience things alongside your characters, it will also help your readers get to know your characters and understand the significance of their experiences."

Show

"For example, let me show you these pages from *Whistling* where the narrator keeps trying to whistle. Elizabeth Partridge could have just told us what the narrator is doing; she could have written, *I try to whistle but can't and I try again.* But look what she writes instead: *I take in a breath . . . let it out, all in a whoosh . . . I gulp in more air . . . make my lips a tight circle . . . my breath blows away on the wind . . . I take in another breath . . .*"

"Do you see how Partridge shows her character trying to whistle by breaking his action into a series of smaller actions? First he inhales. Then he whooshes out his breath. Then he gulps in more air. He tightens his lips. He blows away wind instead of a whistle. Each of those actions is about the boy trying to whistle. Partridge's whole story is about the boy wanting to whistle like his dad taught him, so it's obviously a really important action, which is why she decides to show it.

"I want you to notice how much more we know the character simply because Partridge breaks that action into a series of smaller actions. If she had written, *I tried to whistle but couldn't,* we probably wouldn't think twice about this action. But by *showing* it, she also shows how hard the boy is working; as a result, we really want him to succeed and can imagine his frustration and disappointment when he doesn't. He feels so much more real to us than he would if Partridge simply told us what he does."

Active Engagement

Tell

"Would you all try this now? Read over your drafts and look for the really important things your characters do. Then try to show these actions, rather than quickly telling them, by breaking them apart into a series of smaller actions. This way, your readers will be able to experience these actions alongside your characters and better understand how your characters are impacted by them."

Coach

As I worked with the writers, I helped them with the strategy by saying things like:

- "Get a picture in your head. Now move *really slowly* in that picture. What *exactly* do you see people doing?"
- "Stand up. I want you to act out this action. . . . Now name every little thing you're doing with your body."
- "Instead of writing the action in one sentence, tell me how you could write it in two or three or four sentences. First . . . then . . . next. . . .

Donyelle wrote a story about riding on a boat with her family and realizing that when the tour guide dropped the anchor, he expected everyone to swim ashore. In the middle of her first draft, she moves on to her conclusion (see Figure 4–4).

When I read Donyelle's story, I did get a very general sense of the narrator and of the significance of this event in her life. Because she writes things like, *Although I wasn't sure I jumped in and tried to swim* and *I was so tired but I kept on going,* I can infer that Donyelle was both uncertain about swimming to shore and brave because she did it anyway. And yet, because Donyelle simply tells her readers these things—because she simply

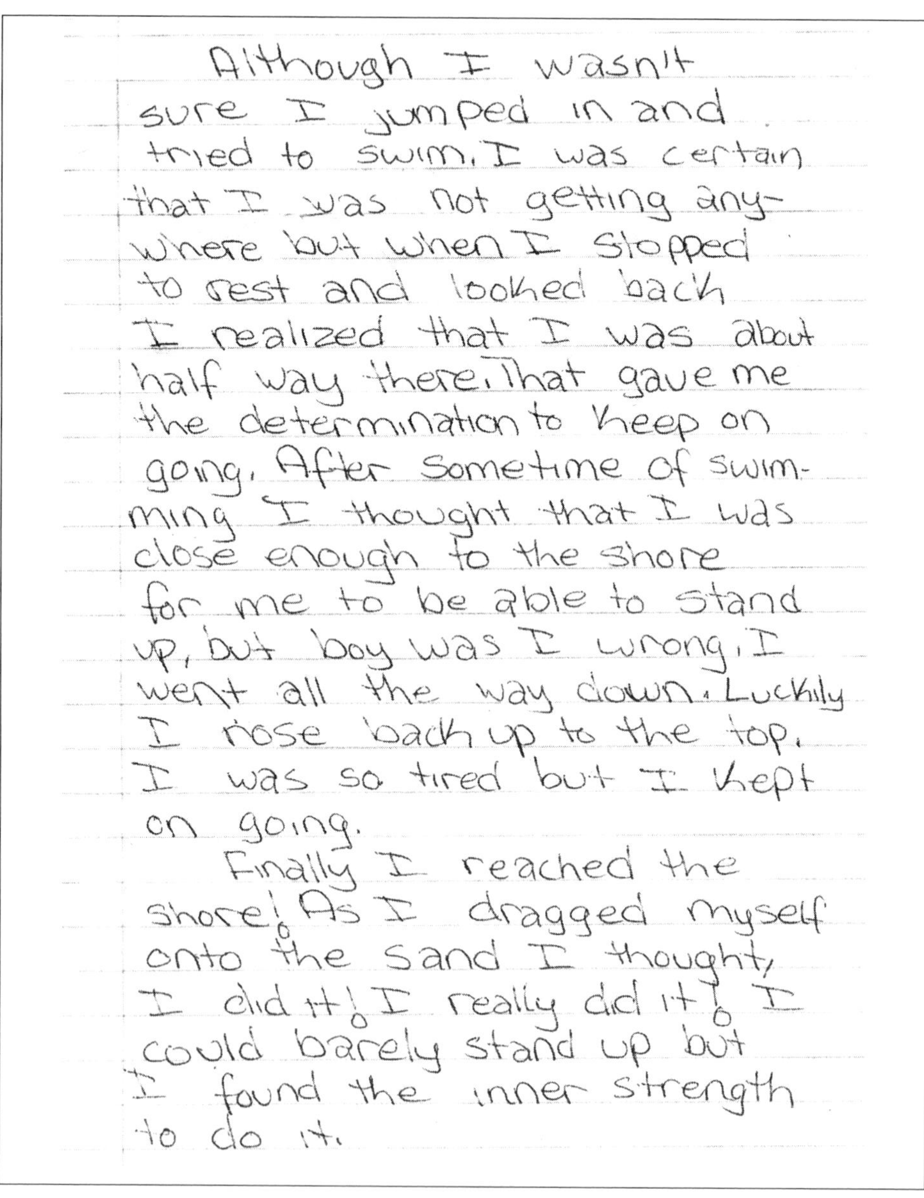

Although I wasn't
sure I jumped in and
tried to swim. I was certain
that I was not getting anywhere but when I stopped
to rest and looked back
I realized that I was about
half way there. That gave me
the determination to keep on
going. After sometime of swimming I thought that I was
close enough to the shore
for me to be able to stand
up, but boy was I wrong. I
went all the way down. Luckily
I rose back up to the top.
I was so tired but I kept
on going.

Finally I reached the
shore! As I dragged myself
onto the sand I thought,
I did it! I really did it! I
could barely stand up but
I found the inner strength
to do it.

Figure 4–4 *Scene from Donyelle's initial draft*

tells us that she tried to swim, that she felt like she wasn't getting anywhere but kept on going—my understanding of the narrator and of the event feels somewhat shallow. If the purpose for writing this story is to show her readers how the moment of swimming to shore impacted her, then I want to see her swimming so I can feel the impact.

Using what she learned in the strategy lesson, Donyelle rewrote this critical scene (see Figure 4–5). Whereas Donyelle once wrote, simply, that she tried to swim and kept on swimming, she now shows her swimming. Because she writes things like, *I drifted down . . . My arms paved a path for me . . . Soon a wave washed over me and I gasped for air,* I can see her in action and experience for myself the significance of the event. Doing so, I get to know the narrator much more intimately; I am no longer told that she is determined, for example, but instead I witness that determination for myself when she kicks and swallows water and pushes forward. By breaking important actions into a series of smaller actions, Donyelle allows her readers to form deeper connections with her characters, thereby arousing compassion and empathy and insight.

Move Between Dialogue, Action, and Inner Thinking: *One way writers show instead of tell about characters is by moving between dialogue, action, and inner thinking.*

Because the same words and the same actions can mean very different things, one way to show readers what we want them to know is by combining words (spoken and/or thought) with actions in order to paint a fuller picture. Imagine, for example, the difference between these two scenes: In one, the teacher stands at the front of the room, one hand on her hips and the other waving furiously at the end of her arm while she screams, "It's time to put your notebooks away and give me your attention!!!" In the other scene, the teacher stands at the front of the room with her arms at her side and a smile on her face, while calmly stating, "It's time to put your notebooks away and give me your attention." Though the words are the same, what each speaker is doing changes completely the meaning and tone of the moment. We can imagine endless scenarios in which the action is the same, but what is said or what is thought is utterly different, and so the meaning and tone are utterly different, as well.

If we agree with Murray that showing instead of telling is about allowing readers to draw their own conclusions, then there are times when we need to give readers as much information as we can to support them with that undertaking. Once students are independently and consistently

"Here I go!" I said to myself. I jumped in the water and suddenly drifted down. When I got back to the top of the water I was in shock. I didn't expect my impact to bring me underneath the water so intensly.

Despite my "surprise" I kept on paddling. I kicked my feet as hard as I could despratley striving for the shore. My arms paved a path for me to swim through. Soon a wave whased over me and I gasped for air. I spat all the water out and used my arms to support me.

When I got tired I stopped to look how far I was from the shore. I have a long way to go still, I thought to myself remembering the conversation I had earlier "About 33 yards".

I can't let myself down, I thought. That gave me the determination to keep on going. I got tired for the second time, but I kept on going knowing that I would someday be proud of myself for it.

Finally, after what seemed like forever, I dragged myself up onto the shore. As I stood

Figure 4–5 *Donyelle's revised scene: breaking apart important actions to show their impact*

using dialogue or inner thinking when they write, we can teach them that one way to convey more information is to weave throughout their most important scenes dialogue, action, and/or inner thinking.

Teaching

Tell

In a minilesson for his third graders, Mark Greller said, "Writers often move back and forth between dialogue, action, and inner thinking. Making characters talk and act lets readers watch them, and making characters think lets readers see inside them. When we do all these things together, our readers really get to know our characters and what they think and feel about what is happening in a story."

Show

"Let me show you what I mean. Here's one part of a story that your classmate Ashley wrote. As I read it to you, I want you to notice how she moves back and forth between her characters' words, actions and thoughts and how that shows us more information about the characters."

> *"Why did I want to get my ears pierced," I thought to myself. I grasped my mommy's hand and said, "Mommy it hurts so much."*
>
> *"I know it hurts but only for a second," my mommy said. Then she squeezed my hand.*
>
> *"You're right," I said.*
>
> *"I know how it feels I got my ears pierced when I was a kid," my mommy said.*
>
> *Then I knew if mommy could do it then so could I.*
>
> *So I sat up nice and tall and crossed my hands in my lap and waited for the lady to pierce my other ear. The needle got closer and closer and I held my breath tight. The lady put the needle in my other ear.*
>
> *"Ouch," I said.*
>
> *Then I remembered what my mommy said it only hurts for a second.*

"Ashley could have simply told us about the characters and events in this scene. She could have written something like: *I was nervous about getting my ears pierced. My mommy told me it would be okay. It hurt when the lady pierced my ear.* But if she did that, we wouldn't be able to see and experience the characters for ourselves.

"Ashley also could have written the whole story with just dialogue between the characters, but again, if she never showed us what the characters did or thought we might miss something important about them. Notice how Ashley often follows what a character says with what a character does, and notice how that shows us so much more about the characters, like when she writes, *'I know it hurts but only for a second,' my mommy said. Then she squeezed my hand.* The fact that the mom squeezes her daughter's hand shows us that the mom isn't saying those things in an impatient voice; it's not like she's saying, 'Ugh! Get over it. It only hurts for a second!' Because Ashley weaves together words and actions, we know the mom says those words in a loving, supportive voice; it's like she's saying, 'It's going to be OK, sweetheart. It only hurts for a second and I'll be right here with you the whole time.'"

Active Engagement

Tell

"Before you go back to your seats, I want you to try this. Let's start a story about when we went to the park and played baseball. I want you and your partner to use action, dialogue, and inner thinking to show readers about the characters in the story—to show what we did and how we felt about what was happening. Our first sentence could be: *Mr. Greller threw the ball across the field.* Tell the next sentence to your partner. Is it going to be action, dialogue, or inner thinking?"

Coach

As Mark circulated the meeting area, he coached into students' work by saying things like:

- "When your character says that, what is she doing? Get a picture in your mind of her facial expressions or body movements and describe exactly what you see."
- "When your character hears that, how does she feel? What thought runs through her mind that will show how she feels?"
- "I want you to slow down what your character is doing so I can see it; instead of summarizing that action in one sentence, can you show it over three or four sentences?"

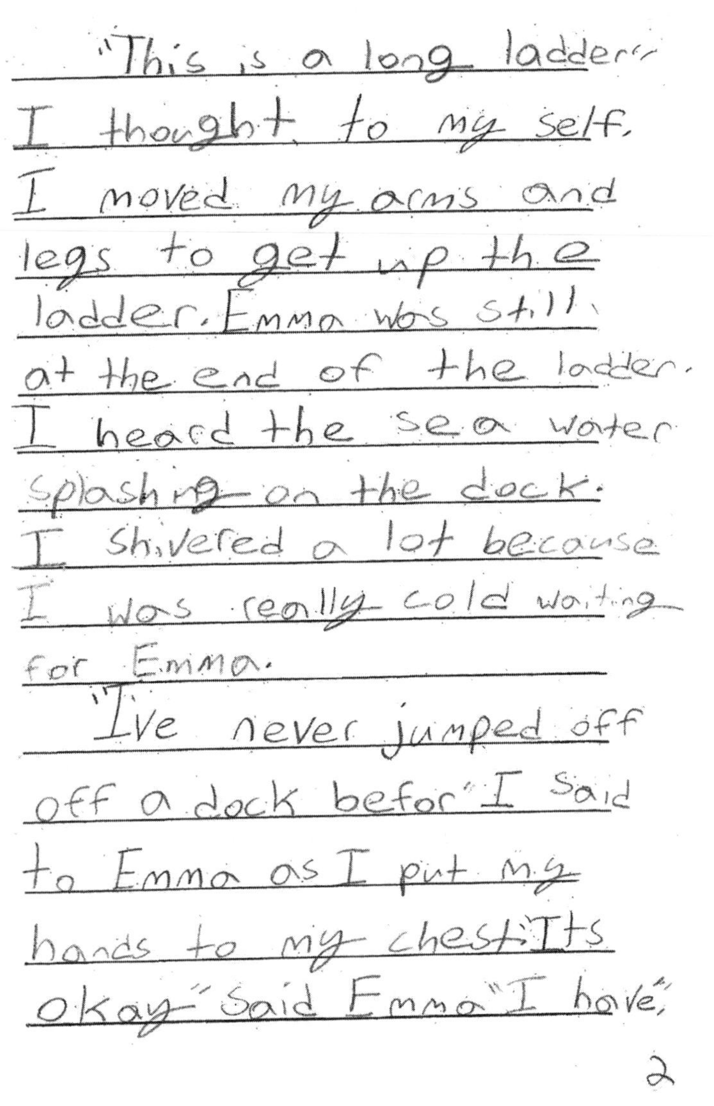

"This is a long ladder" I thought to my self. I moved my arms and legs to get up the ladder. Emma was still at the end of the ladder. I heard the sea water splashing on the dock. I shivered a lot because I was really cold waiting for Emma.

"Ive never jumped off off a dock befor" I said to Emma as I put my hands to my chest. "Its okay" Said Emma "I have,"

2

Figure 4–6 *Excerpt from Julia's draft: weaving together action, dialogue and inner thinking to show character and events*

- "Back up for a minute. Before you jump to the next thing that happens, I want you to show me this important action. Close your eyes and get a picture of what your character is doing. Now, describe all the little things you see her doing. Scan her body, describe every detail."

Following Mark's minilesson, several of his students began to develop their characters by showing their words, actions, and thoughts. The middle of Julia's story can be seen in Figure 4–6. Julia could have told her readers about the narrator and events in this scene by writing something like, *I*

"I dont know if I want
to do this?" I thought
to my self. "IS it scary"
I asked? as I put my
feet together. I didn't think
I really wanted to do
this. "No" Said Emma. "Good"
I Said. I was really nervous
but some how I was really
excited. "It looks really deep"
I thought to my Self.
"I've never done this befor
but Emma has because
she lives here. "IS the
water cold when you jump
in" I asked? "Not really" said
Emma.

3

Figure 4–6 *(continued)*

climbed the ladder to the dock. I wanted to jump in the water but I was afraid. Instead, Julia writes things like: *"I've never jumped off a dock before," I said to Emma as I put my hands to my chest. . . . "I don't know if I want to do this," I thought to myself. "Is it scary?" I asked as I put my feet together.* By weaving together thoughts, words, and actions, Julia shows us what the narrator is doing and how she feels about it; she allows us to draw our own conclusions about the people in her story and how they respond to and are impacted by events.

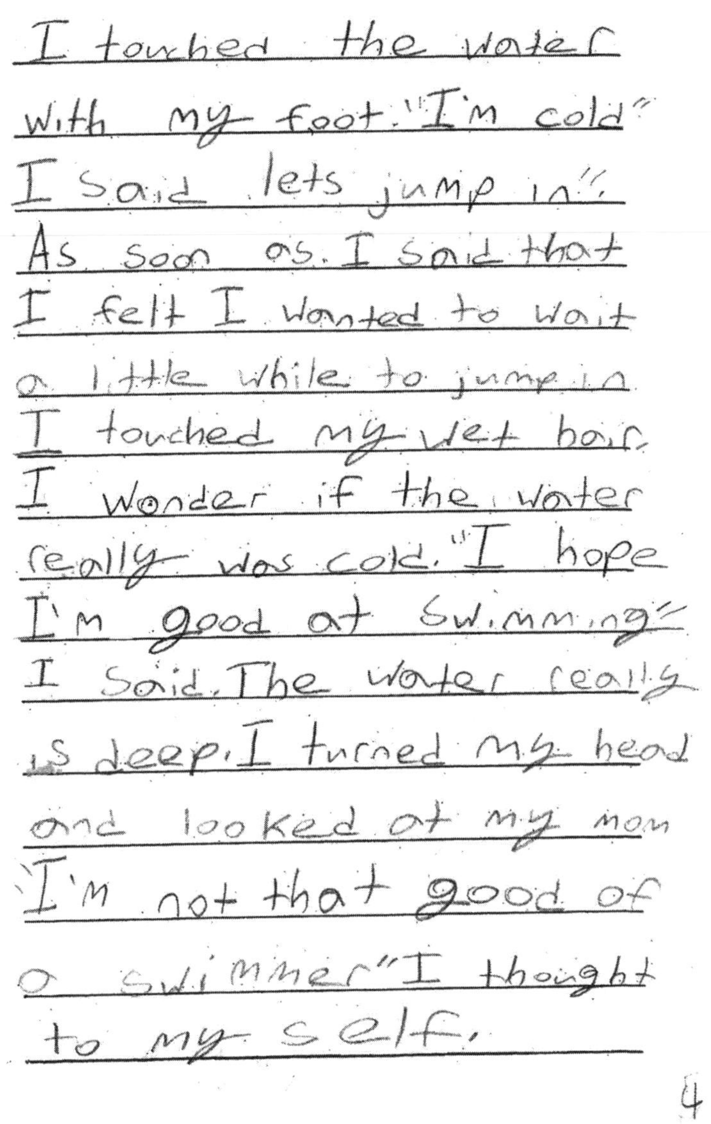
I touched the water
with my foot. "I'm cold"
I said lets jump in".
As soon as I said that
I felt I wanted to wait
a little while to jump in
I touched my wet hair.
I wonder if the water
really was cold. "I hope
I'm good at swimming"
I said. The water really
is deep. I turned my head
and looked at my mom
"I'm not that good of
a swimmer" I thought
to my self.
4

Figure 4–6 *(continued)*

* * *

When we first teach students to show instead of tell about their characters, they will approximate this skill by sprinkling snippets of details throughout their pieces: some dialogue here, a few sentences of action over there. Their writing will be better, but our work as teachers and their work as learners will not be complete until they can truly write their characters into existence. Writing with detail becomes "showing not telling" once writers become adept at transforming the written page into real-time events unfurling in the lives of living, breathing people. We will know that our students have learned how to show instead of tell about their characters when reading their stories feels less like reading a story and more like watching people move around before our very eyes—when suddenly, our lives begin to merge with those of the characters so that we find ourselves thinking and feeling about them much the same way we think and feel about the people with whom we interact every day.

CHAPTER 5

Revealing the Setting

Our actions do not exist in a vacuum but in a particular time and place. As such, our environments add a level of meaning to our daily lives. Think, for example, of all the things you would do in certain places but not others, or of the things you would do in one kind of weather but not another. Imagine fighting with a spouse, walking around in your pajamas, or barefoot: These are ordinary actions when they occur at home, but when they are moved into a public realm, we begin to have dramatic perceptions of people. In the first case we might wonder about marital instability; in the latter, we might infer mental instability.

Knowing the importance of setting in our own lives, it makes sense that when our students write stories, it is not enough for them to simply show us what their characters are doing. They must also show us the environments in which their characters are doing these things so we can make sense of what their actions really mean and of how we are meant to feel about what is happening. If, when you read your students' writing, you cannot envision the context in which characters are moving through events, you might teach the following strategies to give your writers a repertoire of ways to develop setting.

Use Sensory Details: *One way writers reveal the setting is by including sensory details.*

One way we experience the world around us is through our senses. Though we may experience certain senses more or less than others, in any given moment, each of us knows what it is to see or smell or feel or hear or taste. Our senses help us to make sense of our surroundings and, in turn, to make sense of the moment. Sitting here at my desk, I hear large groups of teenagers talking and moving down the street and because I can see that it is middle-of-the-day light outside, I know that schools are just letting out and kids are making their ways home or to after school hangouts. When I look out my window, I see tiny yellow buds popping on the trees and I see a man on his stoop wearing a sweatshirt, no jacket; I know spring is somewhere close. My senses allow me to assess my environment and then make sense of what is happening in that environment. One way to show our readers where our stories take place, then, is to consider the significant details our characters see, hear, feel, taste, and smell.

Teaching

Tell

"Story writers show the setting of our stories so our readers can feel more inside each moment," Aliki Giakas said in a minilesson for her fifth graders. "One way to develop setting is to include important sensory information—information about what the characters see, hear, smell, taste, and/or feel that you want your readers to experience, as well."

Show

"Let me show you what I mean. I'm going to write a scene in which my character Abby gets into a fight with her friend because her friend is mean to the new kid. I think I'll start with Abby and her friend yelling at each other."

> *"I can't believe you said that to me!" Sam yelled.*
>
> *"I'm just being honest," Abby said. "I just don't think it was a very nice way to treat someone."*
>
> *Sam saw the new girl standing alone. "I guess," she said. "I guess I could've been nicer." Sam—*

"Wait, I realize I've written the whole first part of my scene and while I think my readers can figure out what's happening, I don't think they'll be able to get a very clear picture of *where* it's happening. I know that when we write stories, we want to help our readers enter the story and feel like they're right beside the characters, but it's really hard to enter a story when we don't know where we're going! I better back up and weave in information about setting.

"I'm going to try doing that with sensory information: '*I can't believe you said that to me,' Sam yelled.* OK, so now I'm thinking, What might my characters hear, smell, taste, feel, or see in this moment that would reveal the setting to my readers? I guess I need to get clear myself about where they are! I think they'll be at a school like this one, in the middle of a city—oh, so maybe they can hear sirens! And they're on the playground, so they could also hear other kids talking, yelling, running around. I'm going to add some of that in."

> *"I can't believe you said that to me," Sam yelled.*
>
> *Abby heard sirens screeching down the street from the school yard and she felt like screeching, too. "I'm just being honest," she said. She heard other fifth graders talking in groups nearby and wondered if they could hear them. Abby lowered her voice and said, "I just don't think it was a very nice way to treat someone."*

"So now my readers can see that my characters are on a school yard, and they can hear the noise of sirens and footsteps. What other sensory information might I include? Could my characters smell something? Maybe not on the playground. Maybe they could feel something? Like what . . . what do people feel on the playground? I'm imagining being on one and touching things, like the fence, which feels sharp, or the benches, which often feel cold when I sit on them. Oh, I like that, they could sit on a bench, let me add that in."

> *Sam felt the cold bench beneath her pants. She looked up and saw the new girl, standing all alone across the yard. "I guess," Sam said. "I guess I could've been nicer to her."*

"Now my readers can really envision where this scene takes place, can't they? Do you see how I develop the setting by imagining what my characters might see, hear, smell, taste, and/or feel, and that I weave those details throughout my scene instead of just clumping them all in one place? Do you also see how I am careful to include details that connect with the important feelings and ideas in my piece; for example, Abby hears sirens, not chirping birds, because she feels frustrated. And Sam feels a cold bench, not warmth, because she is uncomfortable in this moment.

Active Engagement

Tell

"Now I want you to try it. In this scene, my characters meet in the lunchroom and make up, but I don't have any information so far about their surroundings. I'm going to read the scene to you; then I want you and your partner to discuss what details I could add about what the characters see, feel, smell, taste, and/or hear, and figure out where I could add those details."

> *"I'm sorry," Abby said.*
>
> *"No, I'm sorry," Sam responded. "I was a jerk to that girl and I shouldn't have been. You were right to say something to me about it."*
>
> *"Still friends?"*
>
> *"Absolutely!"*

Coach

As Aliki listened to students' conversations, she coached into those who struggled with the strategy by saying things like:

- "You've been to this kind of place before. What kinds of things do you see and hear when you're there?"
- "Close your eyes. Imagine you're in this place. Nod your head when you see it. Now look around and tell me what you see. . . . Now tell me what you feel or smell. . . ."

When students responded with vague details, such as "It's loud" and "It smells bad," Aliki pushed her writers to be more specific.

- "What kinds of noises do you hear? Name them. What kinds of things do you smell? Name them."
- "Why is it loud? Why does it smell bad? Be very specific about what you hear, smell, and so on."

When students included details that did not match the mood of the piece, she said things like:

- "How do the characters feel in this scene? Keep using your senses to describe the setting, but this time, include details that reflect how the characters feel."
- "How would you feel if you [saw, heard, smelled, tasted, felt] that? Is that how the characters feel in this scene?"

When Aliki's class returned to their seats and to their own writing, Chistina wrote a scene in which her character returns to her childhood neighborhood. (See Figure 5–1)

Especially because the setting is so central to Chrisina's scene, she is careful to develop it fully by drawing from a repertoire of strategies, one of which is to use sensory detail. Christina includes information about what the narrator sees (broken swings and rusty monkey bars; a road with no more pebbles; a hole in the ground where there was once a pond), what the narrator feels (the cold metal gate; dust in her face), and what the narrator hears (the crash of the gate; howling wind). As a result, her readers are also able to see and feel and hear; we can envision exactly where the narrator is and, in turn, are impacted by the setting as if we, too, were returning to that now dilapidated park.

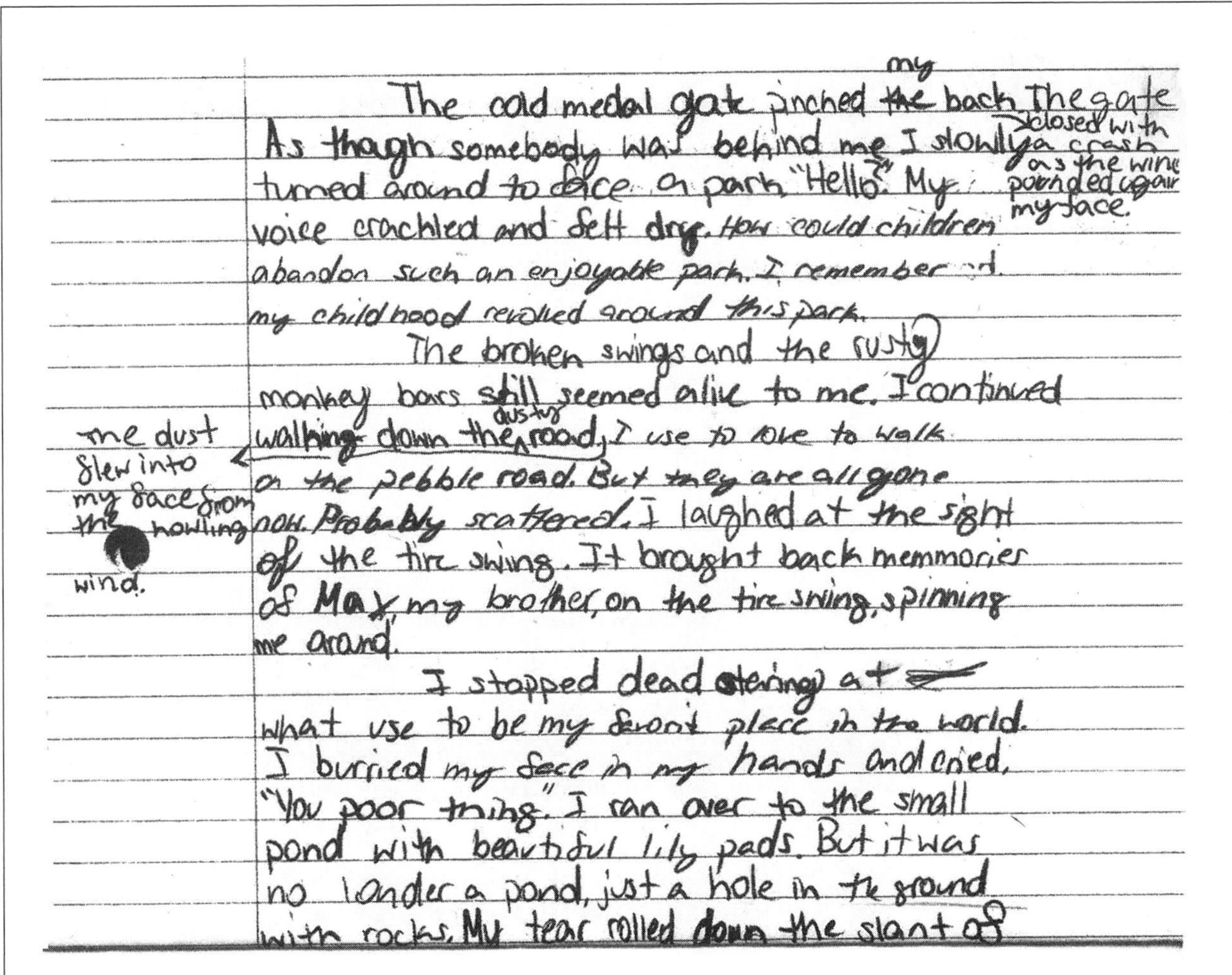

The cold medal gate pinched my back. The gate closed with a crash as the wind pounded agair my face.
As though somebody was behind me I slowly
turned around to face a park "Hello." My
voice crachled and felt dry. How could children
abandon such an enjoyable park. I remembered.
my childhood revolved around this park.

The broken swings and the rusty
monkey bars still seemed alive to me. I continued
walking down the dusty road, I use to love to walk
on the pebble road. But they are all gone
now. Probably scattered. I laughed at the sight
of the tire swing. It brought back memmories
of Max, my brother, on the tire swing, spinning
me around.

The dust flew into my face from the howling wind.

I stopped dead staring at
what use to be my favorit place in the world.
I burried my face in my hands and cried.
"You poor thing." I ran over to the small
pond with beautiful lily pads. But it was
no londer a pond, just a hole in the ground
with rocks. My tear rolled down the slant of

Figure 5–1 *Christina's notebook entry: using sensory detail to reveal setting*

Show Characters' Interactions with Surroundings: *One way writers reveal the setting is by having characters interact with their surroundings.*

In addition to observing our environments, we interact with our environments. I may know school is out because I see large groups of kids moving down the street and hear them yelling on corners. But I also know school is out when I get stuck behind one of those groups of young people and have to slow my pace as we all move down the street. I may know it is spring because I see trees blossoming, or perhaps it is because I step outside and shed my layers, carry my coat and sweater in my hands. Another way, then, to show our readers where our stories take place is to have our characters interact with their surroundings.

Teaching

Tell

In a conference with fifth grader Tara, I said, "Writers usually weave information about the setting all the way through a piece so our readers can imagine exactly where the characters are and lose themselves more easily in the story. One way to show the setting is to have the characters interact with their surroundings."

Show

"For example, on the first page of *Fireflies!,* Julie Brinkloe writes, *I looked up from dinner, through the open window to the backyard.* Right away, we get a sense of the setting because of what the character is doing; when the narrator looks through the open window, we know it must be somewhat warm out because the window is open. We also know he's in a house because there is a backyard, and of course we get a picture of a yard.

"Later in the story, Brinkloe writes, *I ran from the table, down to the cellar to find a jar. I knew where to look, behind the stairs.* And toward the end she writes, *I climbed the stairs to my room and set the jar on a table by my bed.* Again, because of the narrator's actions, we can see where he is: in a big house, for one, with several different floors. We can also see specific details about the setting, like a table in the narrator's bedroom.

"Do you see how Brinkloe weaves setting throughout her story by having her characters interact with it? Do you also notice how she has them interact with the setting in ways that reveal the general location (a big house with a yard in this case), but also specific details (like the table in the boy's room)?"

Active Engagement

Tell

"Can you look over your piece—start with just the first half of the page while I'm here—and find more places where you could add details about the setting by having your character interact with it just like Brinkloe does in her story?"

Coach

To support Tara, I said:

- "We know where your characters are, but now we want to see that place. Close your eyes and put yourself where your character is. Now look around in your mind and name everything you see. What might your character do with some of the things you're naming?"
- "What are the important things your characters do? How could you add onto those actions in a way that shows your characters interacting with their environment?"

When I followed up with Tara after our conference, she had successfully developed the setting throughout her piece; as shown in the first part of her story in Figure 5–2, one way Tara accomplishes this goal is by adding in details that show her character interacting with her surroundings.

Though Tara's last addition seems somewhat extraneous to the driving idea in her piece (reading that the cat *banged herself lightly on the clear glass window* does not contribute crucial information about the cat, the fish, or their relationship), most of her revisions do convey important details. For example, when Tara writes things like *her tail softly hit a small wooden table holding the lamp that lit its prey,* she does not simply develop the setting of her story; she develops parts of the setting that are integral to the plot: by allowing her readers to see the table and the lamp that lights the cat's prey, we get a much better sense of where the cat is in its mission, and the cat's mission is the whole point of the story.

Overall, Tara's revisions not only lift the quality of her piece, they also demonstrate that she is now smarter as a writer; she understands the importance of developing the setting in her stories, and she has at least one strategy for doing so.

Reflect to a Similar Setting: *One way writers reveal the setting is by having characters reflect to a similar environment.*

My longtime friend searched through my room. She was my cat, Vegas. Her eyes moved around warily. Looking at the white walls and the tall bookshelves, her eyes landed on my long desk. Her eyes continued to search, her pupils getting larger.

But something had changed.

Her paws seemed to sink into the green rug as she slowly padded across the floor. Then I realized that there was still time to save them. Vegas was only half way there. She walked faster and faster until she broke into a trot. She quickly swiveled around as her tail softly hit a small wooden table holding the lamp that lit her prey. You see, my cat hates all other animals. What would she think of the fish?

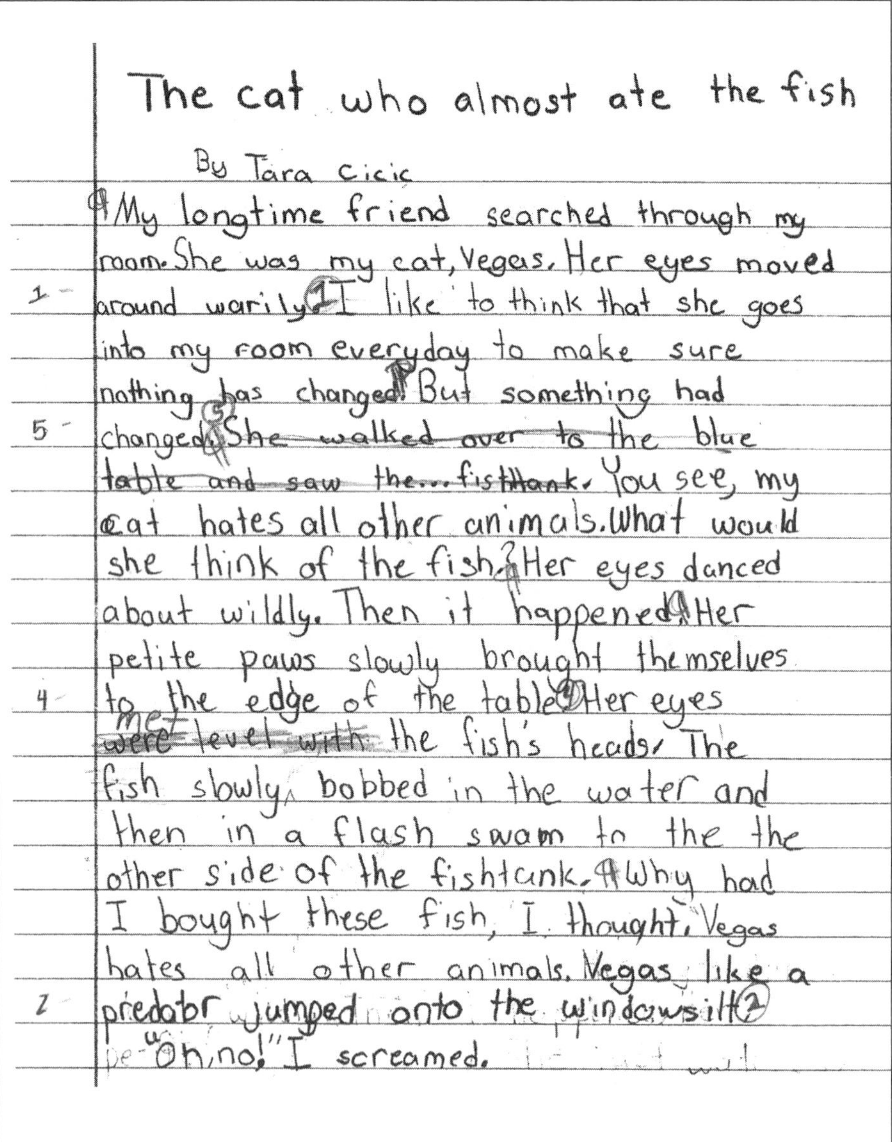

The cat who almost ate the fish

By Tara Cicic

¶My longtime friend searched through my
room. She was my cat, Vegas. Her eyes moved
1 around warily. ① I like to think that she goes
into my room everyday to make sure
nothing has changed. ¶ But something had
5 changed. ③ ~~She walked over to the blue
table and saw the... fishtank.~~ You see, my
cat hates all other animals. What would
she think of the fish? ¶ Her eyes danced
about wildly. Then it happened! ¶ Her
petite paws slowly brought themselves
4 to the edge of the table. ④ Her eyes
~~were level with~~ met the fish's heads. The
fish slowly bobbed in the water and
then in a flash swam to the the
other side of the fishtank. ¶ Why had
I bought these fish, I thought. Vegas
hates all other animals. Vegas, like a
2 predator jumped onto the windowsill ②
"Oh, no!" I screamed.

Figure 5–2 *Tara's revised draft: revealing setting through character interactions with the environment*

All of us make connections to make sense of things. When I read, I understand what characters are doing because I have done, or at least seen people doing, something similar. When I teach, I understand why my students struggle because I have struggled in similar ways, or because I have witnessed other students struggle. Making connections is a way of life, and so it should be a way of life for our characters, as well. Being strategic about the kinds of connections characters make can help us convey important information to readers about who our characters

1 looking at the white walls and the tall bookshelves her eyes landed on my long desk. Her eyes continued to search, her pupils getting larger.

2 eyes wide as she banged herself lightly on the clear glass window.

3 ~~Her bog she leaned on the soft, white, embroidered~~

4 After looking for the fish frantically, confused by the largeness of the tank

5 Her paws seemed to sink into the green rug as she slowly padded across the floor. Then I realized that there was still time to save ~~the~~ them. ~~she~~ Vegas was only half way there. She walked faster and faster until she broke into a trot. She quickly swiveled around as her ~~tale~~ tail softly hit a small wooden table holding the lamp ~~on what seemed to be it's back~~ - that lit her prey.

Figure 5–2 *(continued)*

Her eyes danced about wildly. Then it happened.

Her petite paws slowly brought themselves to the edge of the table. After looking for the fish frantically, confused by the largeness of the tank, her eyes met the fish's heads. The fish slowly bobbed in the water and then in a flash swam to the other side of the fish tank. Why had I bought these fish, I thought. Vegas hates all other animals. Vegas, like a predator, jumped onto the windowsill, eyes wide as she banged herself lightly on the clear glass window.

"Oh, no!" I screamed . . .

are, but also about *where* they are. Once your students are at least beginning to develop the setting in their stories, you might add to their repertoire of strategies by teaching them this more sophisticated way to reveal time and place.

Teaching

Tell

When I conferred with fifth-grader Emma, I said, "Another way writers reveal details about the setting is by having characters reflect in the moment to a similar environment. We might do this when a character goes somewhere similar to or even the same as where he or she has been before. It allows readers to understand how the character's experience of the place compares or contrasts to past experiences, but it also allows readers to better picture and thus enter the character's surroundings."

Show

"For example, I wrote this story about a little girl who is teased by her supposed friends. You see how in the beginning, I let readers know where the character is by writing: *Kassy walked across the playground to an empty bench, trying not to look at the group of girls playing hopscotch at the other end of the yard.*

"One way to give my readers even more information about the setting would be to have the narrator reflect to a similar time or place. I might write something like: *Kassy walked across the playground to an empty bench. The last time she sat here, Wendy sat next to her and we etched our names into the wood. This time, I ran my fingers over the words:* Wendy and Kassy are friends. *Kassy tried not to look at Wendy and the other girls playing hopscotch without her across the yard.* Or I could write: *Kassy walked across the playground to an empty bench and thought about how in the movies, there are always shiny swings and friends holding hands and yelling as they run around slides. Here, all she could see was concrete, broken-down seats and slides, and no friends.*

"Do you see how I reveal details about the setting by having the character reflect to a similar time or place? Do you see how the character can reflect to a time she was in that same place (like when I write about the last time I sat on that bench). Or the character can reflect to another place altogether (like when I write about how things are in the movies)? Do you also see how, when I compare the settings, I am careful to include small, specific details about where the character is (like when I write about the words carved into the bench, or the broken-down swing seats), and that by doing that, you're better able to enter my story?"

Active Engagement

Tell

"I want you to try this now with the story you're writing. See if you can reveal more details about the setting by having your characters reflect to a similar time and place. This is another way for your readers to get an even better sense of where your characters are and be there with them."

Coach

As Emma worked, I supported her by saying things like:

- "Remember you want to include more information about the setting, so when your character reflects, she should think about how the things she sees or hears or feels compares to that in another time or place."
- "Think of different times you've been in a place like this. What are some of the differences about these similar places or similar times?"
- "What are some small, specific details about the place that stand out in comparison to similar settings?"

Following our conference, Emma added information about her setting to different scenes in her story. See Figure 5–3 for excerpts from her revised draft.

Emma uses character reflection to give us a better sense of the narrator as well as a fuller picture of place. For example, when she adds information to her opening scene about the last time the narrator was in the cafeteria, we discover that she and Meygan once enjoyed their time together there, which makes this moment extra painful. Because we can also see more of the place (the red doors and green walls and groups of friends sitting at round tables) we are also better able to feel ourselves in that cafeteria alongside Meygan.

Emma does an even better job revealing the setting of her next scene. Because her character reflects on specific details (the spitballs on the ceiling; the clogged sink), we can feel ourselves not just in any bathroom, but in a very particular bathroom, which again allows us easier access to the moment.

* * *

In *Writing Fiction: Big Dreams, Tall Ambitions* (2006), Lucy Calkins and Colleen Cruz write, "Once your children begin to ground their stories in precise settings, all of a sudden it is as if the stories become real. Everything becomes grounded" (114). Even when we can hear characters talking and see them moving, it is very difficult to enter their world if we do not know exactly where their world is. Furthermore, just as in life, if we do not know

Last time I had walked into the cafeteria, Meygan was at my side giggling as we pushed open the red plastic doors, into the ugly, nasty green cafeteria. Cliques were gathered around round tables and people were going up to get hot lunch. That day it was like a mush.

I crashed into the cafeteria with a boom. An angry boom for goodness' sakes. Anger bubbled up inside me as I remembered what had happened last night. Last night I had stood outside in the freezing cold for an hour! I winced at the memory of the pain that my skate laces had made, digging into my left shoulder. I was supposed to go ice-skating with Meygan, but Meygan never showed up.

speak to you?"

"Sure." Everyone stared as we walked out of the cafeteria. I led Meygan into the bathroom.

It seemed like ages ago, when I had last been here with Sarah when she was mad at me. She had been staring out of the window, while I gazed at the spitballs on the ceiling and the clogged sink.

Once we were in the bathroom, Meygan walked over to the sink. She sat on the edge and I stood facing her.

"Meygan, where were you yesterday?" I demanded, hands on my hips.

"What do you mean?" I could see the anxiety in her face.

"WHAT DO YOU MEAN, WHAT DO YOU MEAN! WE WERE SUPPOSED TO GO ICE-SKATING!!" I exploded

Figure 5–3 *Emma's revisions: revealing setting through character reflection to a similar time or place*

where characters are, it can be difficult to impossible to truly grasp what is happening, or the *significance* of what is happening. Because setting gives readers perspective and gives characters and events meaning, where a story takes place should be as integral to a piece as the characters and events themselves.

CHAPTER 6

Developing Tension

I love roller-coasters. I love the excitement of standing in line knowing something big is soon going to happen. I love the anticipation on the way up, the release on the way down, and the relief when it is all over and done. Being on a really good roller-coaster is like being in a really good story. My breath tightens as I go up, up, and up—or as I flip pages in anticipation of what is to come. My eyes pop in wonder as I go down—or as I uncover the latest plot turn. When I reach the end, even though I know it won't be the same, I wish I could do it all over again; I envy the people who are about to get on the ride, or read one of my most beloved books, for the very first time.

Of course, not everyone loves roller-coasters the way I do, and not everyone responds to books in the same way. But a good story should take us on a ride of some kind. The tension need not be a negative experience; I might feel tense because something bad is about to happen, but I might also feel tense because I have been holding my breath waiting for something wonderful to occur. Furthermore, the tension may exist because of an external or internal problem. Lost homework and a fight with a friend are examples of external problems, problems that occur outside the character. Internal problems, on the other hand, occur when we gain insight into a character's inner struggle; such problems are usually developed by more sophisticated writers and often unfold alongside an external problem.

Whether a love tale or a scary tale or a tale that makes us laugh, whether a problem unfolding outside or inside the character, we should experience places of tension when we read—places where we are not quite sure how the characters will react or what turn the plot will take. If your students' stories seem flat and predictable, without turns or dips, it is probably because they do not yet understand how to build tension. Most likely, they simply state or summarize the desire or conflict at hand. Though introducing a problem of some sort is a good first step when writing stories, we eventually want to teach students to take their readers on a journey from the discovery of the desire or conflict on to the character's response to the issue, and then on again to the resolution. To help your students accomplish this goal, you might teach the following strategies.

Use Repetition: *One way writers build tension is by repeating the problem or a character's attempts to attain a desire.*

It is easy to recall the myriad ways in which repetition causes tension in our daily lives: the child who asks again and again to do something we keep refusing; the student who never completes her homework; the days that pass one after the other as we eagerly await a vacation.

In a minilesson Rebecca Victoros did with her fifth graders, she used an everyday experience from her own life to introduce her students to the notion that repetition causes tension: She told them a story about how she waited and waited for the subway to come, and then when it finally did, it was too packed with people for her to get on. "It made me think about how in life, things get tense when we want something and are waiting and waiting to get it (like our birthday party), or when there is a problem and it keeps coming up again and again (like a little sibling who keeps getting in the way). The exact same thing is true when we write stories."

Teaching

Tell

"No matter what our stories are about, we always want to develop tension of some kind because it keeps our readers hooked into our stories, waiting and wanting to find out what will happen. Because repetition often causes aggravation and anticipation, one way to develop tension is to repeat the problem or to repeat characters' attempts to reach their desire."

Show

"Let me show you how, in one of the stories we love, the author uses repetition to build tension and keep his readers hooked into what's happening, eager to discover the resolution," Rebecca said before pulling out a copy of *Wings,* a picture book by Christopher Myers. "Remember how first, on this page," Rebecca said as she placed a copy on the overhead, "everyone in the neighborhood points at Icarus flying above the rooftops and shouts that he's strange? Then the problem repeats itself on this page: *The whole school was staring eyes and wagging tongues. They whispered about his wings and his hair and his shoes.* The problem repeats itself on this page when the teacher complains that Icarus is a distraction and tells him to leave. And again on this page: *At recess, the snicker grew into a giggle and spread across the playground.* On and on this goes until almost the end of the book, and each time the problem repeats itself, the more tense we get, right? The more we worry about Icarus and the more we wonder what is going to happen.

"Imagine if Myers instead wrote, simply, that everyone in the neighborhood points at Icarus and shouts that he's strange, and then resolved the problem. Not only would there be no tension, we probably wouldn't love this story like we do because we would never get a chance to actually engage with it. It would be over before we ever really cared about the character or what happened to him!"

Active Engagement

Tell

"I want you to try this now with your partner. Most of you were here for the fire drill this month, and even if you weren't, you can imagine how it went. I want you to take a couple minutes to write the story of what happened, focusing on a part where you could build up the tension through repetition; remember, tension keeps readers reading to find out what's going to happen, so with your partner, figure out the exact words you could write to build that tension."

Coach

"Let me get you started: *All of a sudden, we heard the fire alarm! First, we. . . .* OK, turn to your partners and write the first problem that happened, and then build the tension by writing the next problem and the next and the next." To support students, Rebecca said:

- "What is the problem in this story? Remember, the central problem usually arises when the characters want or need something but obstacles get in their way, so what do the characters want or need to do in this situation?"

- "Would it make sense for your characters to do this same thing multiple times?"
- "What else do the characters do to try and overcome the problem or reach the desire?"
- "What might get in the way as characters are trying to overcome the problem? What do the characters do in response to these new obstacles?"

Before Rebecca sent everyone back to their seats, she reminded her class that everyone should be building tension in their stories in order to keep their readers engaged and waiting to find out how characters overcome the problem. Rebecca told them to add "repetition" to their repertoire of ways to build tension, reminding them that they now had several ways to move toward their goal. For the next day and night after the minilesson, Faizah drafted the story in Figure 6–1.

Faizah successfully draws from a range of strategies for building tension, including using repetition. She could have very quickly solved the problem in her story by having Masrur break the vase as soon as the narrator asks him to give it back. Instead, Faizah keeps her readers in suspense by repeating the narrator's attempts to solve the problem: first she jumps off the couch and insists Masrur put down the vase; then she chases him; eventually she catches hold of his sock, but he breaks free; finally, she takes his favorite toy and uses it to bribe an exchange. On and on the problem goes, keeping us in suspense as we journey alongside Faizah's characters, wondering what will become of this precious vase.

Include Clues About How the Story Will Go: *One way writers build tension is by using setting, characters' feelings, and/or verb choice clues that hint at the problem.*

Like many people I know, I often get a little anxious or blue toward the end of a vacation. I start to think about going back to "real life"—to cleaning house and waking up early in the mornings, to hours of emailing and late-night planning for work—and my stomach tightens. But usually, once I get settled back into my home and my work, I find that things are not so bad after all.

In my experience, fear, anxiety, sadness often come with the anticipation of something to come, rather than with the "thing" itself. Knowing this, it makes sense that when we write stories, we can create tension through the buildup of some unknown to come. There are several different kinds of clues we can leave readers, but generally I only teach one or two at a time.

The Broken Vase

I was sitting on the fluffy couch on that blazing afternoon, trying to focus on my homework, but my eyes were glued tight on my brother.

"What are you doing with Mom's GLASS vase, Masrur? You know how important it is to her!" I cried. Give it to me before it breaks and the flowers get destroyed!" I was ready to run after Masrur. To me it felt like a daily chore.

I hopped off the couch and took a step forward. My brother moved back and a frow spread across his face.

"Mom's not home now so no one is going to stop me," he barked as he turned his back at me. This was one of the times I wanted to strangle Masrur

"Mom may not be here, but I am. And if that breaks, I'm gonna break you!" I roared.

Masrur just looked at me with a what-ever stare. Before I could blink, he was lost.

I raced to the bottom of the staircase and glared at that ferocious boy. I took a few steps pretending I never saw Masrur. He came up just one itty-bitty step

Figure 6–1 *Faizah's draft: using repetition to develop tension*

Teaching

Tell

When I conferred with fifth-grader Tywynn, I said, "Another way writers build tension and hook readers into our stories is to hint at before actually

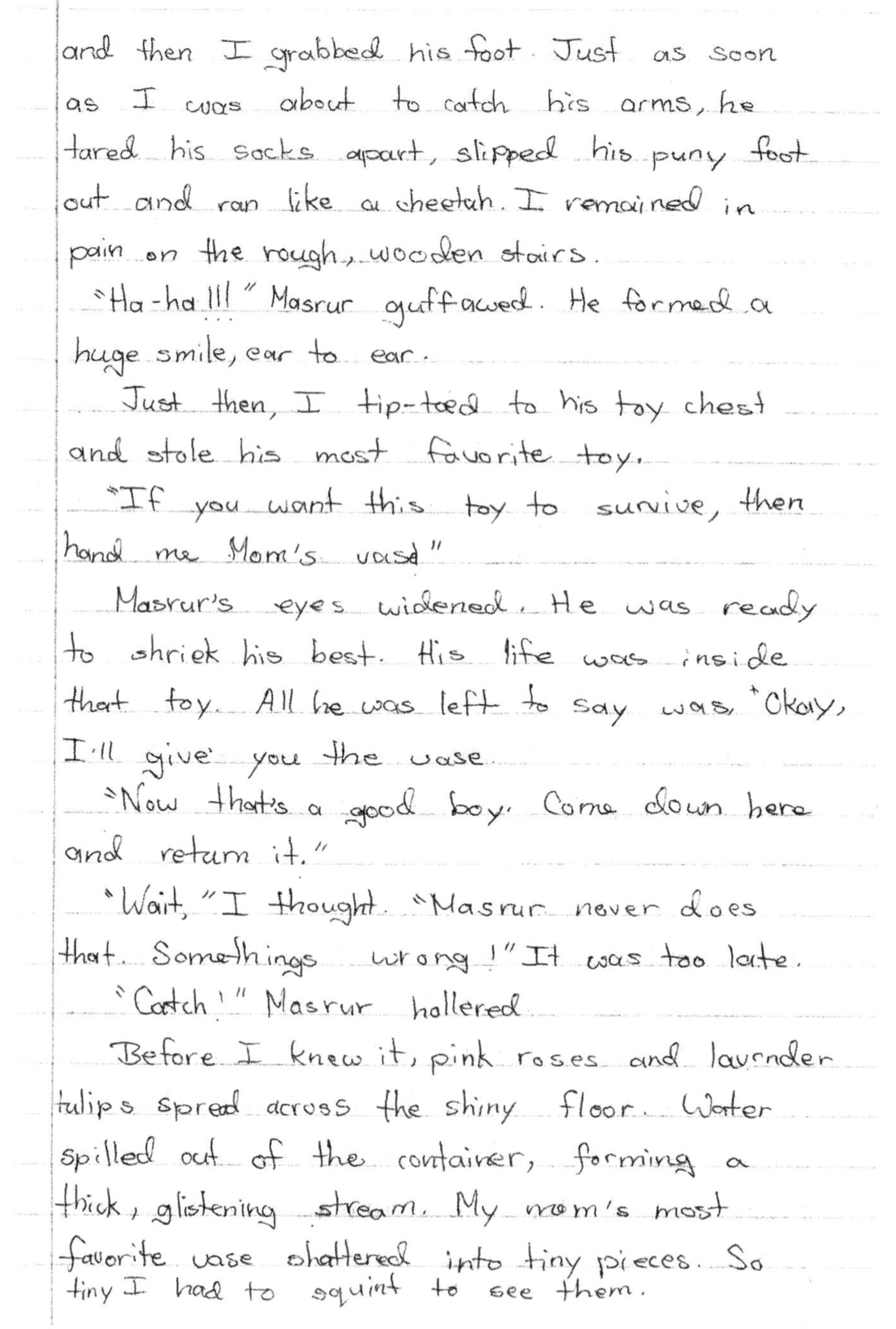

and then I grabbed his foot. Just as soon as I was about to catch his arms, he tared his socks apart, slipped his puny foot out and ran like a cheetah. I remained in pain on the rough, wooden stairs.

"Ha-ha!!!" Masrur guffawed. He formed a huge smile, ear to ear.

Just then, I tip-toed to his toy chest and stole his most favorite toy.

"If you want this toy to survive, then hand me Mom's vase"

Masrur's eyes widened. He was ready to shriek his best. His life was inside that toy. All he was left to say was, "Okay, I'll give you the vase

"Now that's a good boy. Come down here and return it."

"Wait," I thought. "Masrur never does that. Somethings wrong!" It was too late.

"Catch!" Masrur hollered.

Before I knew it, pink roses and lavender tulips spread across the shiny floor. Water spilled out of the container, forming a thick, glistening stream. My mom's most favorite vase shattered into tiny pieces. So tiny I had to squint to see them.

Figure 6–1 *(continued)*

revealing a problem. There are several ways to do this, such as choosing very specific action words or letting reacers know how characters feel before we know why they feel that way. These kinds of clues build tension because they string readers along, leaving them uncertain yet eager to find out what's going to happen."

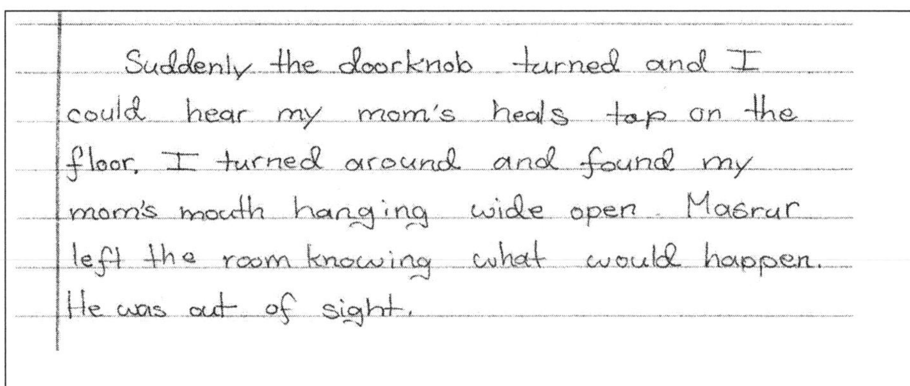

Suddenly the doorknob turned and I could hear my mom's heals tap on the floor, I turned around and found my mom's mouth hanging wide open. Masrur left the room knowing what would happen. He was out of sight.

Figure 6–1 *(continued)*

("In a separate conference with Tywynn, I reminded him of my earlier teaching, after assessing that he internalized it, and I said, "Writers can also use setting details to hint at a problem to come and build tension.")

Show

"For example, here's a draft of my story about a girl who is teased at school. I start my story on the playground with her being bullied. But another way to build the tension would be to start before the problem occurs and leave some feeling and word choice clues that hint at something about to happen. To leave a feeling clue, I might have my character say or do or think something that shows her mood. So in my story, since Kassy is being bullied, I might start with a clue that she feels sad or afraid or anxious. I'm thinking about what Kassy might do before even getting to school, or before she even comes face-to-face with her bullies that would show these kinds of feelings. Maybe I could write: *As soon as Kassy woke up, she rolled over and pulled the covers over her head. She wished and wished that she would disappear.* Writing that would let readers know that Kassy feels bad about something, and it would be a clue that something not too good is going to happen in this story.

"I could also think about word choice clues, like really strong and specific verbs that also hint at the mood. So down here, where I write that Kassy walked onto the playground, maybe I could think of a different verb to show she hated going to the playground. I'm trying to think of other verbs that mean something similar to walked but send a different feeling. *Ran?* No. *Skipped?* Definitely not! *Skipped* feels happy, upbeat. *Dragged?* Oh, that could work because it feels negative and would show that she really doesn't want to go. Or *trudged,* or *forced.* So I could write: *Kassy dragged herself onto the playground.* Or: *Kassy forced herself onto the playground.*

"Do you see how I'm building tension by showing how my character feels and choosing very specific words that hint that something is going to happen? In my story, it's something bad, but in another story, I could hint that something wonderful is going to happen. Clues get readers wondering and reading on to find out how the story will turn out."

(The next time I conferred with Tywynn and taught him how to use setting details to hint at something to come, I said, "In my story about Kassy being bullied at school, I could write toward the beginning that she watched the sun move through the trees and felt its warmth on her arms, but that would set my readers up to feel good because don't we usually feel better when it's warm and sunny outside than when it's cold and gray?

"Since I want my readers to know that something bad is going to happen, I might instead write something like: *A chill moved through the air. Kassy looked up at the trees and wished they hadn't lost all their leaves.* Don't those setting details create a gloomy feeling? They are clues of a problem to come.")

Active Engagement

Tell

"Can you practice these strategies in your draft? Try revising your piece by building even more tension, adding in feeling and/or word choice clues about what's to come. How might that go?"

Coach

To support Tywynn further, I said some of the following:

- "What's the problem in this story? Point to where readers first discover the problem. Now rewind in time and think about what might happen before this that would show how the characters feel without showing why they feel that way."
- "Underline your verbs—your action words—in the first few sentences. Brainstorm words that mean the same thing, looking for one that will make your readers feel what you want them to feel."

(1) All of a suddent the boat ~~pulled~~ screcced right in front of us. (2)
Me and my cousin Dimitri Got on.

Then, Like in 2 minutes the steal bars ~~went~~ crasched down ~~slowly~~. Then the boat started rocking back and forth very slowly then the boat specded up. (5)

(1) It was a hot saturday night. I was scared I was terrified. I was frightened. (4)
(2) The boat had scary designs. It felt like the boat was breathing on us.
(3) The bumper cars the horsey ride and the motorcycles.
(4) The Air smelled like blood.
(5) I could fell the sweat running down my chest.

It was a hot Saturday night. I was scared. I was terrified. I was frightened. The air smelled like blood. All of a sudden the boat screeched ~~pulled~~ right in front of us. The boat had scary designs. It felt like the boat was breathing on us. Me and my cousin Dimitri got on. Then in like 2 minutes the steel bars crashed ~~went~~ down ~~slowly~~. Then the boat started rocking back and forth very slowly then the boat speeded up. I could feel the sweat running down my chest.

Figure 6–2 *Tywynn's revisions: using setting, feeling, and word choice clues to develop tension*

- Close your eyes and paint a detailed picture of where your characters are. What's in your picture that reflects how your characters feel?
- How do your characters feel? What kind of weather makes you feel that way?

When I left Tywynn, he revised the beginning of his piece as shown in Figure 6–2.

Tywynn began to build the tension in his original piece, but now that he has more strategies from which to draw, he is able to take the tension to a deeper level. In his first draft, Tywynn relies on repetition alone to build the tension: first the boat rocks violently, later Tywynn screams, even later his cousin feels like throwing up. With repetition, the tension unfolds along with the events themselves.

With Tywynn's revisions, however, he sets up the tension before the problematic event even begins. Tywynn uses setting clues (*It was a hot Saturday night. . . . The air smelled like blood*), feeling clues (*I was scared. I was terrified.*), and word choice clues (*the boat screeched*) to put his readers on edge before we even know why we are on edge—before we know anything about the actual events.

Show Indecision Around a Choice: *One way writers build tension is by showing a character's indecision around an important choice.*

Mary Ehrenworth taught me that we can develop ideas about the stories we read and the world in which we live by considering and exploring a range of questions about choice: Are characters conflicted about choices they make in the face of struggle, and if so, why? How do their choices affect them and others? What do their choices tell us about the choices we make, or could make, or *should* make in our own lives? Especially (but not only) if we are having these conversations with our students as readers, it makes sense to have similar conversations with them as writers. As our students compose stories, we can teach them that being thoughtful about the choices they have their characters make means being thoughtful about the messages they want to send to readers. We can also teach them that one way to reveal and build tension is to show their characters struggling with difficult decisions.

Teaching

Tell

In a minilesson for my seventh graders, I said, "One way to build tension is to show your characters indecisively moving back and forth between possible ways to respond to a central problem. The more a character struggles, the more the reader worries and wonders about the outcome, which engages readers with the story.

"When you use this strategy, you want to think long and hard about what you want your readers to think is possible *and moral* in the face of certain problems, and have your characters make their decisions accordingly; the outcome of a story inevitably sends a message to readers about people and the world."

Show

"Let me show you how Lana does this in her story," I said before showing them one part of a student draft.

I was in the mall with Tiffany and Maryana today. We were going down the escalator when I saw Jenna and Carolina and Ali. Lately, I've been thinking about them a lot. I don't know why. I mean, I've been having a great time with Tiffany and Maryana, but something is missing. We never laugh like I did with Jenna, Carolina and Ali. It's always about looking pretty and new styles, it's not about real friendship.

So, Tiffany and Maryana and I got off the escalator and I waved at Jenna, Carolina and Ali. Tiffany and Maryana scowled. For a second I thought I shouldn't have waved, but then I just ignored them. Jenna and Carolina and Ali walked over to us and said, "Nat, we need to talk." I swallowed hard. I thought about how much I wanted to talk with my old friends, and also, about how much I wanted to stay popular.

"She is not talking to you," Tiffany spat.

"Don't talk for her," Ali shot back.

"Ugh, at least my 'friend' didn't pick someone over me."

"You little . . ."

"Stop! Listen, what do you guys want?" I said.

"What do we want?! We want you to look in the mirror! Jeez Nat, do you get it? You're about to make the ultimate sacrifice. You're on the brink of being sucked in." Carolina was bright red.

Part of me wanted to go with Tiffany and Maryana. Part of me knew they were right. I took a step towards them, but then I stepped back towards my new "friends" and said, "I think you should go."

"Do you see how the narrator in Lana's story is struggling with her decision, wanting and thinking she should do one thing, but then also wanting and thinking something very different? Notice how Lana shows the narrator waffling around her decisions when she writes things like, *For a second I thought I shouldn't have waved, but then I just ignored them,* and, *Part of me knew they were right. I took a step towards them, but then I stepped back towards my new 'friends' and said, 'I think you should go.'*

"We really feel the narrator's struggle because of that waffling, don't we? We really wonder what she'll decide in the end, how she'll feel about her decision, what will happen as a result, all of which keeps us hooked into the story, right? If she just made a decision right way, decided in the first paragraph or two to choose one group of friends over the other and was fine with it, we probably wouldn't think twice about the issue.

"Now Lana needs to decide what she wants her readers to think when they read her story. If the narrator happily chooses her new, popular friends, the story will send a very specific message to readers about what we could and should do in similar situations, whereas if she chooses her old and true friends, the message will obviously be different."

Active Engagement

Tell

"I want you to try this now. Think about your own characters and talk briefly with your partner about the choices your characters might make when they come face to face with their problem. Also discuss what you want your readers to think is possible and moral in the face of a certain problem, and how the choice your character ultimately makes will convey this."

Coach

As I listened to my students work, I said things like:

- "Brainstorm a list of possible choices. Now pick one to start. What are the pros and cons of that decision?" You could show your character struggling by having them think or talk about those pros and cons.
- "What might your character think or say or do that shows him or her veering toward one decision? Now, what's the next thing they might think or do to show they are second-guessing themselves?"
- "What message will that decision send to your readers? Is that in line with what you want them to think about the problem and how one should respond in a similar situation?"
- "Fill in the rest of this sentence: *He thought to himself, On the one hand. . . .* Now fill in the rest of this sentence: *But then he thought, On the other hand. . . .*"

Before I sent students back to their seats, I reminded them that they knew a variety of ways to develop tension in their stories, and that it was their job to draw from that knowledge in ways that made the most sense for them as writers and for their current stories. Over the next two days, Dean drafted a story about a boy whose peers tease him by calling him gay. One way Dean builds tension and lures his readers into the life of his character is by having his character struggle with and change his mind about how to respond to the problem. Excerpts from Dean's story are shown in Figure 6–3.

When I read Dean's story, I feel Luis' torment and am tormented in turn. In the first scene, when Luis wonders whether he should try acting like a regular guy, lies there "thinking and thinking" and then, "feeling ashamed and scared" tells Miranda and Lizzy that he can't hang out with them anymore, I feel the familiar knot in my stomach that comes when I have a hard decision to make. In the middle scene, when Luis questions what he's doing on a baseball field, we again sense his uncertainty and

'What the hell is wrong with these people. I mean C'mon I'M NOT GAY. What makes them think that?' Then, when Luis thought about it, he wasn't a regular guy, he wasn't into sports, that much, and he hadn't had a girlfriend yet and the fact that the only people that he talked to were two girls was different than the other guys who only talked to girls when they were hitting on them.

'You think they would stop if I became just like them and acted like a regular guy? I guess it's worth a shot. Right? I mean I really cannot stand this anymore.' Luis kind of just laid there thinking and thinking until eventually his eyes closed and he fell asleep.

The next morning Luis bumped into Lizzy and Miranda walking down the halls. Luis was done thinking and really need to talk to them about a bunch of things.

"Hey Luis," said Miranda "how's it hangin'?"

Luis turned around and just stood there as billions of thoughts went in and out of his head," Miranda, Lizzy I don't think we should hang out anymore. Well at least not as much as we have been..." Luis said feeling both ashamed and scared of how they would react.

Figure 6–3 *Excerpts from Dean's piece: showing character indecision around an important choice to develop tension*

'What am I doing here? Luis said to himself as he was sitting by himself on the other side of the bench. 'I'm no jock. I look like an idiot with my cap and sweat pants on. God! I guess everybody was right, I have been hanging with girls too much. I'm on a baseball field and while other guys are talking about sports and girls, I am thinking about how I look! Oh man. Think... think like a regular, sports playin', immature regular guy.

Luis twitled his thumbs, stomped his feet, nodded his head to a beat. Trying to look cool when he felt out of place and alone.

'Why am I here I have two perfectly good friends. I'm so stupid. Did I really that kids would willingly come hang out with me if I tried out for the baseball team?'

Figure 6–3 *(continued)*

turmoil. In the last scene, when Luis considers what he would lose if he chose Miranda and Lizzy versus what he would lose if he chose his new, jock "friends," I have the sensation of going up and up on the roller coaster, knowing something big is about to happen. By having his character struggle and vacillate around an important choice, Dean not only takes his character on a roller-coaster, he also takes his readers on one. We experience, alongside Luis, the confusion and uncertainty and anxiety around the problem at hand.

What's more, by thinking long and hard about what choice his character will make in the end, Dean sends an important message to his readers. He lets us know that it is possible to be true to oneself, and to one's friends, in the face of peer pressure, and he encourages us to follow our hearts in situations of similar torment.

Contrast Words and Thoughts: *One way writers build tension is by showing a clear difference between what a character says and thinks.*

A few weeks ago, I was waiting to speak with a principal when a student came into the office. "Hello," I said. "How're you?"

"What the hell Luis?" said Bill one of Luis's new friends. " You back to being a fag. Why would you rather hang out with them than us? What are you guys going to do on Friday? Have a sleep over and talk about boys?" he said in an obnoxious voice

"C'mon guys they are my friends" Said Luis.

"It's either us or them

"What?! Guys you're acting stupid."

"Us or them."

Luis stood there, so many thoughts going through his head. 'If I choose Miranda and Lizzy all the kids will call me gay and I will go back to the life I used to have. All of my friends will begin to hate me again. But if I choose them I will be like all the other kids, I would be known as Luis, not as the fruit cake.

I don't care. These guys are jerks and Lizzy and Miranda have always been nice to me and always have been my best friends!

"Them," Luis said, still with the emotions twisting in his stomach.

Figure 6–3 *(continued)*

"Fine," she said. At first I didn't think anything of the interaction and simply went back to my work. But a couple minutes later, I noticed she was staring blankly at the wall.

"Are you sure you're OK?" I asked again.

"I'm fine," she repeated, trying on a little smile to convince me.

"Are you here because you're in trouble?" I persisted.

"I guess," she said. In that moment, the principal came in and asked the student to wait outside for a few minutes.

"I hope you feel better," I whispered after her as she stepped into the hallway. I thought about how often in life we say one thing but think or feel something very different. How many times have we *all* insisted we were fine when, in fact, we were nothing close to it? I thought about how as writers, we have the power to reveal (and of course to create) the discrepancies between our characters' words and thoughts. Doing so gives readers insight into and builds tension around characters' internal struggles.

Teaching

Tell

When I stopped a fifth-grade class for a teaching share, I said, "You can develop the *internal* tension in your stories as well as the external tension. That's the tension your characters experience on the inside. One way to develop internal tension is to show when your characters say one thing but then think something very different because it shows that the character is conflicted. As you know, when characters face conflict, readers worry and wonder about the outcome, which engages them with the story, and we all want to write stories that engage our readers."

Show

"Alex just tried this. Alex, would you read what you wrote, and class, listen to how he builds tension by having his character say one thing but think something else. He's going to read something from the middle of his story, after two of his characters get into a big fight."

Alex read: *"I'm sorry for yelling," I said to my sister. And then I thought, "But maybe if you weren't so annoying all the time, I wouldn't have to yell."*

"Writers," I said. "Do you see how Alex starts to resolve the external problem when the narrator apologizes to his sister? At the same time, do you see how he builds tension around an *internal* problem by showing how the narrator thinks something different than what he says? Clearly, the narrator has an unresolved, internal struggle about his relationship with his sister. Knowing this, don't you want to find out more about what happens between Alex and his sister? Alex effectively hooks us into the story."

Active Engagement

Tell

Remember, many of my teaching shares simply have a "tell" and "show." In this case, I said, "Take a moment to read over your drafts so far, and see whether your characters ever say one thing but actually think something different. If you find a place like that and you haven't yet shown this difference, take a minute to add in what your character says that is different than what he thinks, or add in what he thinks that is different than what he says."

Coach

To coach students, I said things like:

- "You might look closely at places where there already is tension of some kind. Look where the problem first gets introduced, or later in the story where a character faces the problem yet again, and see whether your character might say one thing but think something different."
- "You might look closely at places where your characters interact with one another. Do they ever say something that might be different than what they think?"

When Christina drafted her story, she drew from the myriad ways she had learned to develop tension to craft a piece that draws out the conflict and draws in the reader. Excerpts from her piece are shown in Figure 6–4.

Christina uses several strategies to develop the tension in her piece, one of which is to contrast the narrator's words and thoughts. In the beginning of her story, when her mom asks her to get the pudding, the narrator thinks, *I always get the heavy stuff,* but then without resistance responds, *K, ma!* At the end of the story, Christina again contrasts the narrator's words and thoughts when she writes, *I wanted to yell, tell her no. 'Yeah, I'm fine,' I responded.*

By this time, we already know that getting the pudding creates an external problem for the narrator; she falls, drops the bowl, makes a mess. By contrasting the narrator's words and thoughts, Christina creates and conveys an *internal* problem, as well; she illuminates internal tension between the narrator and her family members. Doing so shows more sophistication on the part of the writer and allows for deeper meaning on the part of the reader. We are no longer merely tense about the pudding; we are also tense about the narrator's relationship with her family.

* * *

Life is a journey, and so our stories about life must also be journeys. And every journey has its dips and turns. Whether our students are writing about falling off their bikes or about waiting to open their presents at a birthday

"CHRISTINA!!!! Don't forget the pudding!" my mom reminded me. I always had to get the heavy stuff. . .

"K, ma!" I shouted in response. I went to get the bowl from the 3rd floor fridge.

"Christina!!!!!!" It was my little sister, Stephanie. "Mom said if you don't hurry up you're gonna be in trouble!"

"Okay!" I said.

What does she know? She's the one who's always getting in trouble, I thought. I picked up the bowl.

Suddenly my legs gave way. In less than 20 seconds, I was tumbling down the seemingly-endless stairs. I thought I was going blind.

I shrieked. What was I supposed to do?

My mom was at the bottom, helping Stephanie down the last step. They both looked up, only to see me tumbling down the stairs. A few stairs in front of me, was the 3ft. by 3ft. stair. My savior. I landed on my side.

"CHRISTINA!!!! Are you okay?" My mom asked.

I wanted to yell, tell her no.

"Yeah, I'm fine," I responded, in a harsh voice.

My family still laughs about it . . . *I don't understand what is so funny!!!!!!!*

"CHRISTINA!!!! Dont forget the pudding!" my mom reminded me. I always had to get the heavy stuff...

"K, ma!" I shouted in response. I went to grab the bowl from the 3rd floor fridge.

"Christina!!!!!!" It was my little sister, Stephanie. "Mom said if you don't hurry up, you're gonna be in trouble!"

"Okay!" I said.

What does she know? She's the one who's always getting in trouble, I thought. I picked up the bowl.

Suddenly, my legs gave way. In less than 20 seconds, I was tumbling down the seemingly-endless stairs. I thought I was going blind.

I shrieked. What was I supposed to do?

My mom was at the bottom, helping Stephanie down the last step. They both looked up, only to see me tumbling down the stairs. A few stairs in front of me, was the 3ft by 3ft stair. My savior. I landed on my side.

"CHRISTINA!!!! Are you okay?" My mom asked.

I wanted to yell, tell her no.

"Yeah, I'm fine," I responded, in a harsh voice.

My family still laughs about it... I don't understand what is so funny!!!!!!!

Figure 6–4 *Excerpts from Christina's piece: contrasting character's words and thoughts to develop tension*

party, we, their readers, should feel a rising and falling of emotion as we move from beginning to end. Just as in life, there should be places in the stories we read where we hunch forward, hold our breath, move quickly to discover what happens next; and there should be places where we sit back, sigh in relief, or laugh out loud with a joyous discovery.

CHAPTER 7

Crafting Leads

When I was still a classroom teacher, someone told me that on the first day of the school year, I should do a little bit of everything that would be most important to me during the year. "If you want your students to read, then have them read on day one. If you want them to write, have them write, even if only for ten minutes. *And* do it with passion so students come back the next day hoping for more." As many of us have come to learn, the first day of school is one of the most important days of the year because it sets students up for all the days to come. The first day not only introduces students to their new teacher and classmates, it introduces them to the tone, rituals, and expectations within their new class community.

The beginning of a story carries a similar importance. The lead can break a good story, turn readers away before they get past the first couple paragraphs, or it can lure readers in, eager for more. The lead can introduce readers to the world of the story, setting them up for the pages ahead, or it can introduce characters that suddenly disappear or events that never come to fruition. If, when you read your students' leads, you feel uninspired to keep going, or you are introduced to characters or events that are not, as it turns out, central to the world of the story, you might teach the following strategies.

Introduce the Problem: *One way writers begin our stories is by introducing the problem.*

Toward the beginning of every writers' workshop, once students leave the meeting area and get settled into their independent writing, I watch and listen. I notice who gets back to their seats first, who is among the first to open their notebooks or get out their drafts. I also notice who lingers in the meeting area, who digs around in their desks for as long as possible before finding a pencil, a piece of paper. I notice who stops to talk to peers, and then I eavesdrop: are they discussing what they wrote for homework last night and whether they can read each other's stories, or the game they'll play at recess?

One reason I observe my students closely during workshop is so I can uncover problems and plan for conferences and minilessons that address these problems. Just as identifying central problems in the classroom provides a context for my teaching, identifying central problems in a story provides a context for reading. Once we know the obstacles characters face, we can begin to seek out the ways they respond to and overcome those obstacles, which focuses and engages our attention.

Teaching

Tell

When I gathered a group of fifth graders who were struggling with how to begin their stories, I said, "Writers often begin our pieces by introducing the problem to our readers. This is one way to pull readers into the story right away and help get them ready for what is to come."

Show

"For example, I wrote a story about the day my parents separated. I start my piece by introducing the problem to my readers which is that my parents are getting a divorce, but more specifically, that I really want my dad to come home. Here's my lead: *I tried to wipe away my tears as I dialed my dad's new number, no longer* my *number. Just thinking about that made me cry harder. As soon as I heard my dad's voice, I begged, 'Daddy! Please come home!'*

"Do you see how I have my characters say and do things right away that introduce the problem to my readers? For example, when I dial my dad's *new* number, my readers can figure out that my dad just moved out—that my parents just separated. When I try to wipe away my tears and say, 'Please come home!' you also know how upset I am. By introducing the problem in my lead, don't I get you interested in reading more? I also get you ready for what is to come in the story."

Active Engagement

Tell

"I want each of you to use your own pieces to practice what I just taught you; I want you, on one of these pieces of draft paper, to start your story by introducing the problem in the first couple of sentences. Once you think you've done a good job of that, you can try other ways to begin your piece or you can keep drafting your story."

Coach

I supported students as they worked by saying things like:

- "Is the problem external—something that has gone wrong or that your character wants on the outside? Or is it internal—something your character struggles with emotionally, on the inside? Or is it both? If the problem is internal, your beginning could show how the character feels as a way to reveal the central issue in the story."
- "If the problem is more external, you could still show how the character feels, but you will also want to show what is happening outside the character that is problematic. What might your characters say or do or think to show this problem?"
- "You don't want to give away the whole story, which means you don't want to say how the problem gets resolved. However, you might begin with what causes the problem."

During the strategy lesson, Vincent wrote the beginning of his piece as shown in Figure 7–1. Vincent's lead introduces readers to an internal problem, which is the narrator's struggle to deal with the loss of his grandmother. By introducing his readers to the central issue in his story in the first couple of paragraphs, Vincent prepares us for what will unfold. He allows us to get our minds ready and to make predictions from the very beginning about how this story will go, namely, that the narrator will find a way to feel better about his grandmother's passing. By pulling his readers into the problem from the very first sentence, Vincent allows us to be on the same journey as the character, a journey to find some sort of resolution to the central issue in the piece.

Reveal a Character: *One way writers begin our stories is by revealing important details about a character.*

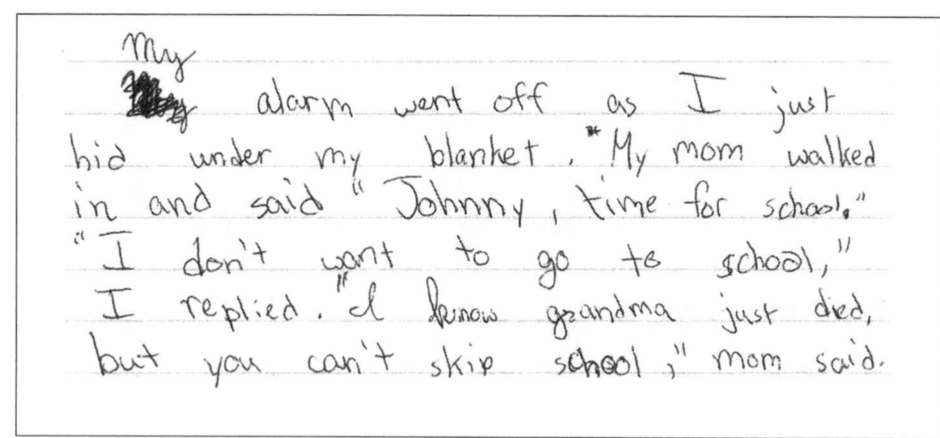
My alarm went off as I just hid under my blanket. My mom walked in and said "Johnny, time for school." "I don't want to go to school," I replied. "I know grandma just died, but you can't skip school," mom said.

Figure 7–1 *Vincent's lead: introducing the problem*

With certain students, it does not matter what I am doing as long as I am doing it with them. For example, some are so hungry for knowledge, so willing to take risks, so ready to collaborate with their peers that any activity is a pleasure. Regardless of the events or the end results, what matters is that we are working and exploring and learning together.

Similarly, in the best stories, characters, not plot, drive the piece. This is not at all to say that the events in a story are irrelevant. But because people, or characters, determine the cause or effect of events, it usually matters *less* what is happening and more *to whom* it is happening. Especially when pieces contain characters that make up the story as much as or more so than the actual events, writers often lure readers in with compelling character description.

Teaching

Tell

When I conferred with fifth-grader Kevin, I said, "One way you can begin your stories is by relaying important information about one or more of your characters. The best stories are about people as well as about events, and introducing characters in the lead lets readers know they will be important to how the story goes."

Show

"Let me show you what I mean. In *Oliver Button Is a Sissy,* Tomie dePaola tells a story about a boy who gets teased because he likes to do things some people think only girls should like to do. DePaola starts his story by writing: *Oliver Button was called a sissy. He didn't like to do things that boys are sup-*

posed to do. Instead, he liked to walk in the woods and play jump rope. He liked to read books and draw pictures. He even liked to play with paper dolls.

"Do you see how dePaola's lead gives his readers information on his central character that is important to the story? Notice that he doesn't write things like, *Oliver has a backyard,* or *Oliver loves chocolate,* because even though those things could be true, they don't connect with the central ideas and events in the story."

Active Engagement

Tell

"I want you to practice this strategy with your piece. Try a lead that introduces important things about one or more of your characters. Remember, you only want to include details that connect with and set readers up for the big things that happen in your story. This can help your readers understand how important the characters are, and how who they are actually determines how the events unfold."

Coach

To support writers further with this strategy, I say things like:

- "What are the really important things that happen in your story? What are the things about your character that influence the cause or impact of these events?"
- "You don't want to say everything about your character, even if the information is true; you only want to include character description that connects with what your story is about."

After our conference, Kevin started his story as seen in Figure 7–2. Kevin makes smart choices about what details to include in his lead. Though he starts to write things like, *Sometimes he is good to me,* he realizes that this information is not important to, and even contradicts with, the central events in his story. In the end, Kevin includes only the character description that introduces readers to the overarching problem in the narrator's life. Doing so helps him craft a cohesive narrative that is about his ski accident on one level and about his relationship with his brother on another.

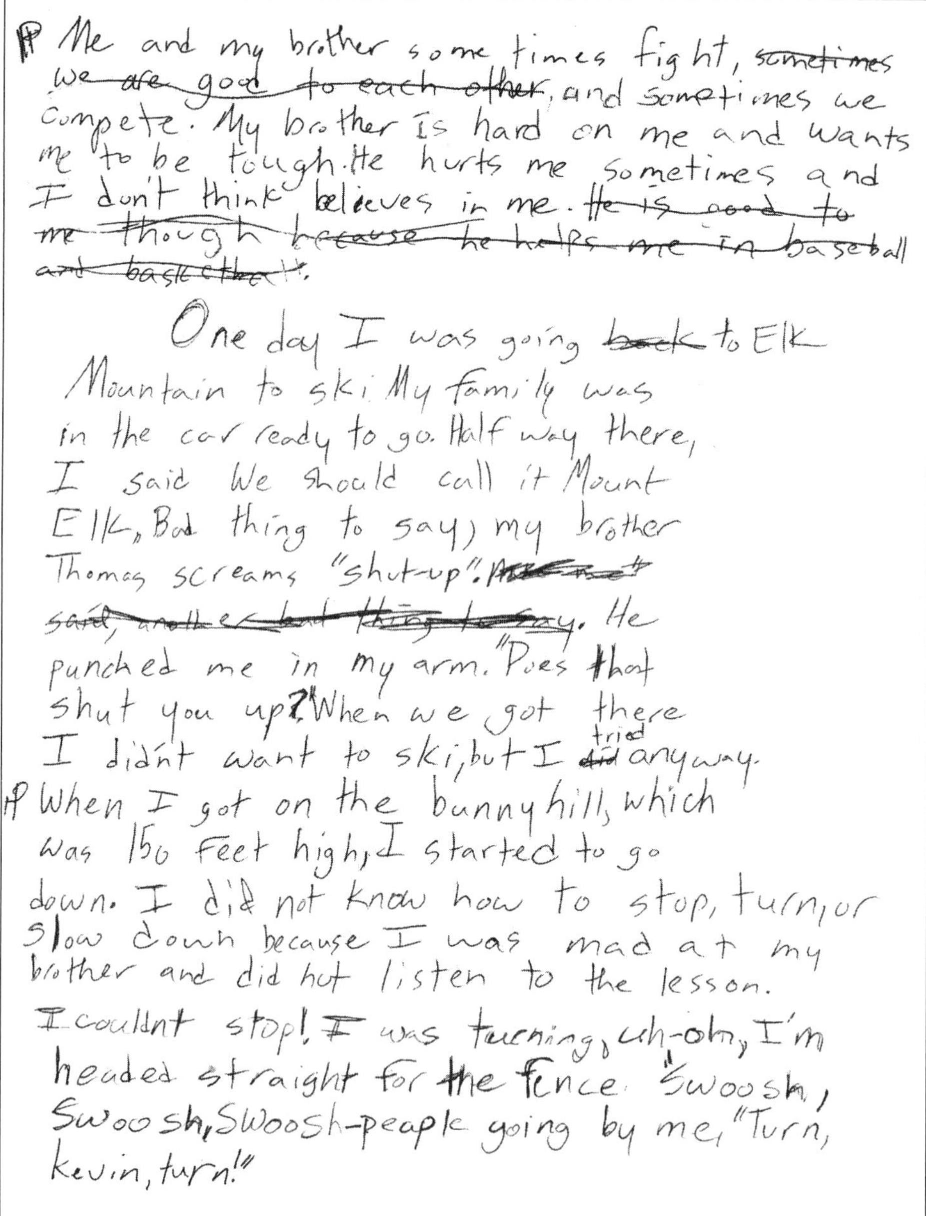

¶ Me and my brother some times fight, ~~sometimes we are good to each other~~, and sometimes we compete. My brother is hard on me and wants me to be tough. He hurts me sometimes and I don't think believes in me. ~~He is good to me though because he helps me in baseball and basketball~~.

One day I was going ~~back~~ to Elk Mountain to ski. My family was in the car ready to go. Half way there, I said We should call it Mount Elk, Bad thing to say) my brother Thomas screams "shut-up"! ~~[illegible] said, another bad thing to say~~. He punched me in my arm. "Does that shut you up?" When we got there I didn't want to ski, but I ~~did~~ tried anyway.

¶ When I got on the bunny hill, which was 150 Feet high, I started to go down. I did not know how to stop, turn, or slow down because I was mad at my brother and did not listen to the lesson. I couldnt stop! I was turning, uh-oh, I'm headed straight for the fence. "Swoosh, Swoosh, Swoosh-people going by me, "Turn, kevin, turn!"

Figure 7–2 *Kevin's lead: introducing character*

Flash Back to Another Time: *One way writers begin our stories is by flashing back to a time that connects with what the story is about.*

As much as we may aim to live in the present, for most of us, the present is intricately tied to the past. Every moment tends to be impacted by the ones that have come before, which means that what we do and how we feel right now is also about what we have done and how we have felt before. Beginning stories with a flashback that connects with the central events and ideas in a story can deepen and give readers further insight into the significance of the current moment.

Teaching

Tell

When I conferred with fifth-grader Rose, I said, "Sometimes writers begin our stories with a flashback that connects with and sets readers up for the central story. When the story is bigger than just this one time—when it is part of and connected to things that have happened before—a flashback can help readers see why the events are so important to the characters."

Show

"For example, I'm writing a story about the night my dad moved out of our house when I was eleven years old. Right now, I start right in that moment like this: *'Come home, daddy!' I cried. 'Can't you please come home?' I gripped the phone with so much force my nails dug into my palm.*

"My beginning is a perfectly good way to begin a story. It shows how devastated I was when my parent's separated. But if I wanted, I could also begin with a flashback to show how hard this night was for me. I might write:

> *I picked up the phone and remembered the last time I talked with my father. It was just last night, and we sat together on this very couch in our living room. He put his arm around me and said, "I love you so much, Pumpkin. Don't ever forget it."*
>
> *But now it wasn't our living room anymore. I dialed my dad's new number and I cried into the phone, "Come home, daddy! Can't you please come home?"*

"Do you see how, by beginning with a little flashback, I show that my story is part of something bigger, connected to things that have happened before? By showing and reminiscing on tender moments my father and I shared in our home, my readers get an even deeper sense of the grief I experienced when he moved out.

"Do you also see that I don't have to tell the whole story of what happened in the earlier moment? In this case, I only share enough for my readers to understand how the current moment is affected by moments that have come before."

Active Engagement

Tell

"Flip through your notebook and find a place where you can practice this strategy. Look for a story that you can lure readers into with a flashback; so look for a story in which the central events are actually part of and connected to something that has happened before."

Coach

To help students with this strategy, I say things like:

- "When was your character in a similar situation? It may have turned out differently or the same. Flash back to that time and highlight how the important events and feelings compare or contrast to *this* time."
- "When did you experience a similar problem or a similar feeling? Flash back to that time to get readers ready for what is to come."

After our conference, Rose wrote the lead in Figure 7–3 for the entry she chose from her writer's notebook, which is shown in Figure 7–4. Rose's

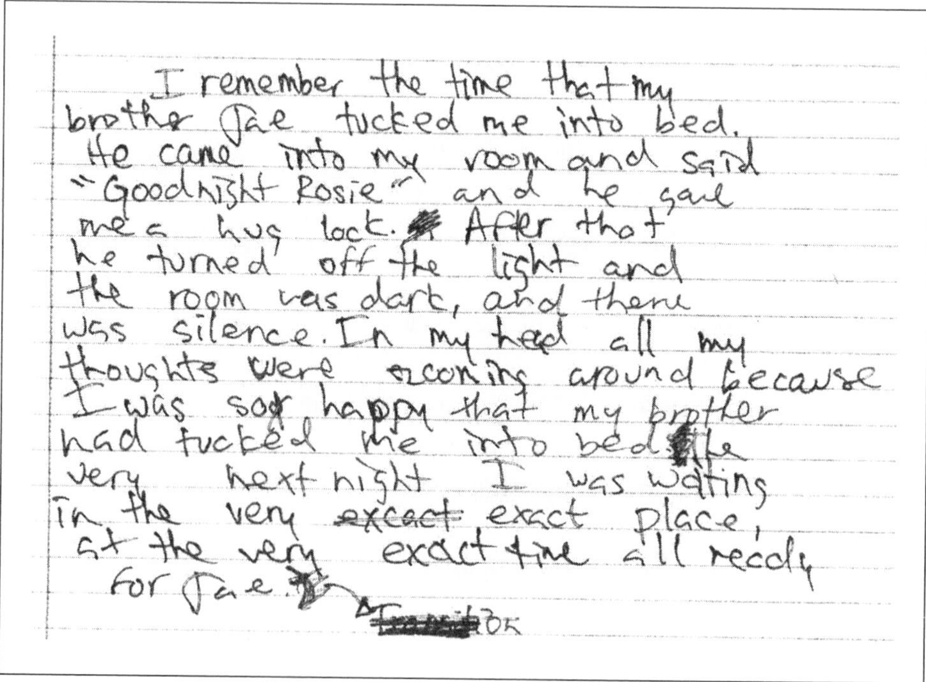

I remember the time that my brother Jae tucked me into bed. He came into my room and said "Goodnight Rosie" and he gave me a hug back. After that he turned off the light and the room was dark, and there was silence. In my head all my thoughts were zooming around because I was so happy that my brother had tucked me into bed. The very next night I was waiting in the very ~~excact~~ exact place, at the very exact time all ready for Jae.

OK

Figure 7–3 *Rose's lead: flashing back to a connected time or place*

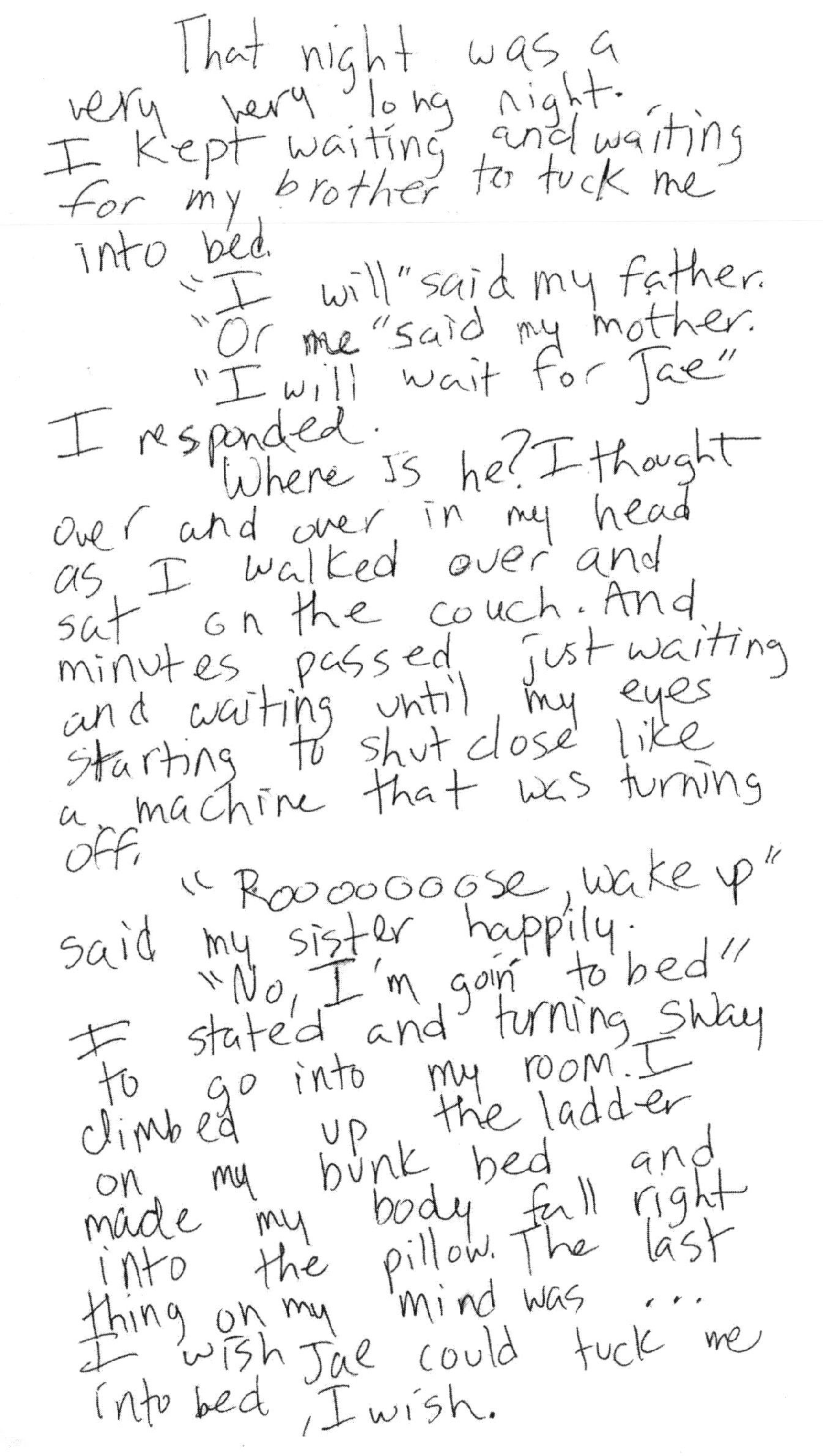

That night was a very very long night. I kept waiting and waiting for my brother to tuck me into bed.

"I will" said my father.

"Or me" said my mother.

"I will wait for Jae" I responded.

Where is he? I thought over and over in my head as I walked over and sat on the couch. And minutes passed just waiting and waiting until my eyes starting to shut close like a machine that was turning off.

"Roooooose, wake up" said my sister happily.

"No, I'm goin to bed" I stated and turning sway to go into my room. I climbed up the ladder on my bunk bed and made my body fall right into the pillow. The last thing on my mind was . . . I wish Jae could tuck me into bed, I wish.

Figure 7–4 *Rose's original notebook entry that follows her new lead*

original entry, which is now the second half of her story, certainly stands on its own without the added lead. However, by opening with a flashback to a comparable moment, Rose highlights the feelings in and meaning of her story. In this case, the contrast between the comfort and happiness she felt when her brother *did* tuck her into bed and the disappointment and loneliness she felt when he did *not* tuck her in emphasizes for readers the depth of her relationship with her brother. One can imagine that if Rose flashed back to a different kind of moment in which her brother once again did not tuck her in, she could emphasize something very different for readers, perhaps that she is regularly disappointed by her brother. Regardless of the content, beginning with a flashback is another way to lure readers into and make the meaning of a story.

* * *

I am awed by the fact that once upon a time, it was possible to have read everything that was ever written and made public. Every story, every poem, every theory. One of my frustrations is that I can never seem to catch up. My shelves are lined with unread novels, half-read teaching texts, collections of essays and poems that have never seen daylight. With so much to read, my expectations are high: if an author does not grab my attention in the first couple pages, I am unlikely to invest more of my time in what they have to share. As writers, then, we need to be especially thoughtful about how we lure our readers into our pieces. We need to do all we can to keep them interested, to keep them wanting more, so that what we write is not lost somewhere on a shelf or in a folder among other passed-over texts.

CHAPTER 8

Crafting Endings

When I first started teaching, there were various points across the day when my room felt like utter chaos, one of them being the last ten minutes of school. Suddenly, students were tripping over one another as they transferred books and binders into backpacks. Suddenly, every boy and girl seemed to be talking at once (What's the writing homework again? Do you want to come over tonight? I can't find my pencil case anywhere!). Suddenly, I was frantically trying to locate lost books and pass out announcements and answer last minute questions. These last minutes of the day always drained whatever energy still remained.

Until one afternoon when I decided to try something different. "I just got this new picture book," I said to my class, "and I cannot wait to share it with you! I'm going to read it aloud as you get yourselves ready to go." From then on, in addition to whatever else we read and discussed during the day, I wrapped up our time together with a read-aloud. I let my class know they should pack their things quietly so everyone could hear the story or poem or article, and that whenever they were ready, they should just as quietly join me on the rug for the rest of the read-aloud. What a transformation. Now, the last ten minutes of the day were an opportunity for all of us to take a collective breath and to come together as a community one last time before heading out into our individual lives. They were also a final opportunity in the school day to listen and ponder and connect.

When we teach our students to write, we want to teach them to end their stories with a similar level of consideration. Reading aloud to my students during those last minutes of school helped us end the day with the same things that were important during all the hours before: community, literature, reflection. Similarly, we want to end our stories with information that connects with and makes a final effort to convey what has been so important in all the preceding sentences and paragraphs. If your students' stories end without warning or without thought, you might teach the following strategies.

Reflect: *One way writers end our stories is with narrated reflection that brings readers a deeper clarity about the meaning of a piece.*

I think reflection is a necessary tool for growth. As a teacher, I only get smarter when I reflect on my practices: What exactly have I done here and how has it affected, or not affected, my students? Is there something else I could try? As a reader, I only get smarter when I take the time to stop my reading and reflect: Why is a character acting this way? What does it mean about people, the world? As a friend and wife and mother and daughter, I only get smarter when I reflect on my actions: Why am I behaving like this? How are my actions impacting others? What other choices do I have here? Regardless of the situation, we learn and grow and make meaning through reflection. As writers, we can use reflection to help our readers learn and grow and make meaning from our stories.

Teaching

Tell

When I conferred with fifth-grader Leeyah, I said, "One way writers convey meaning to our readers is by ending our pieces with narrated reflection. Usually, the reflection shows how our characters have been impacted by events because this allows us to make explicit for our readers the meaning of the story."

Show

"For example, remember how in the first part of *Big Sister and Little Sister* by Charlotte Zolotow, the big sister always takes care of the little sister? She helps her cross the street and teaches her how to sew and whenever little sister cries, big sister puts her arm around her, holds out a handkerchief and says, 'Here, blow.' But then there's the day that big sister cries and little sister puts her arm around her, holds out a handkerchief and says, 'Here, blow.' Zolotow ends her story with a reflection; on the last page, she writes: *And from that day on little sister and big sister both took care of each other because little sister had learned from big sister and now they both knew how.*

"Do you see how the narrator looks back on the events in the story and lets readers know how the characters were impacted by them? From that last sentence we know without a doubt that this is a story about how when an older sibling takes good care of a younger sibling, the younger sibling learns how to take care of others; we know this is a story about how when we treat people well, they learn to treat us, and others, well in return. By ending with reflection, Zolotow gets across to readers the significance of her story and what she wants us to think as we walk away.

Active Engagement

Tell

"I want you to try this now with your piece. You can always choose a different way to end, but for now try ending with reflection that shows how the events have impacted the narrator and thereby gets across the meaning of your story."

Coach

As Leeyah worked, I coached her by asking some of the following questions, and I told her to use her answers to guide her reflection.

- "Why is this story so important for you to tell?"
- "What do you want your readers to know and think and feel when they read this?"
- "How does the narrator/character change by the end of the story and what causes the change?"

Leeyah's story is about a girl whose mother has a new baby and is suddenly less available; in the first part of the story, the girl feels resentful of her sibling and hurt by her mother. After our conference, Leeyah wrote the ending to her piece (see Figure 8–1).

Leeyah clearly understands that as writers, we want to send a message to our readers and that the message is tied to how characters respond to the central problem. In this story, when the narrator overcomes her resentment and settles back into a sense of love and security, an overarching idea seems

I didnt know babes were so much trouble."

"Neither did I love... neither did I." my mom kissed my head and smiled.

I thought to myself, was it THAT hard for my mom? No dad, 2 kids, big struggle? I felt bad, as if I had no heart, but then I thought, my mom did care for me, it was hard to care for us both. She loves me equally, ~~but I was pushing her to love me more? was that happening?~~ I felt tears in my eyes, and tried blinking them away. They glistened and I let them run down my face. I. was just talking to my mom, and we settled it ~~but I was still thinking. I was in my room, and it was 12:00 midnight,~~ ~~and~~ I came to a conclusion. I WAS pushing her TOO hard. I could Sleep now. I knew that my mom loved me and I loved her too. And then I fell asleep.

Figure 8–1 *Leeyah's ending: using reflection to convey meaning*

to be that though new siblings demand extra attention, parents love their children equally. Leeyah now knows that ending with reflection is one effective way to cement the meaning she wants to convey.

Use Action or Dialogue: *One way writers end our stories is with a character's words or actions that show change and significance inside the moment.*

One of the most valuable things we can teach our students about writing narrative is the importance of moving back and forth between character's words, thoughts, and actions. As readers, unless we see what characters are doing and hear what they are saying and thinking, it is almost impossible to enter into their world—almost impossible to experience for ourselves what they are experiencing. This, in turn, makes us less likely to be impacted by the events and characters in a story.

When we write stories, we certainly do not need to rely on dialogue and action alone. There are times, for example, when we use narration to interpret for our readers the meaning behind our character's words, thoughts, and actions. But when we want to invite our readers into the world of our characters and keep them in that world—when we want to allow our readers to interpret for themselves what to make of the events in our pieces—we can end our stories with something our characters are saying, thinking, and/or doing that connects with the meaning of the piece.

Teaching

Tell

When I conferred with third-grader Nicole, I said, "When writers want to end our stories in the moment, we often end with action and/or dialogue that show the significance of the story. In other words, the action and dialogue should get across what we want our readers to know and feel about what happens."

Show

"For example, in my story about the day my dad moved out and I called and begged him to come home, I want to show my readers that I was devastated but also angry. I want my readers to know how on that night, I felt like my whole life and my whole family was falling apart. I end by writing:

I dropped the phone and slid to the ground. My mom knelt down beside me and I turned away, yelling, "I want to move out, too! I want to run away just like daddy." But then my mom wrapped her arms around me and I let her hold me. I pressed my back into her chest and sobbed, "I miss my family. I miss my home."

"Do you see how my words and actions show what I want my readers to know? When I turn away from my mom and yell that I want to run away like my dad, I show that I was angry about what was happening. When I slide to the ground and sob and tell my mom that I miss my family and my home, I show how sad and scared I was; I show how I felt like these really huge things, family and home, were over and gone for me.

"I could write things like, 'What's for dinner, Mom?' or do things like scratch my back. Even though I might have said or done exactly that, those details don't connect with my story and what I want my readers to know and feel, so I leave them out."

Active Engagement

Tell

"Would you practice this strategy with your story? Reread the last couple paragraphs of your piece and try an ending that uses action and dialogue to get across what you want your readers to know and feel."

Coach

To support students with this strategy, I say things like:

- "What do you want your readers to know or feel? Now reread what you've written so far and see whether your characters' concluding words and actions get that meaning across."
- "Instead of telling me what you want your readers to know or feel, how could you *show* it through something your characters say, think, or do?"
- "What were the *exact words* that you said or that went through your mind? I'm going to start you off: *I said . . . I thought. . . .*" Or, what are the exact words that your character might say or think here?"
- "What do you think your character was doing when she said or thought this—again, something that will show your readers what you want them to know or feel about the change in the story?"

He was so soft and cuddly. He was shaking in my hands. He tried to jump out of my hands too. Then my mom took him out of my hands.
She said "Do you want to get him?"
I beamed with supprise and said "yes of course!"
Then my mom asked how much money he was.
The lady said "500 dollars."
Then all the dogs started barking.
Then my mom said "OK! I'll get him!"
She said "When can we buy the dog?"
The lady said "Tommrow at 12:00"
So we said good bye to the puppy and left.

Figure 8–2 *Nicole's initial ending*

Before my conference with Nicole, she drafted the ending seen in Figure 8–2. Though Nicole uses action and dialogue in her original end scene, she includes everything her characters say and do, rather than the words and actions that will convey her intentions for writing this story. Finding out that the dog cost five hundred dollars and that they can pick it up at noon the following day does not help me feel Nicole's excitement about or love for the puppy. After our conference, Nicole revised her final scene as shown in Figure 8–3. With her new ending, Nicole lets her readers know the significance of her story. Using dialogue ("*Oh My God! I just got a puppy!*"), she shows that she was excited to finally get her pet, and through action (*The puppy drifted off to sleep right in my arms. I felt my heart beating*), she shows how much she loves him.

Leave Readers Hanging: *One way writers end our stories is with a cliffhanger that leaves readers to imagine for themselves possible outcomes.*

Little upsets my equilibrium more than unresolved conflict. When I fight with my mother, my husband, a friend and we agree to take some time to think, I always spend our time apart torturing myself with how things might unfold: What will I say? How might she respond? What if I said something else instead? Round and round I go in my mind, writing different scripts for the different ways our conversation might unfold. I think it is the unknown that keeps me so preoccupied during times of conflict. Because I want

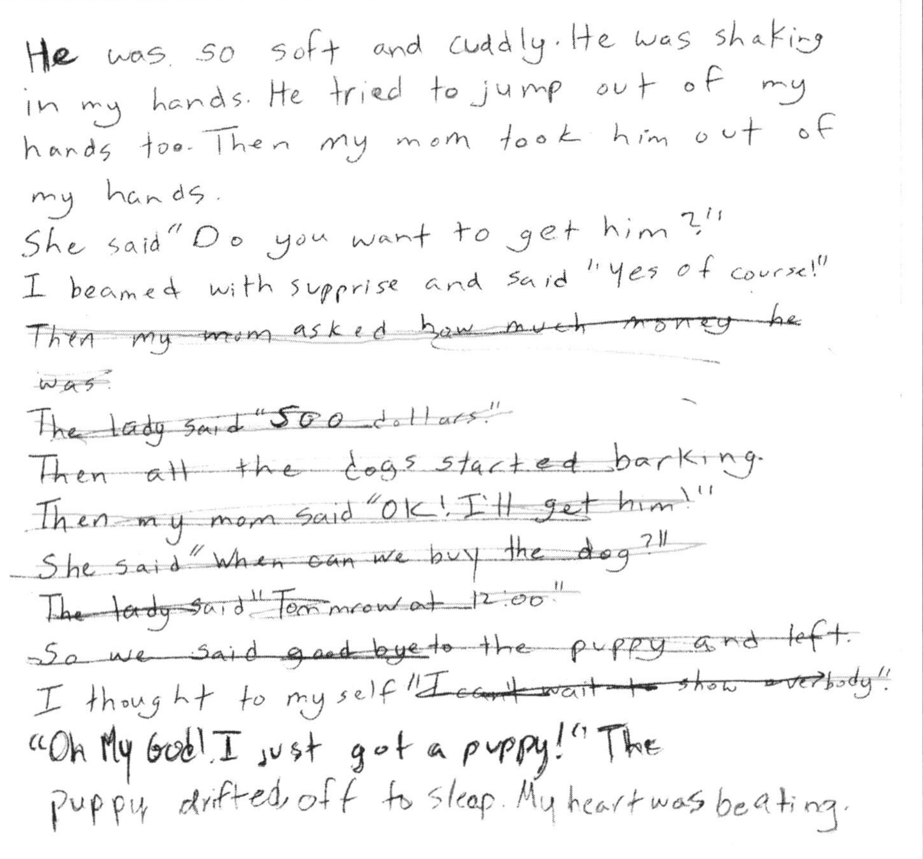

He was so soft and cuddly. He was shaking in my hands. He tried to jump out of my hands too. Then my mom took him out of my hands.
She said "Do you want to get him?"
I beamed with supprise and said "yes of course!"
~~Then my mom asked how much money he was?~~
~~The lady said "500 dollars"~~
~~Then all the dogs started barking.~~
~~Then my mom said "OK! I'll get him!"~~
~~She said "When can we buy the dog?"~~
~~The lady said "Tommrow at 12:00"~~
~~So we said good bye to the puppy and left.~~
I thought to myself "~~I can't wait to show everbody~~"
"Oh My God! I just got a puppy!" The puppy drifted off to sleep. My heart was beating.

Figure 8–3 *Nicole's revised ending: using action and dialogue to convey meaning*

answers, because I want clarity and resolution, I find it nearly impossible to focus my attention on anything other than the impending interaction.

Stories that end with a cliff-hanger have a similar effect on readers. Facing unanswered questions, our thoughts tend to linger; they tend to return again and again to the issue at hand in an attempt to find resolution. As writers, we sometimes choose to present our readers with an unknown, both so they will keep coming back to our stories, and also so they will take the time to interpret and imagine for themselves possible outcomes.

Teaching

Tell

"Sometimes writers end with what we call a cliff-hanger," I said in a conference with fifth-grader Tara. "That means the writer never actually says what happens with the problem, but instead leaves readers to imagine for themselves different possible outcomes. Doing this allows writers to keep the tension going and to keep readers hooked into the story even after the story is over."

Show

"For example, I'm writing a story about a girl who is teased by her friends at school. When I think about what could happen at the end, I think of several possibilities: she might decide to tell her teacher and the teacher might suspend the girls; or she might make a new friend and stop caring what anyone else thinks; or maybe an older student intervenes, tells the girls to stop being so mean.

"But if I want to end with a cliff-hanger, I can't resolve the problem for my readers; I need to make it possible for them to come to their own conclusion. So let me think . . . I could show the problem about to get resolved without letting readers know what happens in the end. Like maybe I could have Kassy introduce herself to a new girl without telling my readers whether they actually become friends. Or I could end with Kassy in the midst of deciding whether to tell her teacher or just ignore the girls and make a new friend instead. Let me see . . . I think I'll have Kassy trying to make a friend while considering her other options, as well.

> *"Hi, my name is Kassy," she said. She knew that if she didn't make a new friend, she would have no choice but to tell her teacher what had been happening. She simply could not take one more day of being all alone and at the mercy of the other girls.*
>
> *The new girl was silent. Kassy held her breath, then exhaled and asked, "What's your name?"*

"With an ending like that, some readers might think that Kassy and the new girl become friends and everything is better as a result. But other readers might think that they don't become friends, or that even if they do, Kassy still tells her teacher what's been happening and her teacher is the one who solves the problem. It's really up to my readers to decide for themselves.

"Do you see how I first thought about different ways I could solve the problem, and then imagined a scenario in which either of those solutions could come true?"

Active Engagement

Tell

"Why don't you try this as a possible conclusion for your story. See if ending with a cliff-hanger, where you let readers imagine for themselves different possible outcomes, helps you stretch out your tension even more."

Coach

To support Tara, I said things like:

- "First imagine what the possible outcomes are. Now, how might you write the ending in a way that leaves open those different possibilities?"
- "You might end your story just before the problem is resolved. Instead of letting your readers know what actually happens, you can show the character about to do something in connection with the problem."
- "You might end your story long after the problem is resolved. You could show your character doing something in the future that could be the result of many different things happening."

After our conference, Tara tried a couple different endings for her story about the day she watched her cat move across her bedroom toward her new fish. In her final piece, she decided to use the one in Figure 8–4 in which she ends with a cliff-hanger. The impact of Tara's ending is quite significant. By simply using an ellipsis and "that time," she leaves readers pondering a range of options: that her cat has not yet eaten the fish, but still could; that she did eventually eat them; that fish and cat coexist peacefully despite what people assume about cats and fish. Because of Tara's conclusion, the tension never really ends. As a result, readers are hooked into the piece even after

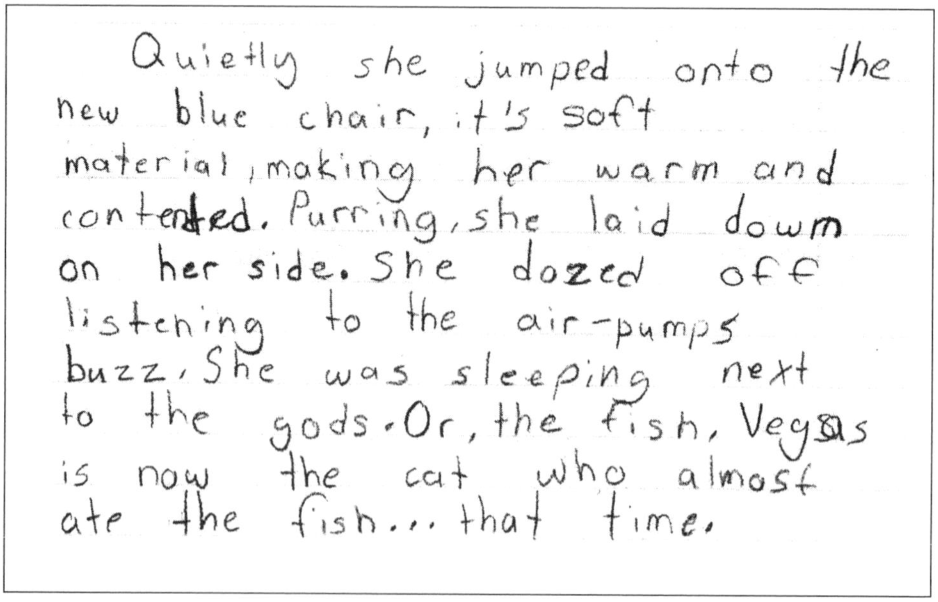

Quietly she jumped onto the new blue chair, it's soft material, making her warm and contented. Purring, she laid down on her side. She dozed off listening to the air-pumps buzz. She was sleeping next to the gods. Or, the fish, Vegas is now the cat who almost ate the fish... that time.

Figure 8–4 *Tara's ending: using a cliffhanger to keep the tension going*

finishing the last word because they are left to forever wonder what really happened between cat and fish.

* * *

The end of a story is like end punctuation. Question marks, explanation marks, ellipses, and periods—they direct us, give us clues about how to make sense of and feel about the information in a sentence. Is the information a certainty? A cause for anxiety or anticipation? Something urgent or exciting?

Similarly, the end of a story is a clue; it lets us know, when all is said and done, what we should make of the characters and events about which we just read. A return to the beginning, a reflection, or a cliff-hanger—they are a writer's last attempt to impact our readers. The more thoughtful our students are about how they conclude their pieces, the more likely that their writing will mean something in the world and the more likely it will leave a lasting impression long after their readers have moved on to new stories.

INTRODUCTION: TEACHING NONNARRATIVE WRITING

Unless we happen to write stories or poems for a living, or for a passion, most of the writing we do as we move through the world is nonnarrative. When we write letters to friends, emails to bosses; when we write memos to parents or comments on report cards, we are writing nonnarrative, a listing of information organized by category. If most of the writing we do is nonnarrative, then we need to teach our students to write it well so they can move through school and beyond with success.

Based on the work of Lucy Calkins and colleagues at The Teachers College Reading and Writing Project, I understand and define nonnarrative writing as category-based writing: writing that is categorized by subtopics or subideas. It includes expository or idea-based writing like essays and speeches, informational or fact-based writing like travel guides and brochures, and procedural writing like cookbooks and manuals. Though nonnarrative writing may contain stories inside of it, the piece as a whole is not structured as a story. Instead, information is grouped together by categories, and any stories that may be included fall into or introduce one of these categories.

When we teach nonnarrative writing, the first thing we need to consider is genre: do we want to teach the entire class to write in the same genre? Consider, for example, whether you want everyone writing personal essays or feature articles or informational picture books. Or do you want to teach students to choose their own genre? Consider whether you want some students writing personal essays; others, feature articles; still others, persuasive letters or speeches or travel guides.

Next, we need to decide whether we want the writing to be research-based or based on personal expertise. If your students are newer to non-narrative writing, you might consider teaching them to choose topics about which they already know a lot so you can focus on the structure of non-narrative writing. Otherwise, you will need to devote a fair amount of time to teaching students how to actually do research and organize their research.

Regardless of the genre, if your students are writing nonnarrative pieces like the ones mentioned above, they will need to draw upon the skills included in the following chapters, skills that will enable them to craft non-narrative pieces that empower them as writers and make a lasting impact on their readers.

CHAPTER 9

Finding Nonnarrative Topics That Matter

Whenever I write with an end goal in mind (a paper for class, a poem for a friend, a book for publication), what I struggle with most is choosing my topic. I usually agonize for days to months, discussing possibilities over dinner with friends; waking up in the middle of the night with new insights (or else new anxieties); jotting ideas in notebooks and on scraps of paper. For me, finding my topic has always been half the battle because I know from experience as a writer that my end piece can only be as good as my topic.

I also know from experience as a teacher that the end piece is only as good as the topic. Many of our students want to pick something and go; they want to take the first topic that comes to them and draft their piece. Unfortunately, even if they have a perfect understanding of how to structure an essay or can craft an article better than anyone around them, their end pieces will fall flat if they have not been thoughtful about their topics. We need to teach our students to slow down; we need to teach them to try on a range of topics just as they would try on a range of shoes or pants before picking the pair to buy. We need to teach them to think hard about the topic that both means something to them and will generate a lot of writing.

You can use any of the strategies in this chapter to teach your students to generate nonnarrative topics; however, you will need to angle the strategy to fit the genre in which they are writing. If students are writing informational texts, you can simply teach the strategies as they are written here, and your students will generate more general topics, such as *Fighting with parents* or *Michael Jordan* or *Global warming*. However, if your students are writing essays, you need to teach them to consider what they *think;* their topics need to be ideas, such as, *Fighting with my parents ruins my whole day* or *Fighting with parents is a way for young people to test the boundaries of their independence.* If your students are writing procedural texts, you will need to teach them to consider the steps one can take; their topics need to yield directions of some sort, such as *Navigating fights with parents* or *Ways to win fights with parents.*

As you model and as students collect possible topics, the writing can take two forms: lists and paragraph writing. However, when students begin with a written list, they should quickly move on to picking something from their list and writing about it in paragraph form. When you see a list in this chapter, imagine that paragraph writing followed, and when you see paragraph writing, imagine that the topic could have originated on a list of possible topics.

If you are just beginning a unit on writing informational, procedural, or expository writing, you might teach any of the following strategies in your minilessons. You could also teach any of the strategies in conferences or strategy lessons if you have students who still struggle to find meaningful and generative nonnarrative topics.

Explore Curiosities and Uncertainties: *One way writers find meaningful nonnarrative topics is by considering things about which we are curious or uncertain and about which we want to know more.*

More than anything, writing is about observing; being a writer means living in the world with wide-open eyes, turning over in our minds or in our notebooks the color of the sky, the look on a woman's face, a line in yesterday's paper, or an image in last night's dream. In other words, being a writer means being curious, about everything. About anything. It means exploring the uncertain. Writers live by questioning, exploring, researching the seemingly small (how does a petal feel once it's wilted in the sun?) to the seemingly huge (who were the first African Americans to fight in the Civil War?).

How profound, then, to teach our students to think about and reflect upon their curiosities and their uncertainties. Doing so means teaching them a way to generate meaningful, purposeful ideas for nonnarrative. But in a larger sense, it also means teaching them how to be writers.

When I taught personal essay to my own seventh graders, some of the students struggled to generate meaningful topics in the first couple days of the unit. I shared my concerns with my colleague Audra Robb, who suggested I have them write with the intention of exploring and learning about uncertainties.

Teaching

Tell

After introducing the day's lesson, I named my teaching point: "One way writers find ideas for personal essays is by considering something about which we are uncertain and then writing to explore and learn about those uncertainties. One reason this works so well is because when we truly ponder, we make room for creative new thinking to enter our minds and the written page."

Show

"Let me know show you what I mean. I've been thinking about things about myself that I don't really understand. One thing is my anger; people always tell me I'm loving and kind, and yet, I get angry a lot. I don't like this about myself, and I'd like to understand more about why I am this way. I'm going to freewrite in front of you, and I want you to notice how I use writing to explore this curiosity and uncertainty I have and, in turn, to uncover some possible essay topics. I know the trick will be to keep my pen moving as much as possible—to think in writing. Watch how I do that."

I started my entry on a piece of chart paper by writing, *I get angry a lot and I don't know why.* "Let me imagine why I might do this. I'm not looking for one answer, or the right answer: *Maybe I do this because* . . . Hmm, because . . . because . . . I need to just freewrite, let whatever comes to mind come out; so let me reread to get a running start, and then I'm really going to keep my pen moving. . . . Maybe I do this because . . . *because when I get hurt it is safer to be angry than to get upset. When I'm angry, it's like I'm building a wall around me, but when I'm hurt, it's like the wall is falling down and I am exposed and vulnerable. That is a scary way to be. So maybe I get angry so much because it's safer for me.*

"Wow, that just poured out of me! Look how much I wrote in just one minute! I want to push myself to keep going, and I will later on. But already, I have some possible topics for my essay that really matter to me, topics that I can imagine writing a lot about; for example, I could write about how it's safer for me to be angry than hurt, or I could write about how when I'm angry it's like I'm building a brick wall around myself.

"Did you notice how I got to those ideas? Did you see how I thought of a curiosity or uncertainty and "wrote to learn" by really keeping my pen moving that whole time? Did you see how I thought on paper—how I considered my uncertainty and then simply wrote the first thing that came to mind, and then let that thought lead to the next and the next? Notice how I used the word *maybe* to help me because when we want to learn, we aren't looking for *the* answer, we're looking for a range of possibilities."

Active Engagement

Tell

"Take a moment to try this before you go back to your seats. Think of something you're curious or uncertain about and could explore in a freewrite; when you're ready, open your notebooks, and I'm going to give you two minutes. In that time, push yourself to write at least half a page; push yourself to think on paper and keep your pen moving the whole time."

Coach

As the class tried the strategy, I circulated the group, reading over students' shoulders, kneeling down next to individual writers to coach them, and even saying loud enough for the entire class to hear certain prompts and reminders. I said things like:

- "Keep your pen moving; think as you write!"
- "Write *Maybe it's because* . . . and then finish the thought."
- "Write *It could be that* . . . and complete the thought."
- "If you're stuck, reread a little bit to get a running start back into thinking and writing."

After about two minutes, I asked everyone to put their pencils down. "Raise your hand if you wrote something you never expected to write—if you uncovered a new thought." Most students raised their hands, and I reminded them that what they just did was an excellent way to seek out powerful topics for their essays.

During the two minute active engagement, Katy wrote the entry shown in Figure 9–1. She successfully used writing to explore an uncertainty and a curiosity; she uncovered new thinking about love and why she wants it when she wrote things like, *Maybe, I get kind of envious of other people. . . . Maybe deep inside of me I want to have that feeling*

Love. I don't understand it. I don't think anyone truly understands it.

For me, I'm in this point in my life where for whatever reason it is, hormones or whatever. I really want "love".

Maybe, I got kind of envious of other people. People who have crushes. People crushing on them, boyfriends, girlfriends, a loved one. Maybe deep inside of me I want to have that feeling where I know someone loves me—someone besides family. Maybe that causes me to force myself to have a crush. Or force myself to think someone likes me. Because I do try. However strange it is I try. Even if it isn't love.

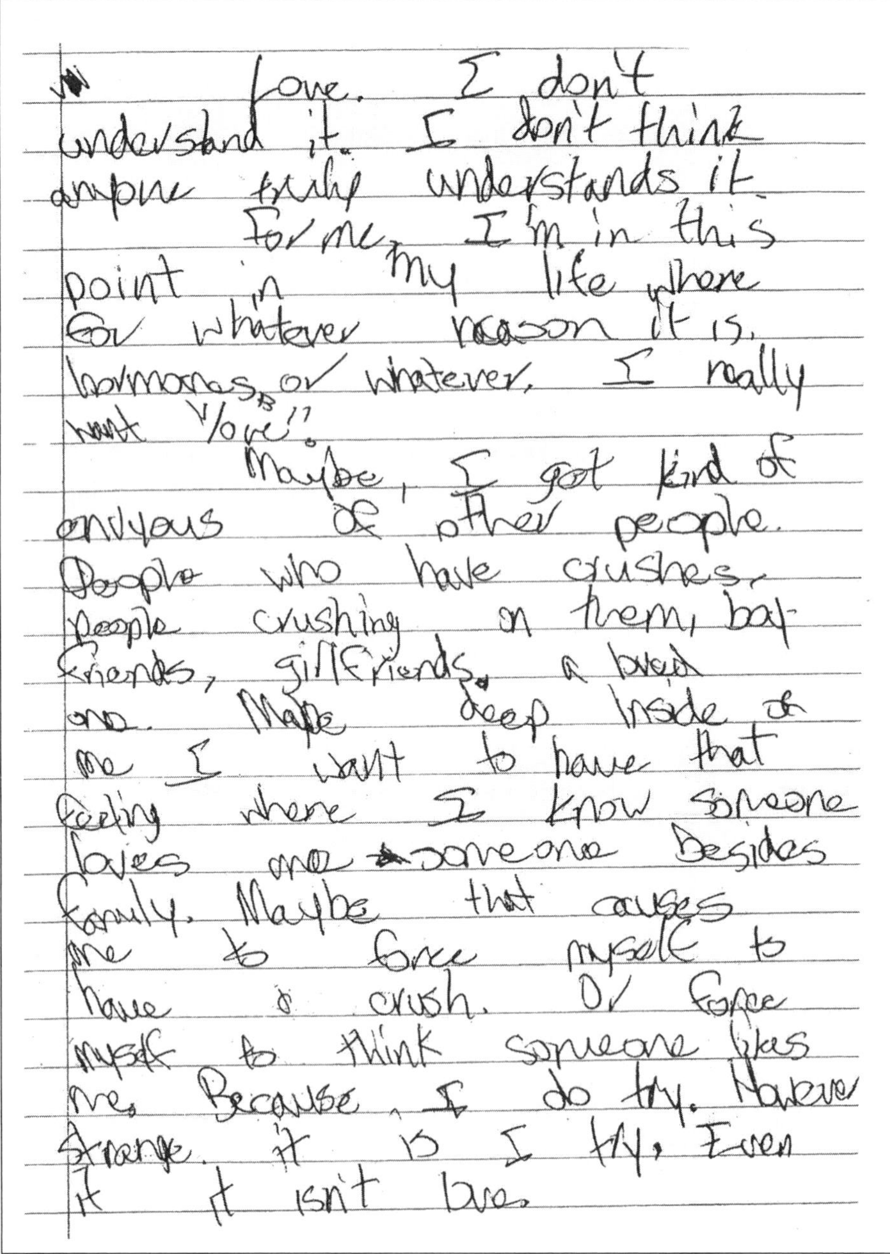

Love. I don't understand it. I don't think anyone truly understands it.
For me, I'm in this point in my life where for whatever reason it is, hormones, or whatever. I really want "love".
Maybe, I got kind of envyous of other people. People who have crushes, people crushing on them, boy-friends, girlfriends, a loved one. Maybe deep inside of me I want to have that feeling where I know someone loves me someone besides family. Maybe that causes me to force myself to have a crush. Or force myself to think someone likes me. Because I do try. However strange it is I try. Even if it isn't love.

Figure 9–1 *Katy's notebook entry of possible topics: exploring curiosities and uncertainties*

where I know someone loves me—someone besides my family. She clearly explored possible topics in thoughtful ways, and as a result, generated possible topics that are deeply thoughtful. Topics that are meaningful for her and that allow her to generate a lot of writing. When Katy returned to her seat after the minilesson, she drew from her repertoire of strategies for generating topics and explored other possible ideas for her essay.

Because my students were writing essay, I taught them to consider their curiosities and uncertainties and what they think about those things; in turn, Katy's entry yielded ideas, such as, *I don't think anyone truly understands [love].* Were my students writing informational texts, I would have simply taught them to consider their curiosities and uncertainties, in which case Katy may have *Love* as a possible topic and an entry in which she gathered initial wonderings and information about love. Were they writing procedural texts, I would instead have taught them to consider their curiosities and uncertainties as well as steps to take around these things. Perhaps Katy would have considered topics like *How to fall in love* or *Attracting your crush* and generated an entry with advice for her readers.

Consider Passions: *One way writers find meaningful nonnarrative topics is by considering the things about which we are the most passionate.*

Our students often bubble over, and at other times lash out with passion. They want to tell us about their pets and how they care for them; they want to tell us about how mean their siblings are and about the book they finished last night. Or, they don't want to tell us anything at all because they are teenagers now and we get in the way of their crushes and their shopping and the time that could be spent in their favorite hangouts; so they are passionate about dating and fashion and local hot spots.

Whether our students are seven or seventeen years old, we can teach them that one way to uncover meaningful topics for their nonnarrative pieces is to search inside themselves and inside their lives for the things that ignite strong feelings; we can teach them to use writing to explore and express their passions.

Teaching

Tell

"One way writers come up with nonnarrative topics is by thinking of things about which we are really passionate," Kathy Racynsky said to her class of third graders who were starting a picture book study. "This is a great way to find ideas because when we feel strongly about something, whether the feelings are positive or negative, we usually have a lot to say or write on the topic. And, we usually say it with a lot of emotion and meaning, which means that what we write will really matter to us and to our readers."

Show

"Watch me as I come up with some possible topics for my nonnarrative picture book by thinking about my own passions. Let me think. . . . What's something that I really love or really hate or really fear or really feel? Right now I'm thinking about things I do. Like teaching! I do that every day and I love teaching, so I can definitely write that on my list of possible topics. I also swim, though not as much as I wish I did because I absolutely love to swim; I'll put swimming on my list, too.

"What else do I feel passionately about? Right now, I'm thinking about things that annoy me because sometimes I get passionate about disliking stuff. Like recycling! I feel passionate about doing it, and I feel passionately upset when people don't do it.

"I bet I could also think about people and places I'm passionate about—like cats! I am passionate in my dislike of cats because they make me sneeze and itch and feel just awful! I'm adding cats to my list of passions. And beaches. I love beaches, am passionate about walking along them and swimming in the ocean.

"Do you see how I'm coming up with possible topics for my nonnarrative picture book by thinking about things I'm passionate about? Do you notice how I'm thinking about things I do (like swimming and teaching), as well as people, places, animals, and objects in my life (like cats and beaches) to help me think about things I feel strongly about? I also want you to notice that passions can be positive or negative because whether we love or hate something (like I love teaching but hate cats), the topic matters to us and we usually have a lot to say about it."

Active Engagement

Tell

"Now it's your turn to try. Take a moment to think of a few things you're passionate about. Put up your thumb when you've thought of at least three things."

Coach

While Kathy waited for the majority of her class to begin in their minds their lists of topics, she helped them by saying things like:

- "Think of things you do a lot: things you do at home . . . things you do at school. . . . Do you really love or hate doing any of those things?"
- "Think of places you spend a lot of your time, or places you wish you could spend more time."
- "Think about objects, animals, relationships about which you feel strongly."

It is important to note that Kathy never prompts students to write about an object or a relationship or something they do often. Instead, she lets them know they can seek out their passions, and she tucks into her coaching that considering things like objects, relationships, and actions are ways to recall passions.

After her minilesson, Kathy sent everyone back to their seats and asked them to start a list in their writers' notebooks of things about which they might want to write a nonnarrative picture book. She reminded them that, as always, they should search for topics about which they care deeply; she also reminded them that *one way* to uncover such topics is to consider one's passions. After Kyriaki made the following list, she picked one of her topics and wrote a new entry with information on one of her passions, as shown in Figure 9–2.

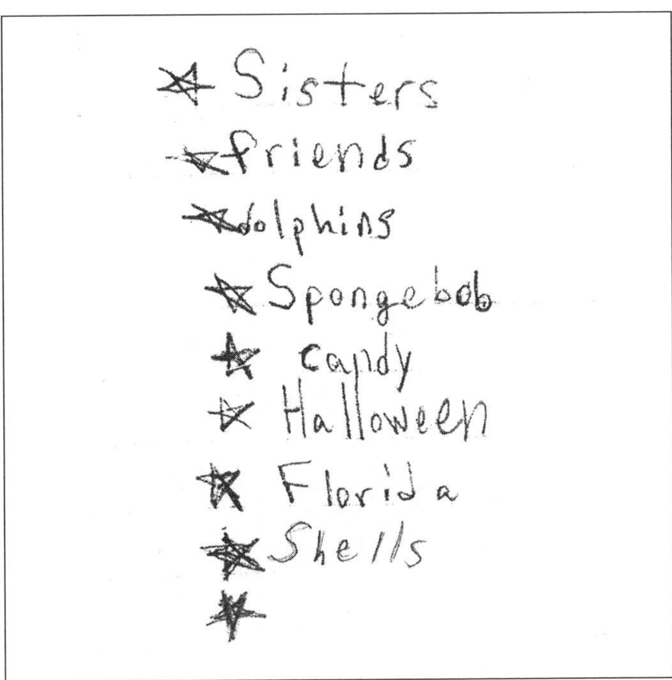

Figure 9–2 *Kyriaki's notebook entries: listing passions and generating information about one of those passions*

SHELLS 11/2

Shells have different shapes and sizes. They are like this because different sea-animals live in them!

For example: hermit-crab shells, have crabs or, hermit-crabs in them. Clam-shells, have clams in them.

DID YOU KNOW?

You can here the ocean from a conch shell!

Figure 9–2 *(continued)*

Everything on Kyriaki's list is a possible topic for a nonnarrative picture book. Over the next several days, she begins to explore possible topics by gathering information on the ones that especially appeal to her, for example, shells.

If Kathy wanted her third graders to write essays instead of nonnarrative picture books, she might have used this strategy to teach students to consider their passions and then to list thoughts about those things. Instead

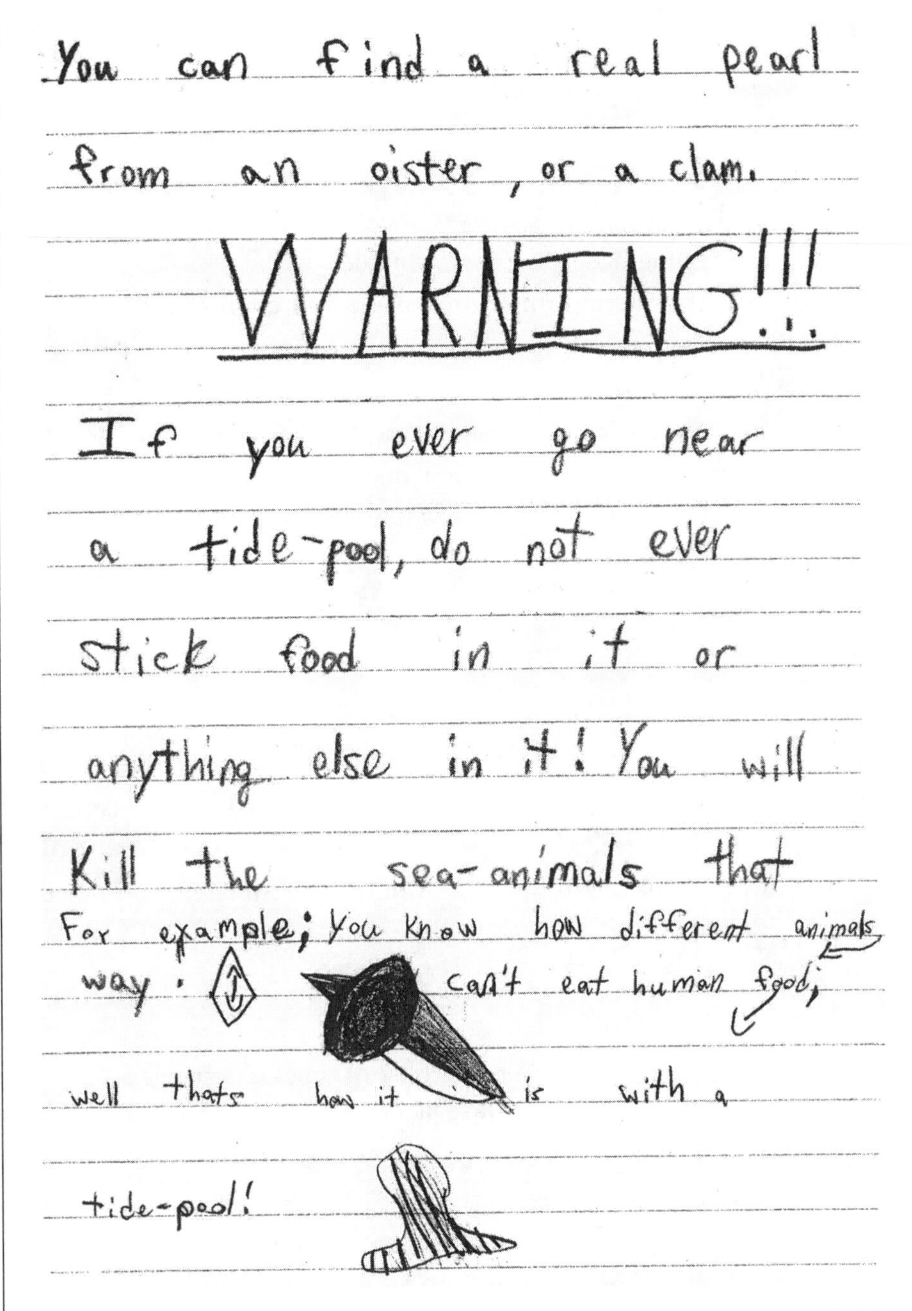

You can find a real pearl from an oister, or a clam.

WARNING!!!

If you ever go near a tide-pool, do not ever stick food in it or anything else in it! You will Kill the sea-animals that way. For example; You know how different animals can't eat human food; well thats how it is with a tide-pool!

Figure 9–2 *(continued)*

of simply writing *Sisters* at the top of her list, Kyriaki might have written, *Sisters are like best friends,* or *My sister is annoying.* If Kathy wanted her students to write procedural texts, she might have taught them to consider their passions and list how to do, or do something in connection with, one of those things. Kyriaki might have written, *How to turn your sister into a friend* or *Getting your sister to leave you alone.*

Consider Times of Struggle and Confusion: *One way writers find meaningful nonnarrative topics is by considering times of struggle or confusion.*

We can teach students to consider times of struggle and confusion in their own lives or in the lives of others, past or present. Either way, doing so means thinking about events that incite strong emotions, and writing about emotional topics almost always means writing about meaningful topics. After all, feeling deeply means caring deeply.

Furthermore, considering times of struggle and confusion often means thinking about the unresolved, which means tapping into a longing to understand. Whenever there is a desire and an ability to deepen understanding, there is an accompanying potential for new insight and information. And new insight and information makes for topics that matter to reader and writer alike.

Teaching

Tell

"One way you can come up with powerful topics is by considering times of struggle or confusion and reflecting on those times," I said to a class of seventh graders. "This is a powerful generating strategy because most of us learn and grow and change in the face of difficulty, which should not only give us a lot to say, but should lead to thoughtful ideas."

Show

"Let me show you what I mean. When I think of times of struggle and confusion in my own life, I think about things like those years in elementary school when my friends repeatedly left me out. Of course I struggled because it was so painful, and I was confused because I didn't understand why they treated me that way, or whether there was something I could do to make it different.

"I also think about my first broken heart. This was another time of struggle for me; it took me a long time to feel OK again. And for so long, I was confused about why my boyfriend broke up with me and what I could do to feel better.

"For now, I'm going to pick one of those times of struggle and confusion—let's say when my friends were so mean to me—and I'm going to gather ideas about that time of struggle and confusion. Hmmm . . . I'm not sure what to write first, so I think to get started, I'll ask myself a question and then answer it in writing: Why was that time so hard? It was really hard for me because . . . because. . . . Let me just start writing: *It was really hard for me when my friends teased me all those years because I felt lonely and afraid all the time.* Why else was it hard for me? *Sometimes I also thought something was wrong with me because why else would they pick on me all the time? I am the kind of person who often finds fault with myself, so maybe that made it easy for them to find fault with me, too.*

"Already I have found some good ideas by reflecting on a time of struggle and confusion. Do you see how I get and keep myself writing and uncovering those ideas by asking and answering cause and effect questions, like when I asked, Why was that so hard for me? I had a lot to say in response to that question which is a sign that this topic matters to me."

Active Engagement

Tell

"Now I want you to try this. Right now, you should be thinking of times of struggle or confusion in your own lives. Some of you might take a moment to jot some of these times down; but very quickly, I want you to pick one of those times and write an entry in which you reflect on that time. One or more of those thoughts might be a compelling idea for a personal essay."

Coach

To help students generate ideas and keep their pens moving, I said things like:

- "In times of struggle and confusion, we usually feel things like anger, fear, disappointment, anxiety, sadness. You might recall times when you felt one or more of these emotions."
- "Answer the question, What caused this struggle? Then answer, What else might have caused this struggle?"
- "Answer, What resulted from this time of struggle and confusion?"
- "Consider how you or others felt about yourselves and others during this time."

When she returned to her seat, Jessica took a couple minutes to finish the entry she started in the minilesson (shown in Figure 9–3), after which she continued to explore possible essay topics in other entries.

Jessica may or may not decide to write an essay on her ideas about divorce. If she does, she may explore ideas like, *My parents probably would*

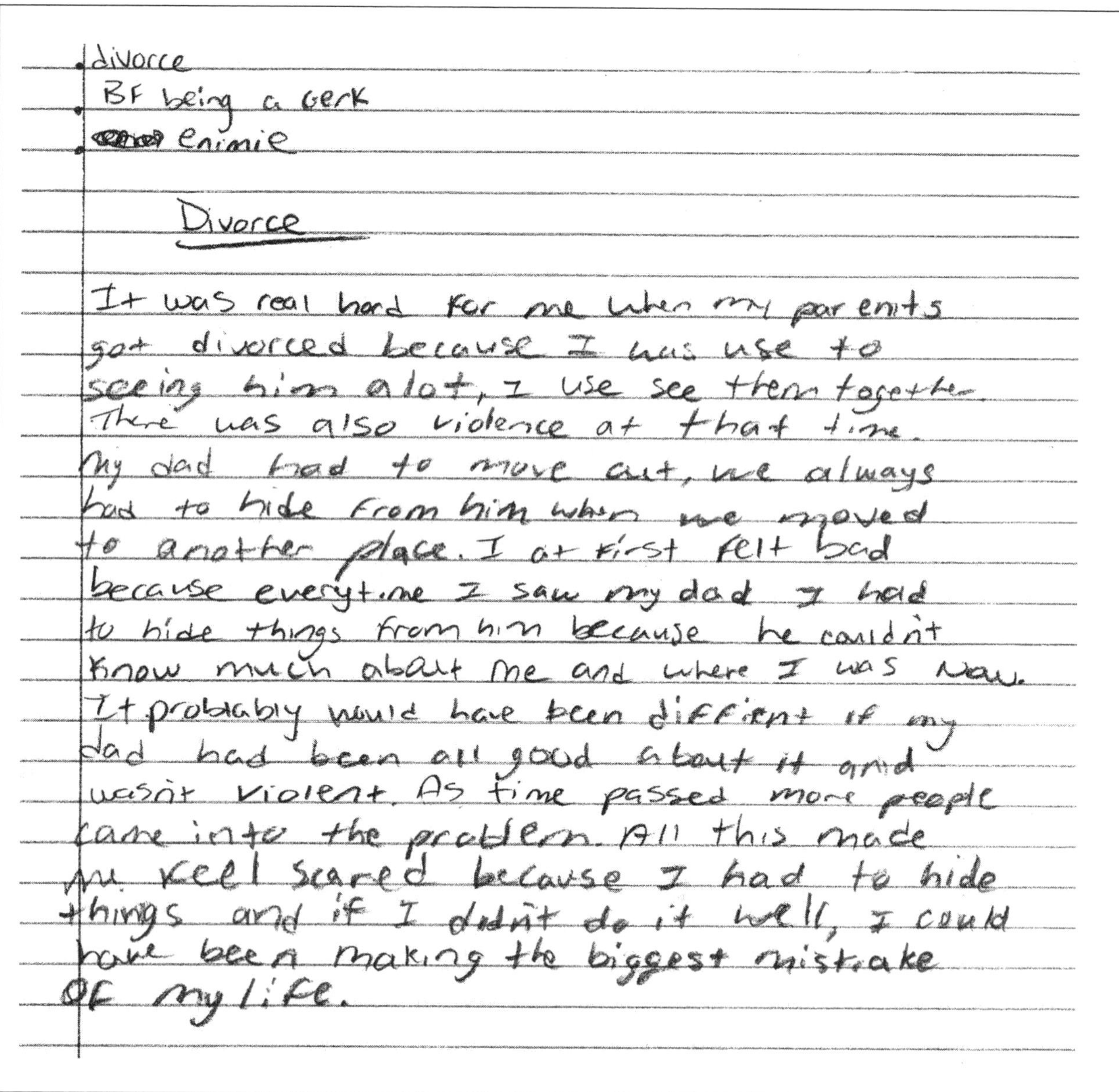

- divorce
- BF being a gerk
- ~~[scribbled]~~ enimie

Divorce

It was real hard for me when my parents got divorced because I was use to seeing him alot, I use see them togethe. There was also violence at that time. My dad had to move out, we always had to hide from him when we moved to another place. I at first felt bad because everytime I saw my dad I had to hide things from him because he couldn't know much about me and where I was now. It probably would have been diffirent if my dad had been all good about it and wasn't violent. As time passed more people came into the problem. All this made me keel scared because I had to hide things and if I didn't do it well, I could have been making the biggest mistrake of my life.

Figure 9–3 *Jessica's notebook entry of possible topics: exploring times of struggle and confusion*

have been different if my dad had been all good and wasn't violent or *I was scared because I had to hide things and I didn't do it well.* By reflecting on a time of struggle and confusion, Jessica begins to access topics about which she has a lot to say and which allow her to produce ideas that truly matter.

Were Jessica writing an informational piece, I could have taught her, very simply, to consider times of struggle and confusion; as she moved from her list to paragraph writing, Jessica might have begun to gather facts about divorce rather than her own feelings and thoughts. Were she writing a procedural text, I could have taught Jessica to consider times of struggle and confusion and then to imagine steps people might take to avoid or respond to such times; Jessica might have collected topics like, *Dealing with your parents' divorce* or *How to make sure you're really ready to marry.*

* * *

When we teach our students to generate writing topics, we want them to understand that ultimately, we write to make sense of and to leave a lasting impact on the world. We write articles to convey important information. We write essays to explore our opinions or to persuade others to share our way of seeing the world. We write procedural texts to give our readers the tools they need to face certain challenges, to accomplish certain tasks.

In turn, regardless of the genre in which they choose to write, we want to teach our students to think deeply about what matters to them. Not only so they will choose topics that will hold their attention, but so they will choose topics that will, in fact, allow them to explore and convey meaning and significance. Topics that will allow them to make a difference in people's lives.

CHAPTER 10

Developing Ideas

When I moved into my first apartment with a backyard, my husband and I cleared out the six-foot weeds and slowly started to transform the stretch of dirt into something grand. We dug holes and planted vegetable seeds. We transferred potted flowers into the ground and collected discarded stones from parks. We watered. We waited. We weeded. By the time we left the apartment three years later, our backyard had evolved into a country oasis in the middle of Brooklyn. In one corner, beneath the shade of a fig tree, we had table and chairs atop a large piece of stone. A garden of herbs flourished in another corner. Rows of carrots, zucchini, squash, tomatoes grew along one side of the yard.

Growing a garden, like developing ideas, is a journey, and the digging and weeding one does along the way determines the end result. Just as we grow gardens one tiny seed at a time, we develop ideas one tiny thought at a time. Just as gardeners usually pull handfuls of weeds for every squash or tulip that pushes its way through ground, nonnarrative writers often have pages of dead-end facts and ideas for every prized one we uncover. If you find a series of unexplored information when you read your students' nonnarrative writing, or you find thinking that feels more like weeds than tulips, you might teach them to develop their ideas.

Teaching students to develop ideas is really about teaching them to uncover and explore more complex, more original thinking and there are different times and reasons for doing this. When students write expository texts, we want them to develop their ideas before settling on a thesis so they can craft more meaningful and memorable pieces. We can teach students to redevelop their ideas once they have drafted expository text so they can conclude their pieces with new insight and send readers away still pondering. When students write informational or procedural texts with their own opinions woven throughout their factual information, we can teach them to develop what those opinions are, again, so they can move away from the kinds of thoughts anyone and everyone might have and toward something more unique.

Whether teaching students to develop a thesis, conclusive thoughts, or responsive thinking, if your goal is to move them beyond ideas that feel flat and predictable, you might teach the following strategies.

Seek the Surprising and Unique: *One way writers develop ideas is by looking for what we think that is surprising or different from what others might think about the topic.*

Seeking the surprising and unique is really the ultimate goal we all have as writers, and the ultimate goal we all have for our students who write. Still, I teach this goal as a strategy because I have found that doing so greatly increases students' ability to uncover new thoughts or new expressions of their thinking. As soon as I tell students that they should write searching for fresh ideas, for something that they alone might say, they more easily move away from the cliché.

Teaching

Tell

When I pulled together a small group of fifth graders, I said, "Good writers move beyond our initial thoughts and develop our thinking into something that will leave a lasting impression on our readers. Writers sometimes do this by holding an end goal in mind, which is to develop original thinking; as we write, we keep asking ourselves, What do I think about this that is different from what someone else might think? What do I think that might even be surprising to my readers?"

Show

"Let me show you how I develop one of my ideas, which is, *My best friend is important to me.* That's an ordinary, everyday statement; any of you would probably say something like that about your best friends, right? So I want to push myself beyond this idea by thinking about what I think that is different or surprising. Watch me do that. I'm going to start with my initial thought: *My best friend is important to me.* Hmm . . . what do I think about my best friend that is different from what other people might think? *My best friend is kind and caring. She always makes time for me.* That still feels like what others would say. How could I write these thoughts in a more surprising way? My best friend always makes time for me. . . . *Sometimes she's so selfless I feel bad about not being more so.* Oh, now that's a little more interesting. Let me keep going with that: *For example, this week she called me every day even though she was really busy and I only called her once because I was so distracted by work. Or this other time—*

Wait, now I'm getting away from my ideas and just writing examples. I don't want to do that yet; I want to try and develop more of my thinking first. So let me get back to that question: What do I think or feel that's different or surprising? Sometimes she's so selfless I feel bad about not being more so. . . . *My best friend shows me the kind of person I want to be. Oftentimes, when I want to work on my behavior, I think about my best friend and how she would act and I use her as a model.* Wow, now I feel like I'm getting to much more interesting ideas. I don't know that any of you would immediately say these things about your best friends. I'm going to keep working on this entry later, but do you see what I'm doing? Do you see how I'm outgrowing my initial thought by asking myself again and again as I write, What do I think that is different or surprising?"

Active Involvement

Tell

"I want you to try this now. You can either start a new entry or pick an idea from one of your other entries. Either way, I want you to develop your ideas by repeatedly asking yourself as you write, *What do I think that is different or surprising?*, so you can move away from your more ordinary thinking and toward something more unique."

Coach

As students worked, I supported them by saying things like:

- "If you asked your classmates what they thought about this topic, would they say something similar to what you're writing here? How could you write your idea in a way that they wouldn't?"

- "What do you think or feel about this topic that you think might surprise the people who know you? What might make them say, 'Oh, I didn't know she thought or felt that way.'"
- "Can you be more specific? What do you really mean when you write that thought?"
- "Reread what you've written so far and underline anything that seems original to you—something different from what other people might write about this topic. Now keep writing and try to come up with more ideas like the one(s) you underlined."

During the strategy lesson, Antonio decided to write a new entry in which he explored his thinking about his father. He started by writing more "ordinary" ideas: that he loves his father, that they have fun together. When Antonio finished his entry, he had pushed beyond his initial thoughts. He underlined ideas that seemed surprising or different to him, as shown in Figure 10–1.

By pushing himself, sentence after sentence, to consider his more original thoughts and feelings, Antonio moves away from everyday ideas like *I love my dad* toward the more unique: *In his arms I'm safe* and *If my dad wasn't my dad I wouldn't be me*. What's more, Antonio is learning how to distinguish between the mundane and the striking, as demonstrated by the fact that he underlines some of his more original thinking as such. Antonio might decide to use one of his underlined thoughts as a thesis for his essay; or perhaps he will use them to write another entry in which he explores his thinking even further. Either way, because he is learning to uncover and recognize more compelling ideas, he is sure to write a more meaningful piece.

Engage in Conversation on Paper: *One way writers develop ideas is by having a conversation on paper. We use phrases common in strong discussions, such as "that makes me think" and "on the other hand" and "I used to think but now I think," to push our thinking.*

The best conversations, like the best nonnarrative pieces, yield new ideas and information. Knowing this, many of us are committed to teaching students how to talk about literature; we know the better their conversations about text, the better their thinking as readers. In most classrooms where my colleagues and I work, one can find a chart that says something

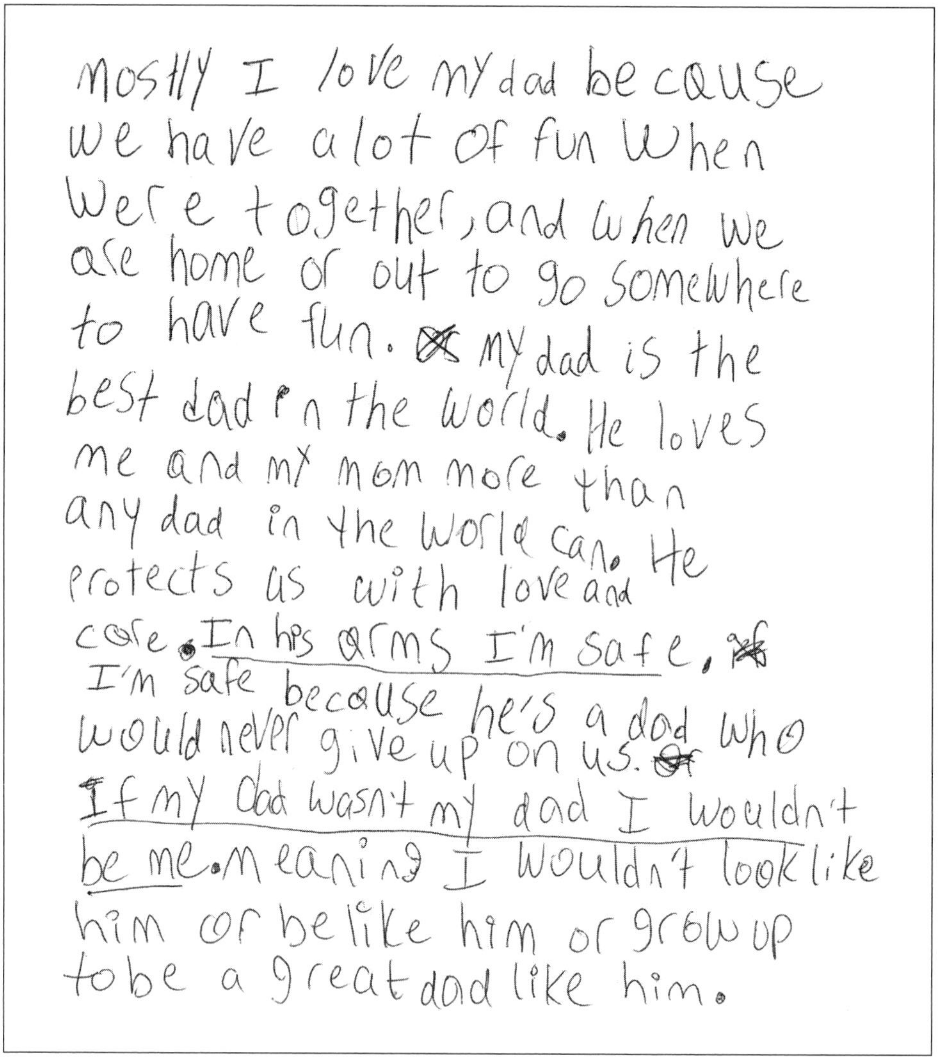

Mostly I love my dad because
we have alot of fun when
were together, and when we
are home or out to go somewhere
to have fun. My dad is the
best dad in the world. He loves
me and my mom more than
any dad in the world can. He
protects us with love and
care. In his arms I'm safe.
I'm safe because he's a dad who
would never give up on us.
If my dad wasn't my dad I wouldn't
be me. meaning I wouldn't look like
him or be like him or grow up
to be a great dad like him.

Figure 10–1 *Antonio's notebook entry: developing ideas by seeking new and surprising thoughts*

like *Talk Prompts* or *Phrases That Push Our Thinking and Talking* with a list of any of the following or more:

- I think this because . . .
- In addition . . .
- This makes me realize . . .
- This is important because . . .
- This connects with . . .
- This is different from . . .

- Maybe it's because . . .
- On the other hand . . .
- I used to think . . . but now I think . . .

Just as students use these prompts to move toward new thinking in a discussion, we can teach them to use the same words and phrases to move toward new thinking on paper.

Teaching

Tell

When I conferred with fifth-grader Tasfia, I said, "Writers often stick with our written ideas by using phrases like 'this makes me think' and 'on the other hand' and 'I used to think but now I think;' in other words, the same things we say to keep a conversation going with other people can help us have and keep a conversation going on paper. It's important to stay focused on our thinking because the longer we stay with an idea, the more likely we'll dig beneath its surface and uncover something really interesting—the kind of thinking that engages our readers from beginning to end."

Show

"For example, notice how in my entry I start out with the idea that friends are important and I stay with that idea, which allows me to make it better."

> *My best friend is important to me. She is kind and caring. She always makes time for me. This makes me think that she's really generous. This is important because she makes me realize that I want to be generous, too. I used to feel bad about not being more so, but now I just try to act in ways that I admire about her. This makes me realize that my best friend shows me the kind of person I want to be. Oftentimes, when I want to work on my behavior, I think about my best friend and how she would act and I use her as a model.*

"After my first sentence or two, I could have jumped to a totally different idea about friends, like 'friends are also mean sometimes,' or to a different idea about what's important to me, like family. But instead, I stick with my idea by using some of those phrases; see how I write things like

This makes me think that she's really generous and *This is important because she makes me realize that I want to be generous, too* and *I used to feel bad about not being more so, but now I just try to act in ways that I admire about her.* Do you see how using those phrases and staying with my idea helps me make my thinking more interesting? Isn't it more interesting to read, 'My best friend shows me the kind of person I want to be' than it is to read, 'My best friend is important to me?'"

Active Engagement

Tell

"I want you to try that now. If you're continuing an entry you already started, look for a place where you jump to a new idea, then back up a little in your entry and use some of these phrases to stick with and grow your original idea. If you're starting a new entry, do the same work of using these phrases to stay with an idea."

Coach

To support students with this work, I say things like:

- "Read your first sentence and paraphrase its content. Now go sentence by sentence and ask, Is this sentence saying something similar or something totally different? When you get to a totally different idea, that's a good place to start revising your entry by lingering with your original idea."
- "Write, *This makes me think* . . . and finish the sentence."
- "Write, *On the other hand* . . . and finish the sentence."

When I collected Tasfia's notebook later that day, I saw that she had crossed out a couple lines where she started to explore entirely new thinking. (*Sometimes I think my sister is also kind of fun. For example she really makes me laugh.*) Instead, she added an entire page and a half of writing that now lingers with her original thought. See Figure 10–2 for her entry.

Tasfia uses several words and phrases that help her linger with her original idea and in turn, she accomplishes the reason for lingering: she deepens and grows her thinking. For example, Tasfia moves from *having a sister is*

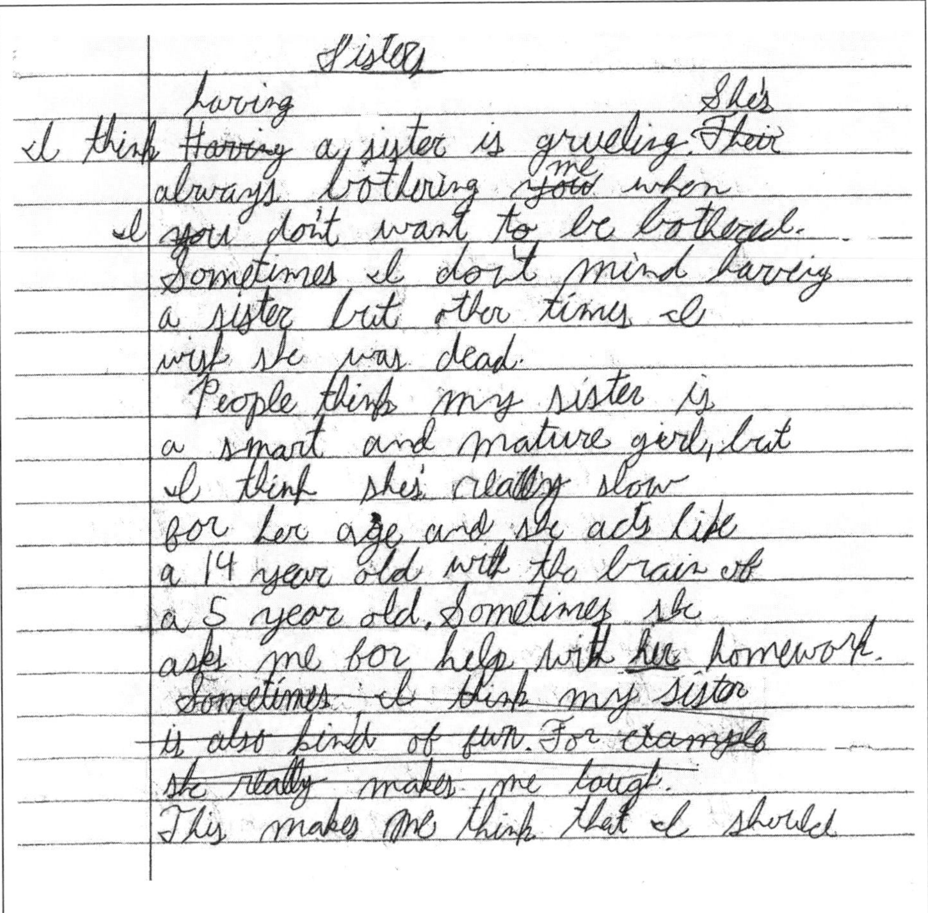

Sisters

I think ~~Having~~ loving a sister is grueling. ~~Their~~ She's
always bothering ~~you~~ me when
I ~~you~~ don't want to be bothered.
Sometimes I don't mind having
a sister but other times I
wish she was dead.
People think my sister is
a smart and mature girl, but
I think she's really slow
for her age and she acts like
a 14 year old with the brain of
a 5 year old. Sometimes she
asks me for help with her homework.
~~Sometimes I think my sister
is also kind of fun. For example
she really makes me laugh.~~
This makes me think that I should

Figure 10–2 *Tasfia's notebook entry: developing ideas using phrases that push our thinking*

grueling. She's always bothering me to ideas like: *I should be the older sister not her,* and *If I could have been born before my sister the things she does might have made sense for her age.* Tasfia is clearly learning that by lingering, we often uncover new ways of saying things, and sometimes, we even uncover new ways of seeing things.

Rewrite Ideas Another Way: *One way writers develop ideas is by rewriting them in as many ways as possible.*

In *A Writer Teaches Writing* (1968), Donald Murray writes:

> *Rewriting is what you do when you are a writer, for it is an essential part of the process of writing. It is the way in which you fit ideas into language. . . . The process of writing and rewriting is very much like the process of developing a picture: slowly it evolves before your eyes. (11)*

be the older sister not her.
~~Another re~~ One reason I think
I should be the older sister
is because she acts like she
doesn't know anything. For example
the other day she was asking
me if I knew how to write a
DBQ essay. Of course I did but
I couldn't believe it.
My sister ~~is~~ if you ask
me is really babyish. Once
she actually scribbled all over
my homework ~~ex~~. It's as if
she doesn't know any better. If
I could ~~b~~ have been born
before my sister the things she
does might have made sense
for her age.
Sometimes I can't believe
that she has any friends. Her
friends seem so much mature
than her.
~~I wish I was older than~~
My sister is so immature
Sometimes I can't believe she's
in highschool.

Figure 10–2 *(continued)*

As Murray teaches us, good revision is not merely inserting and crossing out; after all, revision means to *envision again* how something might go. Teaching students to write the same thinking in as many new ways as possible is an excellent strategy for helping them re-envision their first efforts as something fresh; it is an excellent strategy for "fit[ting] ideas into language"—or for using language to outgrow initial ideas.

When Kathy Racynsky gathered a small group of her third graders, she said, "Writers, I am so impressed by what I see in your notebooks. We're writing nonnarrative picture books, but not only are you collecting facts about your topics, you are also collecting ideas that go with your facts—your own thoughts and opinions about the information you're gathering! You are all ready to learn something new, which is why I've gathered you together."

Teaching

Tell

"When writers start to collect ideas, we often develop those ideas to try to make them even more interesting; the more interesting our ideas, the more likely our readers will remember what we have to say. One way we develop our thinking this is by taking an idea and rewriting it another way and another way to see if we can get to that more interesting, more original thinking."

Show

"Let me show you what I mean. Here's an entry by another student. As I read it, I want you to notice how he's more or less saying the same thing in every sentence, but in different and often more interesting ways."

> *I feel good in school. Being in school makes me happy. I feel comfortable and at home in school. School is like a second home for me. People say home is where the heart is, but I also think school is where the heart is. I love my friends and teachers and I feel loved at school for who I am.*

"Notice how in his first sentence, he writes, *I feel good in school,* which isn't particularly memorable; a lot of us would say that, right? But then notice how he takes that same idea and rewrites it again and again until it starts to get a lot more interesting. For example, *School is like a second home for me* and *I feel loved at school for who I am* are stronger, more original ideas than *I feel good in school,* right?

"Do you see how those ideas are really another way to write the idea that came before them? For example, *School is like a second home for me* is another way to say *I feel comfortable and at home in school,* which is another way to say *Being in school makes me happy.*

"By sticking with his original statement and exploring other ways to say it, this writer uncovered more original thinking. His readers are now much more interested in what he has to say."

Active Engagement

Tell

"I want you to try this now. Look at the last entry or two that you wrote and find an idea you had. I want you to develop that idea by writing it another way and another and another, knowing that what you're doing is trying to write something really original and interesting."

Coach

To support students, Kathy said things like:

- "How else might you say that?"
- "What's another way to describe that feeling?"
- "Write, *Another way to say this is* . . . and finish the sentence."
- "What's a more interesting, more original way to write the same idea?"

During the strategy lesson, Evelyine returned to the entry shown in Figure 10–3. Evelyine gathers facts (*The beach is a place where there is sand and water and rides*), but she also reflects on her facts to gather ideas (*I think the beach is a great place to visit*). However, her idea is predictable; it is an idea that many people would have about the beach. Using the above strategy, Evelyine developed her idea that the beach is fun. See Figure 10–4 for her revisions.

Now Evelyine has an idea about the beach that we would not expect to hear from most people: *I felt like I was free to fly like a bird.* Especially for a third grader, the idea is fresh and rich.

* * *

When I lose something, I cannot rest until I search every corner of my life. Sometimes the pursuit takes minutes, sometimes days. But almost always, I unearth other things along the way: belongings lost long ago and never found, possessions I did not even remember I had. Often, rediscovering these

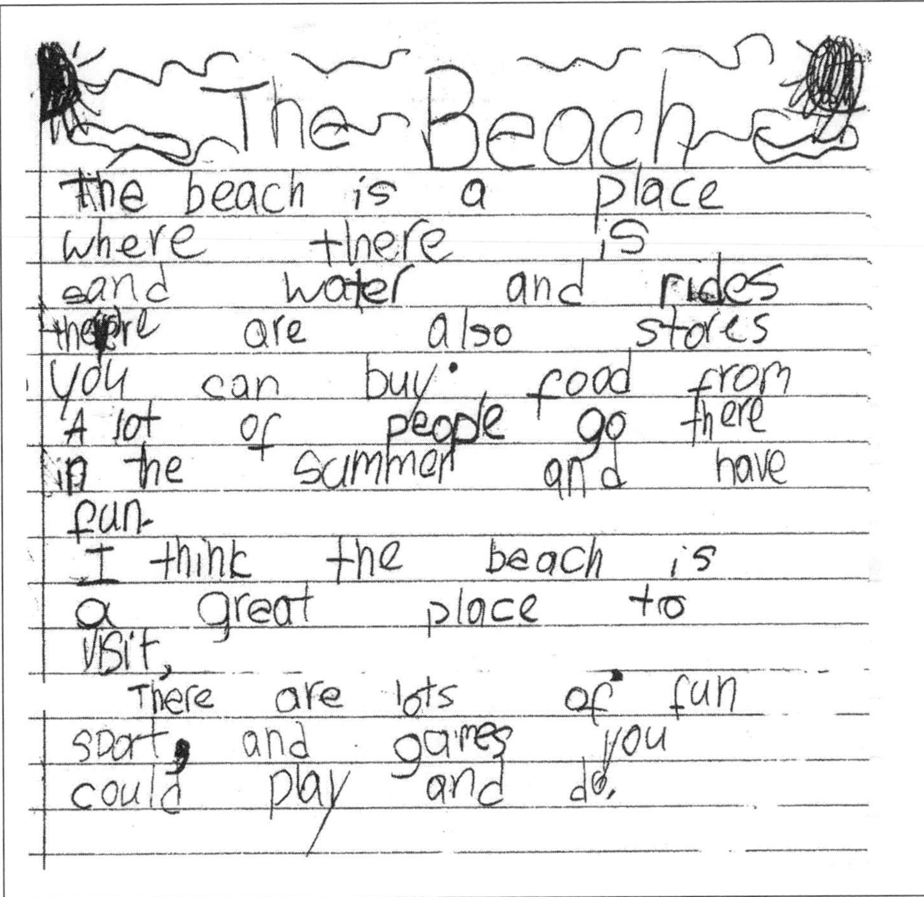

The Beach

the beach is a place
where there is
sand water and rides
there are also stores
you can buy food from
A lot of people go there
in the summer and have
fun.
I think the beach is
a great place to
visit,
There are lots of fun
sport, and games you
could play and do.

Figure 10–3 *Evelyine's original notebook entry*

forgotten objects is more exciting than finding what I originally set out to find.

Developing ideas is somewhat like searching for lost objects in that it almost always leads to something unexpected. When we work on developing ideas, we almost always unearth new insight along the way: perspectives we may have heard, or even held, but have forgotten along the way; beliefs we did not even realize we had; information we never knew to begin with.

Developing ideas is critical when we write nonnarrative because it leads us to new thinking. Hopefully surprising. Hopefully complex. Hopefully something worth writing about.

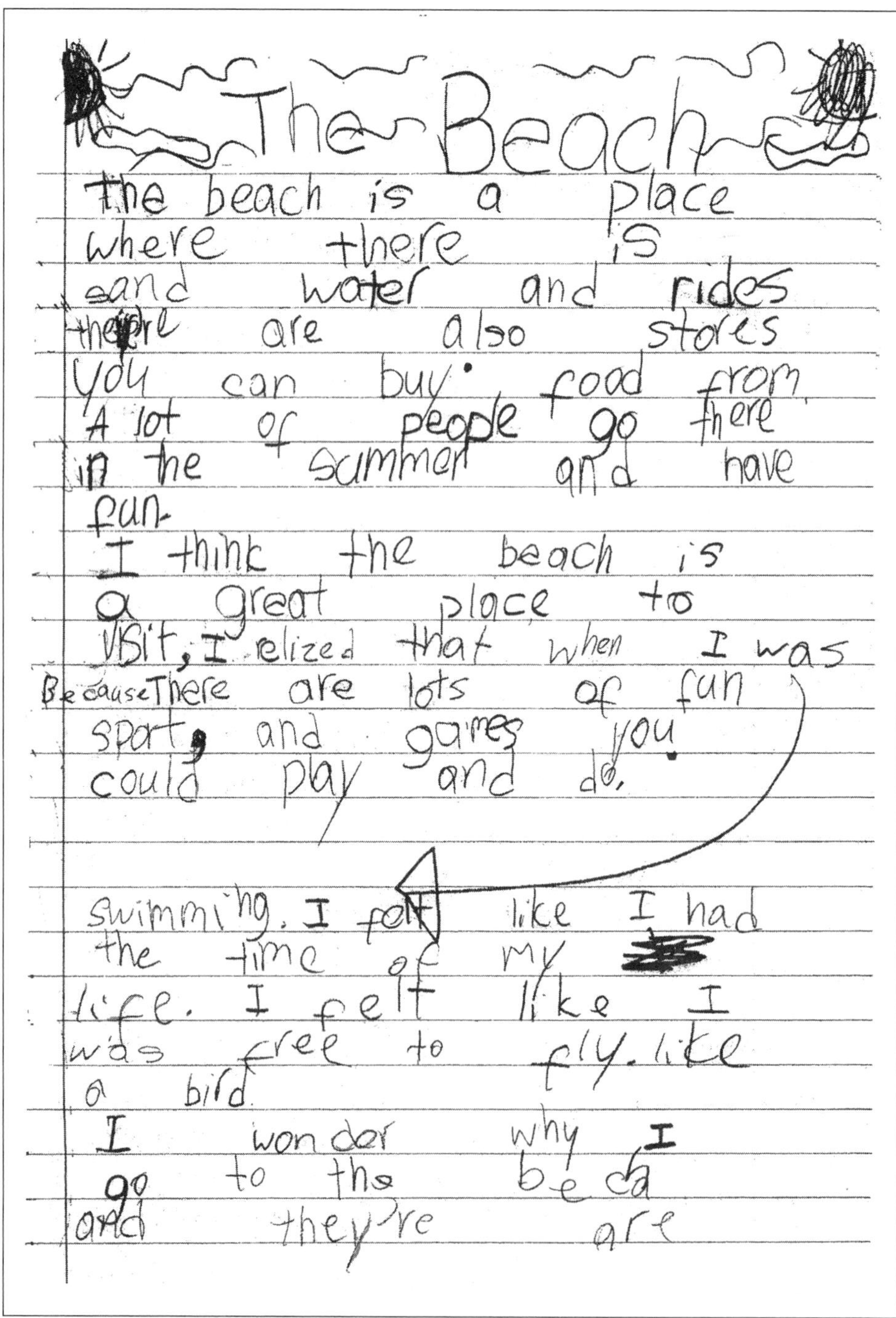

The Beach
The beach is a place
where there is
sand water and rides
there are also stores
you can buy food from.
A lot of people go there
in the summer and have
fun.
I think the beach is
a great place to
visit, I relized that when I was
Because There are lots of fun
sport, and games you
could play and do.

swimming. I felt like I had
the time of my
life. I felt like I
was free to fly. like
a bird.
I wonder why I
go to the beca
and they're are

Figure 10–4 *Evelyine's revised notebook entry: developing ideas by rewriting them in other ways*

CHAPTER 11

Creating Categories Inside of Topics

Just as we organize our world by categorizing the people, places, and things around us, we organize our nonnarrative writing by categorizing the information within a piece. Otherwise, chaos ensues; after all, categories are what allow us to make sense of and manage incoming information. Think about a typical day of teaching. Most of us spend a lot of time thinking about individual students, but we probably spend most of our time thinking about categories of students: those who failed and those who passed the math test; our strongest, our most struggling, and our most resistant writers; the ones that favor science, the ones that favor reading, the ones that favor gym. We certainly have multiple ways of sorting our students, just as we have multiple ways of sorting ourselves, our surroundings, the events in our lives. Clearly, there is no one right way to categorize the world, just as there is no one right way to categorize a topic. But we need categories nonetheless.

When our students write nonnarrative, they need categories before they gather all their evidence to ensure they collect enough information for each one; similarly, they need categories before they draft their pieces so they can envision how those pieces will go. The types of categories students create will depend on the genre in which they are writing. When composing expository pieces, each category needs to be a full-sentence claim that connects back to the thesis; I refer to these categories as supporting ideas. When composing informational or procedural pieces, each category can be written as a word or a phrase that identifies a smaller topic within the piece's overarching topic.

Regardless of the genre in which students write their nonnarrative pieces, they need categories that are independent from one another; in other words, they need to avoid repetition. And, they need categories that either are equal in weight or that strategically grow in weight so that readers finish on something significant to consider. You might use any of the strategies below to teach your students how to generate categories for their topics.

Consider Parts: *One way writers create categories for our nonnarrative pieces is by considering different parts of our topic, much like we would imagine different pieces of a pie.*

Regardless of the genre, writers can create categories for their topics by thinking of the various parts that make up the whole. This does not mean, however, that every topic has but one possible set of parts. Just as there are different ways to cut and eat a pie, there are different ways to envision and relay a topic.

Teaching

Tell

Once Adele Dinstein's seventh graders picked and developed topics for their nonnarrative texts, she gathered them for a minilesson on creating categories for their pieces. "One way writers generate categories for nonnarrative pieces is by thinking of the different parts of our topics. Parts of a topic are somewhat like pieces of a pie: all the smaller pieces fit together to make up the whole. Thinking about the parts of a nonnarrative topic helps writers gather enough information about a topic; it also helps us organize that information so readers have an easier time understanding and holding on to what we want them to know."

Show

"I'm going to show you how I think of the different parts of my topic. You all know that I'm writing a travel guide on Shanghai. I'm going to flip through my notebook as I think about everything I know and wonder about Shanghai to make sure I don't forget anything.

"I see a little information and actually several questions about the history in Shanghai, so that could definitely be one of my categories. If this is my pie," Adele said, drawing a circle and writing *Traveling in Shanghai* above it, "then I'm going to make *History* one of the parts.

"I don't actually see anything on shopping, but I love to shop, and I always shop when I travel, so I definitely want one part of my piece to be on places to do that. I'm going to make *Places to shop* another category, another piece of my pie.

"I have a little information on the temples in Shanghai. Which reminds me that even though there's nothing in my notebook about museums, I

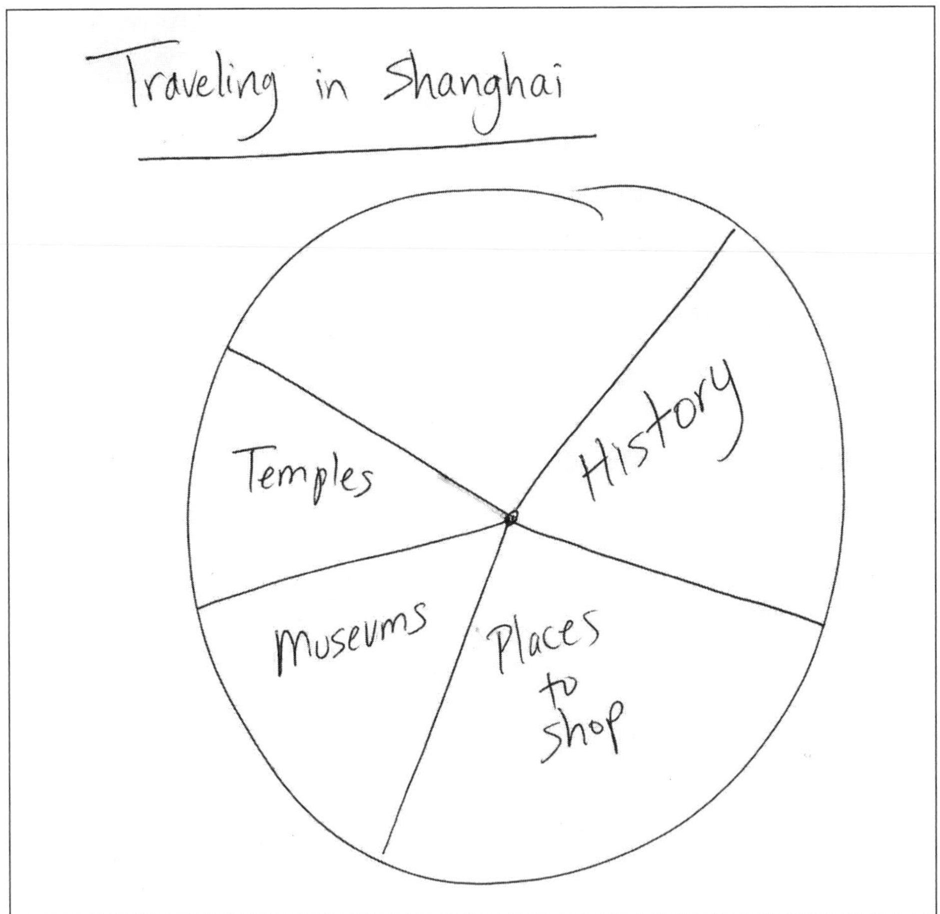

Figure 11–1 *Adele's teaching text*

know people often visit museums when they travel, so I better add *Museums* as well as *Temples.*

"I can worry about the order of my categories later on, and may even add a couple more when I have more time to think about this, but hopefully you understand what I'm doing. Again, I'm thinking of my topic as a pie and using my notebook as well as further reflection to come up with the different parts of that topic. This helps me make sure that when I gather information, I gather enough for my readers, and that I present it in an organized way so my readers can understand what I share with them."

Active Engagement

Tell

"I want you to get started before you go back to your seats. Please take a couple minutes to think of your own topics and their parts. Start a new page in your notebook that has your topic on the top and then your parts below;

you can make a pie, like I did, or a list, or even a web, as long as you're clear about your categories."

Coach

To support students, Adele said things like:

- "If your topic were written about in a book, what would be in the table of contents?"
- "What are some of the things you know, or want to know, about your topic?"
- "Make sure your categories are big enough to hold several different facts. If you realize you have a category that is really more of a fact, think about the heading it might go under."

After the minilesson, Ari planned her brochure as shown in Figure 11–2. Sharon planned the article as shown in Figure 11–3. Though Ari made a

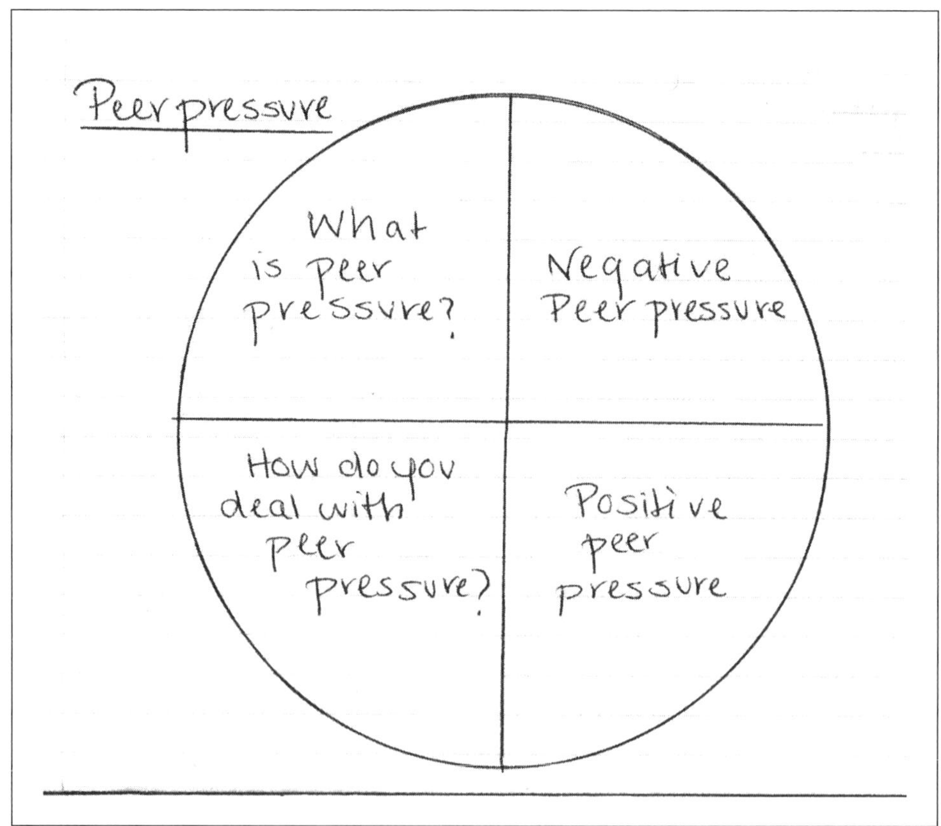

Figure 11–2 *Ari's categories: considering parts*

"pie" and Sharon made a list, both accomplish the same goal: they successfully envision how their pieces will go by moving beyond their overarching topics (*Peer pressure* and *Stonehenge*) and into the specific categories they want to explore as writers. As with any piece, they could have generated very different categories for their topics. What's important is that the parts go together to make the whole, as do Ari's and Sharon's.

Were Ari and Sharon writing expository texts, they would begin with an idea rather than a topic. For example, instead of *Stonehenge,* Sharon's topic might have been, *Stonehenge is a magical place.* To generate categories for this topic by considering parts, she might have written things like, *The land around Stonehenge is magical,* and *The stone configurations are magical.* Were she writing a procedural text, perhaps her topic would have been *Building Stonehenge,* in which case her categories might have been, *Designing Stonehenge* and *Gathering the stones* and *Lifting the stones.* Again, regardless of the genre, students can generate categories by considering parts; the difference will be how they angle their categories.

Consider Times or Places: *One way writers create categories for our nonnarrative pieces is by considering different times or places in connection with our topic.*

In most classrooms, either I teach this strategy in a teaching share to offer the class options for how to generate categories, or I teach it in a conference or strategy lesson to students who need additional support generating categories and whose topics naturally lend themselves to time or place categories.

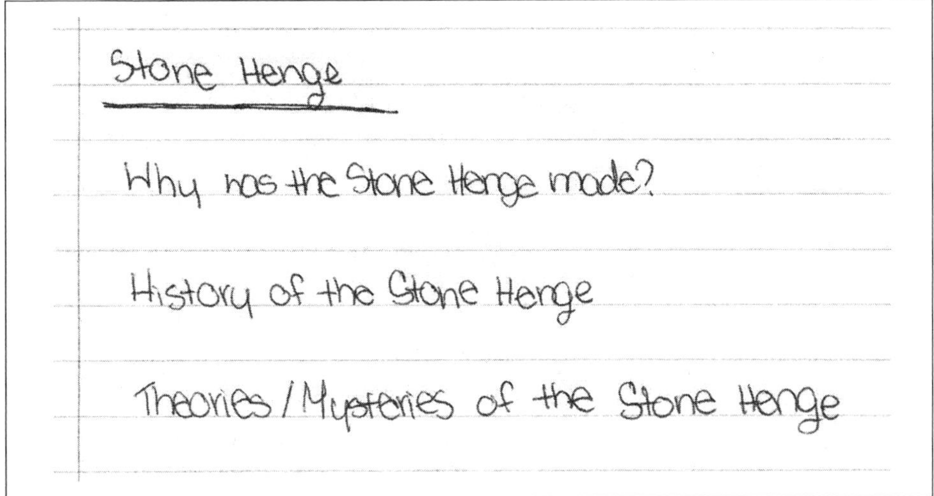

Stone Henge
Why was the Stone Henge made?
History of the Stone Henge
Theories / Mysteries of the Stone Henge

Figure 11–3 *Sharon's categories: considering parts*

For example, if someone were writing about music around the world or the evolution of rock and roll, they could consider reasons or parts as a way to generate categories, but they could certainly consider times or places, as well.

Teaching

Tell

When I stopped a class of seventh graders for a teaching share, I said, "Sometimes writers come up with categories by thinking about whether there are different times or places inside of our topics. This is simply another way to organize our thinking and make sure that in the end, we gather enough information for our readers."

Show

"Two of your classmates are already doing this work. Sarah's topic is the Salem witch trials. She's thinking about time and how it relates to her topic and came up with the following categories so far: *Before the trials, After the trials, Salem today.* Do you see how *before, after,* and *today* are different moments in time?

"Nawar's topic is food from different cultures. She's thinking about place as a way to generate categories. She has categories like: *Thai cooking, Italian cooking, Indian cooking.* (And then she has subcategories within each of those categories, so within Thai cooking, she has a subcategory for Traditional Foods and one for Recipes). Do you see how Nawar is considering how place relates to her topic as a way to come up with her categories?"

Active Engagement

Tell

"So as you all finish generating your categories, know that you can think about parts of your topics, but you can also think about time or place." Because this was a teaching share, I sent students back to work without asking everyone to practice the strategy. However, if I did want students to practice this strategy, I might say, "Now I want you to come up with categories by thinking about how time or place relates to a topic. Pretend for a moment that you are writing about peer pressure. What might be some different times or places when peer pressure would occur? Discuss this with your partner."

Coach

To support students with this strategy, I say things like:

- "Does this topic occur in different places? Of all those different places, are there any in which the information relating to your topic is different?"
- "Has your topic changed over the course of history? Or does it change over the course of a day or year or lifetime? If so, you might create categories along different points of a time line."

See Figure 11–4 for Sarah's picture book categories. See Figure 11–5 for Nawar's cookbook categories. Interestingly, Sarah and Nawar both consider time or place as well as parts of their topic. For example, Sarah focuses on time categories (*Before the trials, Afterwards, and Today*), but she also thinks about other important parts to her topic and decides to include a category that will give her readers some background information on the trials (*What were the Salem witch trials?*). Similarly, Nawar focuses on place to generate her big categories (*Thai, Indian,* and *Hawaiian cooking*), but she creates subcategories within her categories by considering the parts she wants to address about each of these types of cooking (*Traditional foods* and *Recipes*).

Were Sarah writing an expository text on the Salem witch trials, her topic might have been, *The Salem witch trials grew out of people's fear of women's power.* By thinking about time or place, perhaps she would generate categories like, *Leading up to the trials, people were uncomfortable with the ways in which women demonstrated healing powers,* and *After the trials, fear kept women from expressing themselves.* Were Sarah writing a procedural text, perhaps her topic would have been *How to prevent further*

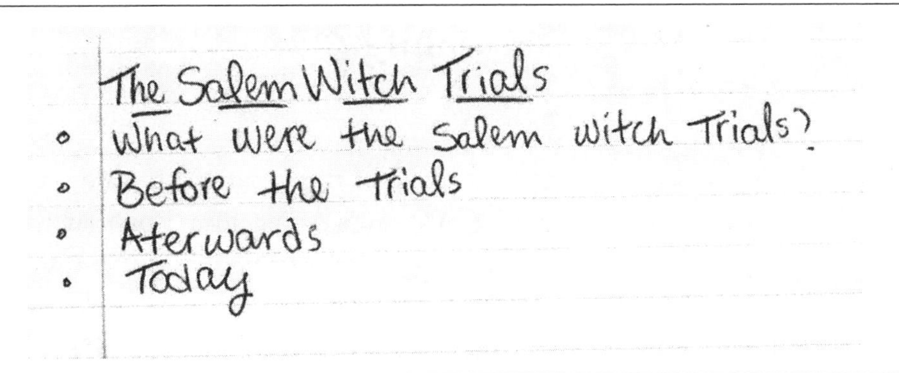

Figure 11–4 *Sarah's categories: considering time*

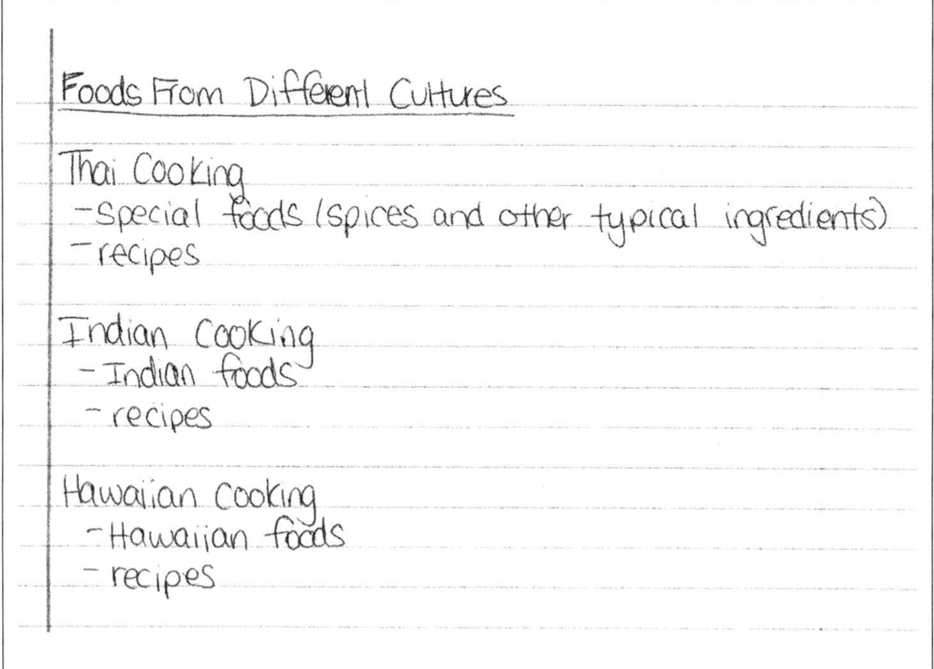

Figure 11–5 *Nawar's categories: considering place*

atrocities like the Salem witch trials. Her categories might be things like, *Liberating women in Afganistan* and *Fighting genital mutilation in Africa.*

Consider Reasons: *One way writers create categories for our nonnarrative pieces is by considering reasons behind our topic.*

Any writer might consider reasons as a way to generate categories for a nonnarrative piece. However, this strategy is especially helpful for students who are crafting expository text, text in which they are putting forth ideas, because students can ask and answer the question, Why do I think this? As Calkins and Gillette (2006) suggest, we might teach students to respond and hence create their categories by writing, *I think this because . . .* "

Teaching

Tell

When Aliki Giakas gathered a small group of fifth graders, she said, "Once writers have a thesis, we come up with supporting ideas for that thesis because they help convince our readers of what we have to say; because our supporting ideas are one kind of proof for our thinking, they have to fit with our thesis statement. One way writers come up with supporting ideas that fit is by asking ourselves, What are the reasons why I believe this? Most essay writers come up with at least three reasons because fewer than that makes our thesis less strong and believable."

Show

"Let me show you how another student writer did this. Faiza read over her notebook entries and realized that what she really wants to say to her readers is that the most dreadful day in her life was when her baby brother got extremely sick; that's her thesis. So then she asked herself, Why do I think this? What are three reasons why that was the most dreadful day? Faiza thought and thought and look what she wrote:

- It was the most dreadful day because I never saw my brother so sick.
- It was the most dreadful day because I was so impatient waiting for him to come home from the hospital.
- Even worse, it was the most dreadful day because everyone tried to make me feel better and it didn't work.

"Do you see how Faiza thought of three reasons why her thesis statement is true? For example, she doesn't write *I was never as sick as my brother was that day* because even though that might be the case, that statement doesn't support her idea that the most dreadful day in her life was when he got sick.

"Do you also see how every one of her reasons is something totally different? For example, she doesn't write *It was a bad day because I never saw my brother so sick* and also *It was a bad day because he felt awful,* because those are really the same reasons. By coming up with three different reasons for her thesis, Faizah is more likely to prove it."

Active Engagement

Tell

"Now I want you to try this. I want each of you to revise your draft plans by thinking about three reasons for your thesis statement; remember, you need to make sure that every reason starts to prove your thesis.

Coach

When Aliki circulated the group, sitting alongside students to help them revise their draft plans, she supported them in different ways. Some students generated supporting ideas (or categories) that were repetitive. For example, Sanzida had two supporting ideas: *My brother is always bothering me* and *My brother is really annoying.* Aliki said:

- "Give me an example, some proof, for this supporting idea. Now give me an example for this next supporting idea. . . . When writers have the same examples for different supporting ideas, it's usually a sign that the supporting ideas are too similar and that we need to come up with a new one. So think of a different reason for your thesis."

Other students struggled to make their ideas equal in weight. Ahmed, for example, decided that his reasons for being good at basketball were that he is good at teamwork, he is good at tricks, and he is good at dribbling the ball. Aliki said:

- "Think about a scale. If you put a really big idea and a really small idea on the same scale, the big idea will be much lower down, which will make the smaller idea feel unimportant. Can you put your supporting ideas on a scale and make sure both sides of the scale stay even? If you find an idea that is too small, think of another, bigger reason for your thesis statement."
- "What makes you think this smaller reason? The answer to that question could become your new supporting idea."

Still other students had supporting ideas that did not actually connect with their thesis statement. Aliki said things like:

- "How does this supporting idea prove your thesis? Since it does seem to fit, can you revise your supporting idea to make that connection clearer to your readers?" Or, "Since it doesn't seem to fit, can you think of another reason for your thesis statement, something that better proves your thesis?"
- "Finish the following sentence: One reason I think [thesis statement] is because . . ."

Because Aliki knew that most of the students would finish generating categories before writing workshop ended, she reminded them of the next step before sending them back to their seats. After recapping her teaching, she simply said, "When you're done revising your draft plans, remember

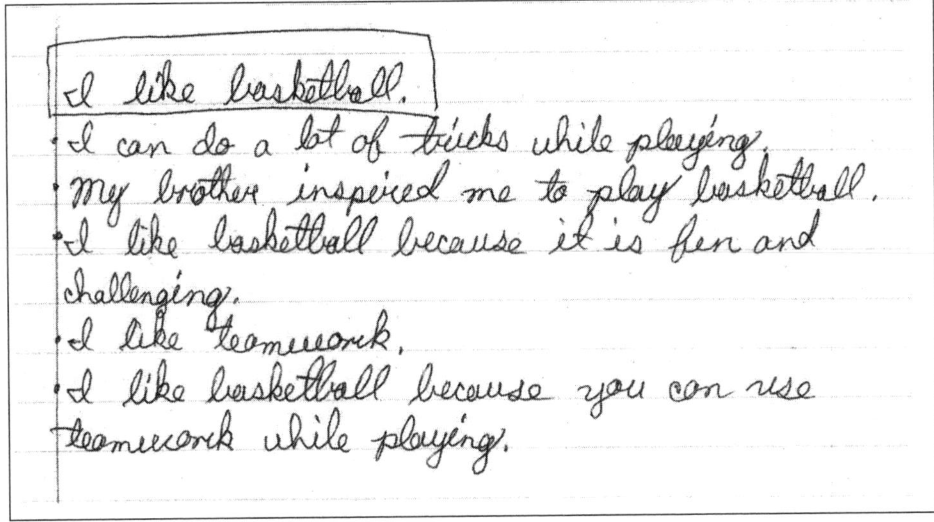
I like basketball.
I can do a lot of tricks while playing.
my brother inspired me to play basketball.
I like basketball because it is fun and challenging.
I like teamwork.
I like basketball because you can use teamwork while playing.

Figure 11–6 *Juan's initial categories*

today's whole class lesson so you can start to gather evidence for one of your supporting ideas."

Before the strategy lesson, Juan's draft plan read as shown in Figure 11–6. Notice that some of Juan's categories do not support his thesis statement. For example, *My brother inspired me to play basketball* is not a clear reason for actually liking basketball. Furthermore, some of his ideas feel repetitive: *I like teamwork* and *I like basketball because you can use teamwork while playing* are very similar categories, so similar that Juan would find it difficult to impossible to find different evidence to support each of those claims.

After the strategy lesson, Juan revised his draft plan as shown in Figure 11–7. Juan now has three categories for his essay—three supporting ideas for his thesis statement—that will effectively convey to his readers what he wants them to know. Thinking of reasons for his thesis helped him generate categories that connect back to and support his overall claim. Because Juan is writing a traditional five-paragraph essay and because he struggles to stay focused on his thesis statement, repeating his stem (*I believe I am good*) and using a starter for reasons (*because*) is a good strategy for helping him generate supporting ideas that truly are supports.

Were Juan writing an informational instead of an expository text, his topic might have simply been *Basketball.* Were he to consider reasons for his topic, he might have generated categories like *The history of basketball* and *What attracts fans.* Were Juan writing a procedural text, perhaps his topic would have been *Becoming a basketball player.* Thinking about reasons for becoming a basketball player, he might have created categories like *Finding the best team* and *Training for the NBA.*

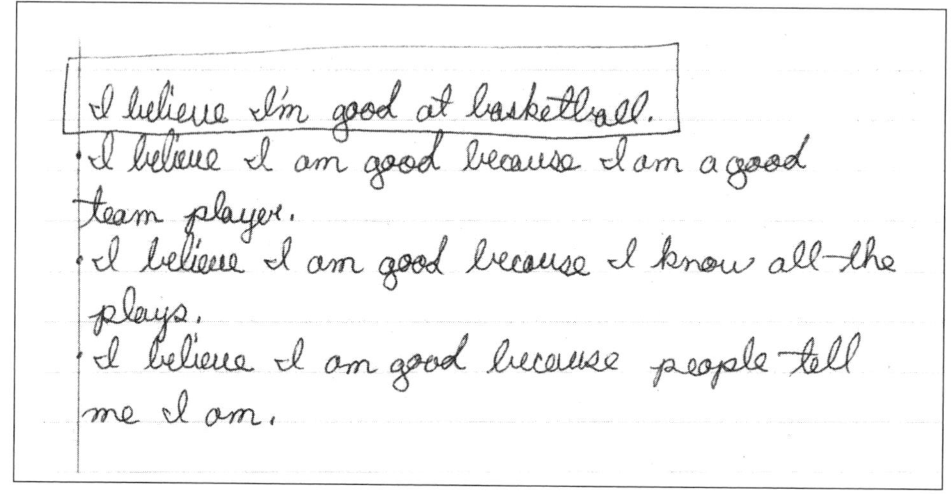
I believe I'm good at basketball.
I believe I am good because I am a good team player.
I believe I am good because I know all the plays.
I believe I am good because people tell me I am.

Figure 11–7 *Juan's revised categories: considering reasons*

* * *

When doctors study broken limbs or troubled hearts, they often take X-rays to see how all the parts fit together, to draw conclusions about symptoms, and to infer how long things will take to heal. When scientists study their environments, they often use a magnifying glass, again to observe parts, causes and effects, elapsing time. When writers study topics, we want, in a sense, to send those topics through an X-ray machine or place them under a magnifying glass. We want to shed light on all the angles and perspectives. Doing so not only gives us insight into the big picture. It also gives us a way to organize our understanding of the big picture; each new part creates a place for us to file away information as well as a system for accessing that information later.

Of course, as with any skill, what's important is the end result, not how students arrive there. When we teach students to create categories, the strategies they use to reach this goal will often depend on their topics; some topics may more naturally yield parts, others reasons, still others time and place categories. Regardless of how students create their categories, doing so will help them better understand, organize, and access different aspects of a topic.

CHAPTER 12

Gathering Information

Most teachers agonize over their bulletin boards. I know I did. Inevitably, when it was time for a new display, I would stay in the school building until six or seven o'clock at night, copying student work, cutting and pasting construction paper, considering exactly how I should lay out and explain the pieces I tacked to walls.

On the one hand, I wonder whether it makes sense for us to pour so much of our energy into the parts of our work that do not directly involve our students; after all, we are neither planning nor teaching nor assessing when designing our bulletin boards. On the other hand, we *are* gathering and presenting evidence of our planning and teaching and assessing; we are saying to all who walk the halls, "Here is what my students and I have been doing together." So of course we agonize. Our bulletin boards are not merely a display of student work; they are our proof that all our agonizing over everything else we do as educators is, in fact, making an impact in the lives of our students.

Just as teachers use bulletin boards to teach others about the quality of teaching and learning that occur inside our classrooms, writers use information to teach our readers about our nonnarrative topics. If your students are just beginning to gather material, or if they have already begun the process but still fail to teach their topics or convince you of their ideas, it is probably because they have not provided adequate or appropriate information. In turn, you might teach the following strategies.

Use Facts and Statistics: *One way writers gather information is by collecting facts and statistics relevant to our topic.*

Though any type of nonnarrative writing inevitably contains facts, some simply contain facts about the writer, whereas others contain outside facts—facts about other people, facts about the world in general. For example, personal essays may include facts like "My mom yells more on weekdays" or "My baby sister cries when my mom yells." But an informational text on stress cannot rest solely on these types of facts; when we read informational texts, we expect to learn information not simply about the writer, but about the world. In *Crafting a Life* (1996), Murray writes, "the reader will not read unless there is an adequate delivery of information to satisfy the reader's hunger for specifics" (62).

Teaching

Tell

When I conferred with seventh-grader Ari, I said, "When you write informational texts like this one, your job is to teach your readers about your topic. One really important way to teach readers is to gather relevant facts and statistics. Gathering facts and statistics also gives us credibility because it makes us seem well informed and usually causes readers to listen more closely to what we have to say."

Show

"For example, I'm writing an editorial on how what we eat in this country is killing us and our children. But if I want my readers to listen, I can't just spew my own beliefs. I need to provide facts so people will believe what I have to say. I have to do more research, but so far, these are some of my facts: 90,000 Americans die each year from food-borne viruses that largely originate because of the unhygienic, not to mention inhumane, conditions in slaughterhouses. One out of two people are getting cancer and one out of four are starting to die from cancer, which is largely attributed to the amount of sugar we consume, the amount of hormones we inject into the animals we eat, and the pesticides we ingest due to nonorganic farming. Sixty-five percent of Americans are obese or overweight and the number one cause is the introduction of corn syrup into our diets.

"When you hear those facts, don't I seem well informed on my topic? Don't you feel like you're learning something and can trust me as an authority?"

Active Involvement

Tell

"I want you to try this with your brochure. I know you may need to do some more research. But to get started, look through your draft and think about where you want to include some facts and statistics and what kind of information you might look for during your research."

Coach

To support Ari, I said things like:

- "Find places where you make claims about something. These are places where you should gather facts or statistics to prove your claim."
- "You want your readers to learn information in every part of your piece, so make sure each of your categories contains facts or statistics. What kind of information might you look for under each of these categories?"
- "Check your information by asking whether it is a fact, something based on research of some kind, or whether it is your own thought and assumption about your topic."

See Figure 12–1 for part of Ari's initial draft. Ari does an excellent job gathering personal experience and opinion as a way to convey information, and yet her brochure is almost void of outside facts. Reading it, I wanted more details about negative peer pressure: What are some common forms of peer pressure? Who does it affect? How many people experience it? Following our conference, Ari revised her piece as shown in Figure 12–2.

Though Ari could do more work gathering a wider range of facts (for example, facts about other groups of young people in addition to Filipino boys), she has already strengthened her brochure by including statistics about peer pressure, as well as facts about the common types of pressure (which she shows in her bulleted list). As a result, I trust her more as an authority on her subject matter. Even more importantly, Ari is now a smarter writer because she understands that when she writes to teach people about something in the world, she needs to include facts on the topic.

Use Quotes: *One way writers gather information is by quoting other sources who have important things to say about our topic.*

Negative Peer pressure

The children sat in a circle passing the bottle from one child to the next, and with each swig of the bitter drink, they laughed and coughed like roaring hyenas. The beautiful girl... hesitated, searching the faces of the others around her. She hid from their smirking lips and drowned in their dark eyes. Their voices echoed through her head— "Do it!" "Come on, we all do it," "Its easy, Do it, Do it!"...

Negative peer pressure is what causes many children to do something that they do not want to do, such as taking drugs, or drinking alcohol. Friends have a great affect on adolescents. They have a tendency to believe that they know what is right for others and they can pursuade them into doing things that they know are wrong.

Figure 12–1 *Excerpt from Ari's initial draft*

I am not proud of it, but in a recent fight with a friend, I said, "I'm not the only one who feels this way about you!" As soon as the words were out of my mouth, I wished and wished I could take them back. But in the moments leading up to my outburst, all I felt was frustration: I seemed unable to convince my friend that my perception was valid. Of course, "he said, she said" is not a game one should play during personal conflict; but the strategy can be a powerful way to convince readers of our point of view and of the importance of our topics.

Teaching

Tell

When I stopped a class of seventh graders for a teaching share, I said, "When writers gather information around a topic, we sometimes quote what another author writes instead of putting the information in our own words. We usually do this when the person we're quoting has said something especially well, especially important, or when the person we're quoting is himself especially important. We obviously can't quote someone else's entire piece, but we can quote key parts, either a phrase or a sentence or a paragraph or two."

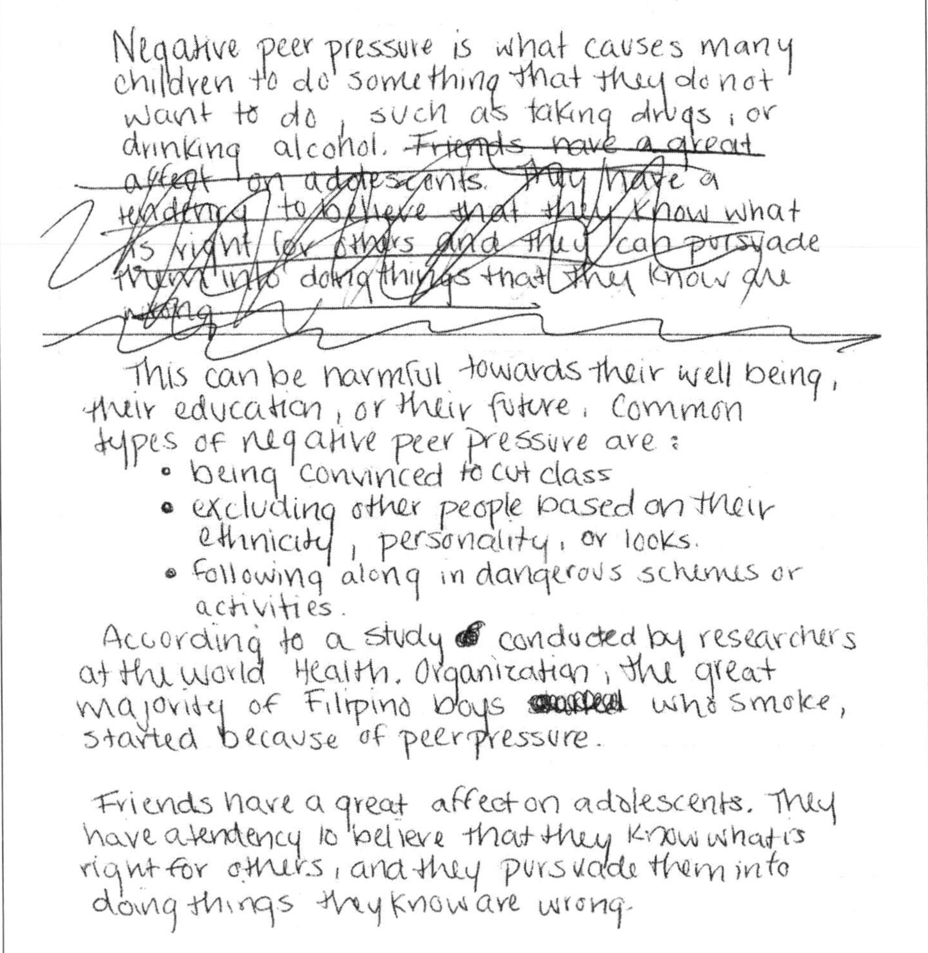

Negative peer pressure is what causes many children to do something that they do not want to do, such as taking drugs, or drinking alcohol. ~~Friends have a great affect on adolescents. They have a tendency to believe that they know what is right for others and they can pursuade them into doing things that they know are wrong~~

This can be harmful towards their well being, their education, or their future. Common types of negative peer pressure are:

- being convinced to cut class
- excluding other people based on their ethnicity, personality, or looks.
- following along in dangerous schemes or activities.

According to a study conducted by researchers at the World Health Organization, the great majority of Filipino boys who smoke, started because of peer pressure.

Friends have a great affect on adolescents. They have a tendency to believe that they know what is right for others, and they pursuade them into doing things they know are wrong.

Figure 12–2 *Revised excerpt from Ari's draft: gathering facts and statistics*

Show

"One of your classmates just did this in her piece. She's writing an article on anorexia, and in one part she writes about societal pressures. Anna, would you read that first paragraph and when you come to the quote, slow down a little so we can really hear it. As she's reading, I want all of you to listen closely to how she quotes something really important that connects directly with her topic."

> *It's hard for girls to turn on the T.V. or open a magazine without feeling bad about ourselves. It's not just that female models and actresses are all beautiful. They are also very thin. Most women don't have bodies like that, but when that's all we see all day long in the media, we start to think something is wrong with us which is why anorexia is such a problem in our society. Susan Bordo is a feminist who says, "What we need to ask is why our culture is so obsessed with keeping our bodies slim, tight, and young*

that when 500 people were asked what they feared most in the world, 190 replied, 'Getting fat.'" Getting fat should not be our biggest fear. Death should be our biggest fear. But instead, so many girls and women are killing themselves because they would rather be thin than alive. We need to change the images we put on T.V. and in magazines so this will stop.

"Did you hear the quote? Anna writes in her piece, *Susan Bordo says,* quote, '*What we need to ask is why our culture is so obsessed with keeping our bodies slim . . . that when 500 people were asked what they feared most . . . 190 replied, "Getting fat."*' Do you see how that quote speaks directly to Anna's topic because it shows what a huge problem body image is—and of course, body image is what causes anorexia?

"I want you to notice that Anna doesn't quote just anything. She doesn't quote someone who says, 'Anorexia is an eating disorder that mostly affects women and girls,' because Anna can write that herself in her own words, and quoting something like that isn't a particularly strong statement so it isn't going to strengthen her piece. Instead, Anna quotes something that is written very well and that drives home the information in her piece. When we hear her quote, aren't we all a little bit shocked and concerned about anorexia?"

Active Engagement

Tell

Because this was a teaching share, I simply said, "As you continue drafting and revising for homework, some of you may decide to use outside quotes to provide information on your topics. If you come across something someone says that is really important to your topic, and the person is an authority figure on the topic, or says what they do better than you could say it yourself, you'll probably quote them in your piece."

Coach

To support students with this strategy, I say things like:

- "Let's look at a text you're using for research. Reread this first part and underline things the author writes that speak directly to your topic. . . . Now, are any of these quotes really big and important; do any of them sum up one of your big points?"

- "Is the person who said this someone of authority? Always think about whether quoting someone gives your piece more credibility or whether it would be just as effective for you to summarize in your own words."

In the days following my teaching share, Jennifer made the decision to quote other authors several times throughout her article on obesity. Under one of her headings, *Leading Causes of Obesity,* Jennifer writes about everything from emotional distress to DNA to lifestyle. She ends one of her sections with the paragraphs shown in Figure 12–3, the last of which includes a quote from an expert.

Probably one of the most important cause leading to obesity is the lifestyle of people. As technology is improving, people nowadays are less active. Televisions, computers, and videogames are dominating our spare time. As lives become busier, people like us are most likely to grab takeout food or eat at a restaurant. These meals are usually oily and fatty and not as healthy as meals prepared at home. If this describes your way of life, then you'll have a higher risk of being obese.

As scientist Martha Williams says, "... with so many factors of obesity, it's nearly impossible to not be at least overweight." Although it can be said as "nearly impossible," and needs a lot of Patience, as long as you try, nothing is ever impossible.

Figure 12–3 *Excerpt from Jennifer's draft: quoting outside sources*

Jennifer makes very good use of an outside quote. Not only does she quote information central to her piece, she also quotes an authority figure. Jennifer successfully validates for her readers the information in her piece by showing that others, scientists even, share her thinking that obesity is a serious problem difficult to overcome in today's society.

Incorporate Different Perspectives: *One way writers gather information is by seeking and incorporating different perspectives on our topic.*

Writing nonnarrative means writing texts that teach. Whether teaching readers about ourselves or about others, incorporating different perspectives inevitably broadens our readers' knowledge on a topic. It gives readers more tools for drawing conclusions, making connections, backing up their own arguments, and refuting others. Once students understand how to gather one perspective—once they know how to teach readers something about a topic—we can teach them to strengthen their pieces by integrating a wider range of viewpoints.

Teaching

Tell

When I did a strategy lesson with a group of fifth graders writing literary essays, I said, "One way writers gather information is by looking for different perspectives on or opinions about our topics. This gives our readers a wider range of information, and it gives us more credibility: the more we know, the more our readers will believe us."

Because the students before me were composing essays, I also said, "When we write essays, talking back to different people's opinions also strengthens our argument; it helps show how our thinking makes more sense than other people's thinking."

Show

"Let me show you what I mean by including multiple perspectives. This student wrote an article on sibling rivalry. In this part of his piece on ways to deal with the problem, he has a whole paragraph on why some people think family counseling is important in cases of sibling rivalry. Then he has another whole paragraph on how other experts say sibling rivalry is normal and that there are concrete things families can do on their own when the problem arises. Do you see how he includes different perspectives, one that encourages counseling and another that encourages families to address the issue on their own? Do you see how that gives his readers a wider range of information with which to build their own expertise on the topic and draw their own conclusions?"

Again, because the students before me were writing expository texts in which they were trying to convince their readers of something, I continued by saying, "Since you are writing essays, you need to do more than simply include different perspectives; you actually need to show how your perspective is the right one, which means writing how the other ones are incorrect. So let's say this student was writing an essay on sibling rivalry and one of his ideas was that families should seek professional help when brothers and sisters compete with one another. He could still write that some experts think families are equipped to solve the problem on their own. But then he might talk back to the idea by writing something like: *What these experts aren't considering is that even when people have a list of things to do, they often need help figuring out how to do them, and how to do them well. Furthermore, though general guidelines can be very helpful, every situation and every family is different, which means different people often need to respond to difficulty in slightly different ways. Seeing a counselor makes it much more likely that families will get the specific support they need.*

"Do you see how in that example, I include different perspectives, but then show how mine is the better one? For example, when I write, *What these experts aren't considering is . . .* and then I give evidence to dismiss the other viewpoint. Do you see how that actually makes my argument stronger? It's like I imagine the different ways my readers might argue with my idea, and then before they have a chance to dismiss that idea, I show them how my thinking is stronger than theirs."

Active Engagement

Tell

"I want you to try this now with your literary essays. For now, pick one of your supporting ideas [categories] and imagine what someone else might think that is different from what you think. Make sure to include why they might think what they do, but then, talk back to that perspective; write what makes your perspective a better one."

Coach

To support students, I say things like:

- "What's another way to think about or respond to this?" (If students are writing essays, we need to follow the question with: "Where's your evidence that this other way isn't correct?")
- "Choose one of your categories and underline the perspective(s) you have so far. If you only have one, you can do some more research looking for a perspective that differs."
- "Finish the sentence, *Some people think . . . but other people think . . .*"
- "Finish the sentence, *Some people think . . . but I think . . .*"

Before the strategy lesson, the beginning of Alana's literary essay read as follows:

> *The story,* The Giving Tree, *is about a boy and a tree's relationship. When the boy is young he comes a lot. But when he gets older, he doesn't come. I think this book by Shel Silverstein is about a change. In the beginning the boy and the tree are friends. In the middle the boy comes rarely. In the end the boy doesn't act like a good friend at all, but the tree still tries to be a good friend.*
>
> *At the beginning the boy and the tree are friends. In the text it says, "Once there was a tree . . . and she loved a little boy." Later in the text it says, "And the boy loved the tree . . . very much. And the tree was happy." The boy didn't grow up yet and be mean. The boy came everyday. The boy would climb up her trunk, gather leaves, play hide-and-go-seek, and sleep in her shade. They had a lot of love for each other. They were best friends and neither of them was greedy, selfish or mean to one another. They had a relationship that was amazing.*

In her original draft, Alana did an excellent job conveying and supporting her ideas. Not only did she quote the text as a way to support her claims, she wrote how these text excerpts are proof for her ideas. It is only because Alana conveyed and supported her thinking with such clarity that I decided to teach her she could further strengthen her piece by incorporating different perspectives. After the strategy lesson, Alana revised her essay as shown in Figure 12–4.

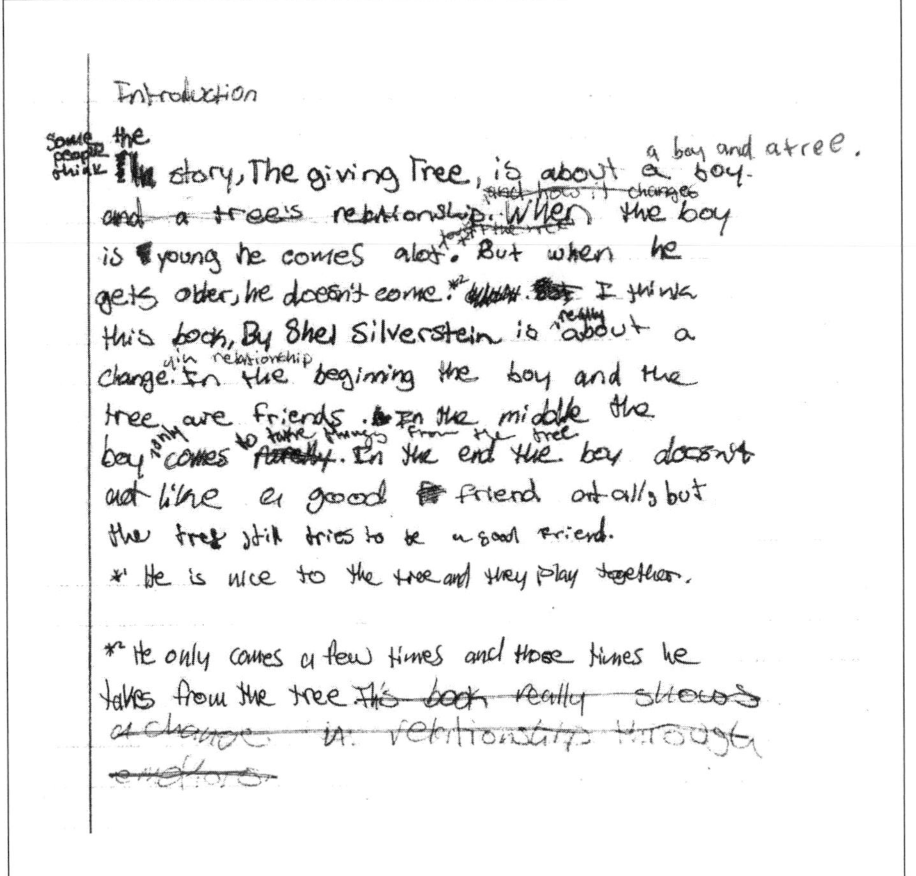
Introduction

Some people think the story, The giving Tree, is about a boy and a tree. ~~and a tree's relationship.~~ When the boy is young he comes alot.*1 But when he gets older, he doesn't come.*2 I think this book, By Shel Silverstein is really about a change in relationship. In the beginning the boy and the tree are friends. In the middle the boy only comes to take things from the tree. In the end the boy doesn't act like a good friend at all, but the tree still tries to be a good friend.

*1 He is nice to the tree and they play together.

*2 He only comes a few times and those times he takes from the tree ~~This book really shows a change in relationships through emotions~~

Figure 12–4 *Revised excerpt from Alana's draft: incorporating multiple perspectives*

Some people think the story, *The Giving Tree*, is about a boy and a tree. When the boy is young he comes a lot. He is nice to the tree and they play together. But when he gets older, he doesn't come. He only comes a few times and those times he takes from the tree. I think this book, by Shel Silverstein is really about a change in a relationship. In the beginning the boy and the tree are friends. In the middle the boy only comes to take things from the tree. In the end the boy doesn't act like a good friend at all, but the tree still tries to be a good friend.

By including and refuting other perspectives, Alana's essay is even stronger than before. Writing things like, *Some people think the story,* The Giving Tree, *is about a boy and tree . . . I think this book by Shel Silverstein is really about a change in relationship,*" Alana right away gets her readers to listen; she lets them know that she has something different to share, and most of us tend to perk our ears when we think we are going to learn a new perspective on things.

Furthermore, when she adds that some people think the boy is greedy and selfish from the start and then spends an entire paragraph challenging that perspective, Alana strengthens her own claim. She shows that her perspective emerges from careful consideration of differing perspectives.

Because Alana is writing an essay, it is important for her to refute any opposing claims she incorporates into her piece. For students writing informational texts, simply including differing perspectives is enough to

At the beginning the boy and the tree are friends. That's what most people think. Other people think the boy was greedy and selfish from the start. In the text it says, "He would climb up her trunk and swim from her branches and eat apples." They think that when the boy came and was friendly, he just wasn't ready to give up on the tree yet. Some people think that the boy eating her apples is a form of being greedy. But I think that in the beginning the boy was nice.

I think that when the boy came and was playing and eating apples that was their way of friendship. The boy wasn't being greedy yet because it made the boy and the tree happy. In the text it says, "Once there was a tree .

At the beginning the boy and the tree are Friends.* In the text it says", Once there was a tree . . . and she loved a little boy". Later in the text it says", And the boy loved the tree . . . very much. And the tree was happy. The boy didn't grow up yet and be mean. The boy came everyday. The boy would climb up her trunk, gather leaves, make crowns, eat apples, swing on brances, play hide-and-go-seek, and sleep in her shade. They had alot of love for each other. They were best friends and neither of them were greedy, selfish, or mean to one another. They had an relationship that was amazing.

Figure 12–4 *(continued)*

strengthen their pieces as well as their own credibility as writers; again, including multiple perspectives leaves readers more informed and also demonstrates more knowledge on the part of the author.

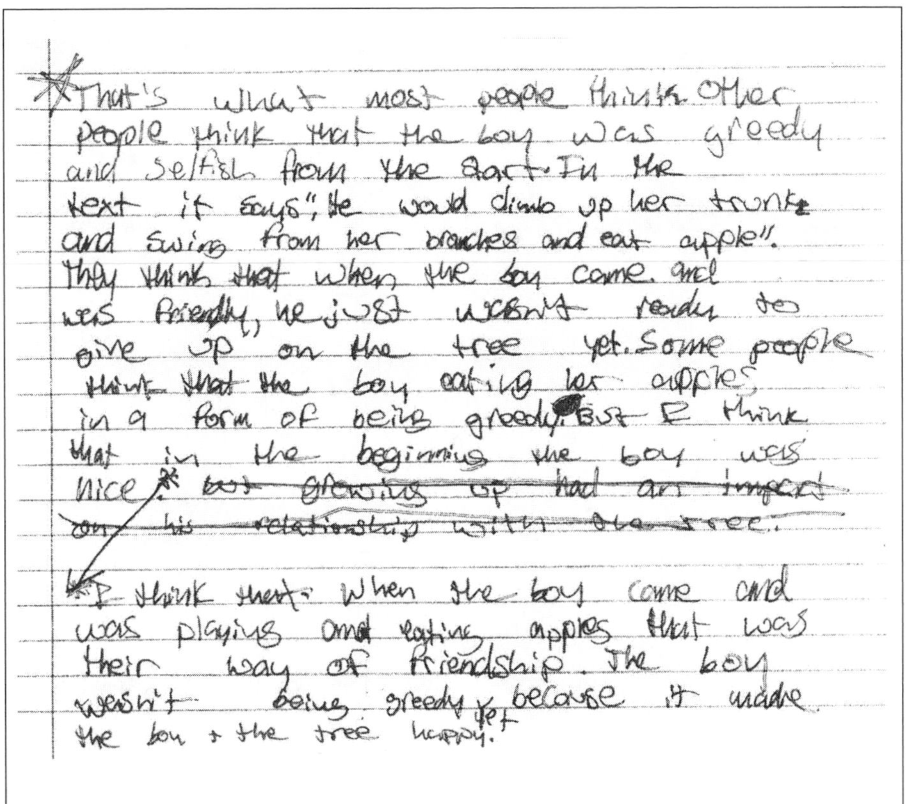

*That's what most people think. Other people think that the boy was greedy and selfish from the start. In the text it says, "He would climb up her trunk and swing from her branches and eat apple". They think that when the boy came and was friendly, he just wasn't ready to give up on the tree yet. Some people think that the boy eating her apples is a form of being greedy. But I think that in the beginning the boy was nice * ~~but growing up had an impact on his relationship with the tree.~~

*I think that when the boy came and was playing and eating apples that was their way of friendship. The boy wasn't being greedy yet because it made the boy + the tree happy.

Figure 12–4 *(continued)*

. . and she loved a little boy." Later in the text it says, "And the boy loved the tree . . . very much. And the tree was happy." The boy didn't grow up yet and be mean. The boy came everyday. The boy would climb up her trunk, gather leaves, make crowns, eat apples, swing on branches, play hide-and-go-seek, and sleep in her shade. They had a lot of love for each other. They were best friends and neither of them was greedy, selfish, or mean to one another. They had a relationship that was amazing.

* * *

Whether crafting texts that are expository, informational, or procedural, our students must back up their topics with information that teaches the reader; that is our job when we write nonnarrative text. Students might gather facts or quotes, personal experiences or differing perspectives, as long as they convey information that will allow readers to make sense of and deepen their understandings of the topic at hand. Otherwise, no matter how profound the topics, readers will have no way to walk away smarter, and no reason to walk away changed.

CHAPTER 13

Crafting Introductions

Most of us learned early on the importance of a strong lead, or introduction. Whether or not we learned how to write one, we most likely know when we cross paths with one; after all, we know when we pick up a book or an article or a letter and from the first paragraph, struggle to put it down. William Zinsser writes (2006):

> *The most important sentence in any article is the first one. If it doesn't induce the reader to proceed to the second sentence, your article is dead. . . . [Y]our lead must capture the reader immediately and force him to keep reading. It must cajole him with freshness, or novelty, or paradox, or humor, or surprise, or with an unusual idea, or an interesting fact, or a question. Anything will do, as long as it nudges his curiosity and tugs at his sleeve. (55–56)*

For some of our students, the problem is less that their introductions are weak and more that there are no introductions at all. Others, of course, write introductions, but fail to craft ones that "nudge [the reader's] curiosity and tug at his sleeve." If either is true of your students, you might teach the following strategies.

Begin with a Provocative Image or Statement: *One way writers lure readers into our nonnarrative pieces is with a provocative image or statement that connects with the information we impart in the body of the text.*

The *New York Post* is infamous for its provocative headlines. Sometimes humorous, sometimes offensive, the front page is often the source of passing conversations and office debates. Which is, of course, exactly the point; the front page is what lures so many of its readers to the stands.

It is no surprise that we can provoke an audience with carefully crafted words. So neither is it a surprise that one way to introduce nonnarrative text is to lure readers in with an image or a statement that arouses emotion and reaction.

Teaching

Tell

When I conferred with seventh-grader Camilla, I said, "When writers want to hook our readers into a piece before getting into the nuts and bolts of our content, we sometimes start with a provocative image or statement—a really interesting, intriguing, emotional image or statement—that connects with the information we plan to convey."

Show

"For example, in his article about an animal called the Tasmanian devil David Gordon (1999), starts with this image: *Blood-curdling screeches during the night frightened early European settlers . . . sounds . . . sent chills down their spines. . . .* Do you see how it's an image about the author's topic? Can't you hear those screams of the Tasmanian devil? Can't you see those settlers in the middle of the night, huddled together, listening to those screams and shaking with fear? Can't you imagine their chills?

"Here's one more example from the article, 'So a Big, Bad Bully Is Coming After You. . . .' by Candace Purdom. This lead is a little different, but still this really powerful image: *Bigger than Shaquille. Meaner than the Wicked Witch of the West. Scarier than a raptor.* The author also could have written the image more in the form of a statement. Something like, *Bullies are bigger than Shaquille, meaner than the wicked witch.* Either way, reading these leads, you can really picture the central content of the piece and because that image is so provocative, you want to read more, right?"

Active Engagement

Tell

"I want you to practice this now with your piece. If you were going to begin with a provocative image or statement that pulls readers into your piece and connects with the information you relay in the body of your article, how might that go?"

Coach

To support Camilla, I said things like:

- "I'm going to repeat what you just said. One way to check whether it's a strong image or statement is to see whether you get a picture in your mind."
- "When something is provocative, it usually arouses emotion. When you read this, do you feel angry or scared or joyful or some other feeling? If not, what could you write that would make you feel a strong emotion?"
- "How do you want people to feel when they read this piece? Close your eyes and get a picture of something about your topic that makes you feel that way."

After our conference, Camilla added the introduction to her article shown in Figure 13–1. Following this image, Camilla moves directly into the content of her piece; she writes, *OCD* [obsessive compulsive disorder] *is a disorder in which people create obsessions, impulses and images that run*

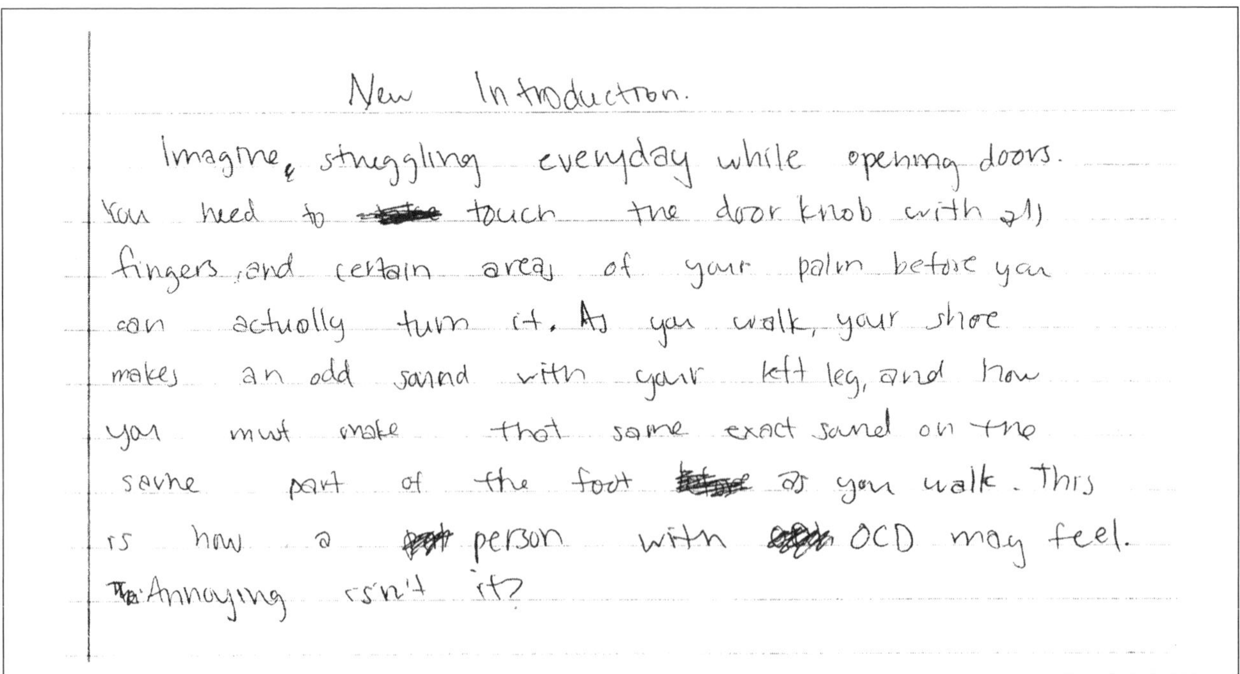

New Introduction.

Imagine, struggling everyday while opening doors. You need to touch the door knob with all fingers, and certain areas of your palm before you can actually turn it. As you walk, your shoe makes an odd sound with your left leg, and how you must make that same exact sound on the same part of the foot as you walk. This is how a person with OCD may feel. Annoying isn't it?

Figure 13–1 *Camilla's introduction: using a provocative image or statement*

through their mind constantly. With her new lead, Camilla still begins her article with an overview of her topic, but now, she does so in a much more interesting way; now, she hooks her readers into her piece by pulling them inside of a provocative image of life with OCD. Not only do we know what her piece is about; we can also see and feel what her piece is about. And thus, we keep reading, to learn more about what we see and feel.

Begin with a Question: *One way writers lure readers into our nonnarrative pieces is by opening with a question that connects with the information we plan to convey in the body of our piece.*

Think about how many of our conversations begin with questions. (How are you feeling? What did you think about that movie, that book, that vacation?) We ask questions as a way to invite people into discussion and spark a back-and-forth dialogue. Because we write nonnarrative text to inform or convince our audience of a particular topic or way of thinking, we often want to create the sense that we are engaging our readers in a conversation; our readers might pose counterarguments or counterevidence to the things we say, but by the end of our "discussion," we hope to convince them how right we are, how right the information we are providing. Knowing all this about conversations and about nonnarrative texts, it makes sense that one way to lure readers into our nonnarrative pieces is by beginning with a question that connects to, and that we plan to address with, the central information in our text.

Teaching

Tell

When Rebecca Victoros taught her fifth graders how to craft the introductions to their essays, she said, "One way to begin your essays is to start with a question that connects with the information you convey in the body of your piece and that provokes emotion in your readers. Doing so arouses curiosity and makes your audience want to read on to discover the answer to your question."

Show

"For example, in my essay on global warming, I write about how the change in temperatures is killing animals, killing plant life, and is going to kill us if we don't do something soon. When I think about questions I might ask readers, again, I want to think about possible questions that both connect with my content and that will hook in my readers. I could ask something like: *How does global warming affect Earth?* That definitely connects with my content. But it's not that interesting a question because it doesn't really arouse emotion. Unless the person reading is really, really interested in global warming, they may not want to keep reading.

"So what does get people to keep reading? Things that are shocking or scary, things that make the reader sad or excited or angry; again, things that arouse emotion of some kind. What are the emotions I want people to feel? Well, scared definitely, because global warming is scary. Maybe angry that things have gotten so bad and that we aren't doing more. So maybe I could write something like: *Is our time on planet Earth running out? Or, Did you know that you may be partly responsible for the end of life as we know it?*

"I think either of those questions would work because they both connect with the content of my piece: In my essay, I write about the things we are all doing, or not doing, that are endangering our planet. And, I think both questions arouse emotion: certainly fear, even shock. The second question, when I ask readers whether they know they might be responsible for ending life as we know it, might also make readers defensive or angry, which might make them keep reading to find out how to argue back."

Active Engagement

Tell

"I want you to try this now by writing a new lead for the essay we've been studying. As you know, this author begins his piece by stating his ideas. Take a minute to jot in your notebooks a couple of questions this author could have used instead to begin his essay on divorce and star the one you like best. Remember, the one you star needs to connect with what the author addresses in the body of the piece, and it needs to arouse emotion in the reader."

Coach

To support her writers, Rebecca said things like:

- "What questions did you have, or do you have now, in relation to this topic?"
- "How do you feel about the topic and what makes you feel that way? Turn those feelings into a question to your readers."

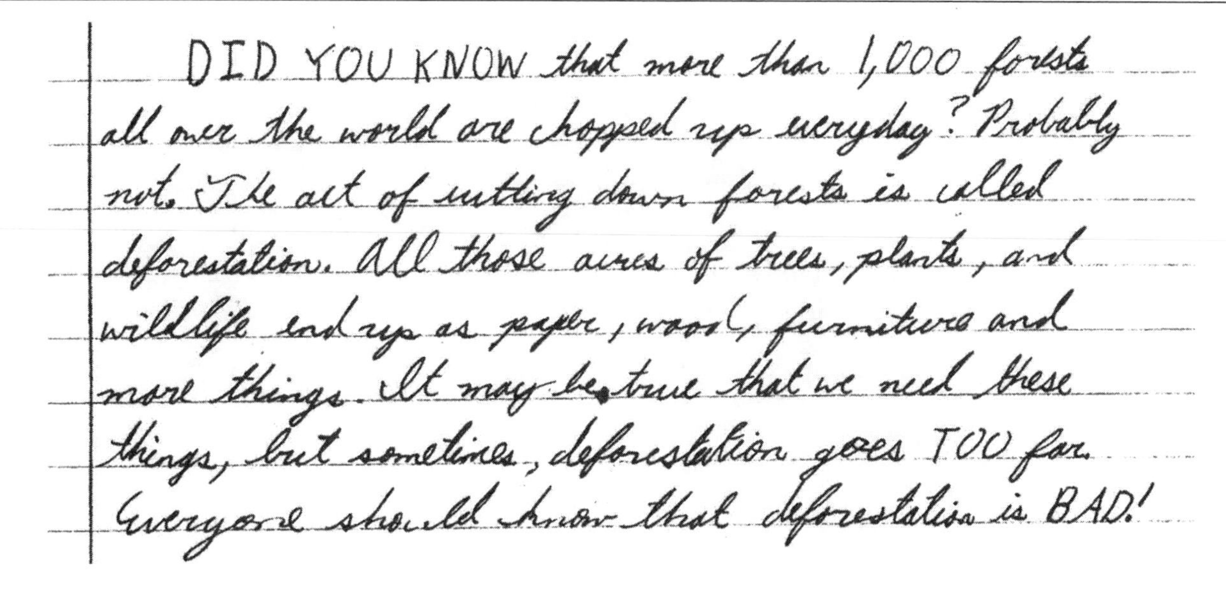
DID YOU KNOW that more than 1,000 forests all over the world are chopped up everyday? Probably not. The act of cutting down forests is called deforestation. All those acres of trees, plants, and wildlife end up as paper, wood, furniture and more things. It may be true that we need these things, but sometimes, deforestation goes TOO far. Everyone should know that deforestation is BAD!

Figure 13–2 *Trieu's introduction: using a compelling question*

- How do you want your readers to feel about this topic? What is a smaller detail about the topic that might cause readers to feel that way? Try presenting that detail as a question."

After Rebecca's minilesson, Trieu, who was writing an essay on why deforestation is harmful to our planet, wrote the introduction shown in Figure 13–2. In the body of his essay, Trieu writes how deforestation is bad because it destroys medicine, prevents certain species from living, and takes away oxygen for everyone to breathe. His opening question (*Did you know that more than 1,000 forests all over the world are chopped up everyday?*) certainly connects with that content in that he addresses the implications of destroying all those forests. Furthermore, his question provokes emotion; personally, I was shocked when I heard just how many forests are cut down each day. And following my shock, I felt outraged, afraid, sad. Like a thrilling or tragic book I can't put down because I need to find out how things turn out, I kept reading Trieu's essay because I wanted to follow my feelings to the end and learn more about the destruction of all these forests.

Begin with a Story: *One way writers lure readers into our nonnarrative pieces is with a story that reflects the information to come.*

Stories are a powerful way to prove a point; regardless of how we feel about a topic and whether or not we agree with a claim, we cannot easily refute someone's personal experience. Stories are also a powerful way to conjure empathy, to make our readers care about the information we relay; when information is personalized, it usually carries more of an impact. Knowing this, nonnarrative writers often weave throughout our pieces stories that connect with and convey the information we want to impart. Similarly, we often use stories to lure readers into our pieces from the very start and to lay the groundwork for what is to come.

Teaching

Tell

When I gathered a group of seventh graders for a strategy lesson, I said, "One way to begin your nonnarrative pieces is with a story that connects with your topic. As we know, a good story grabs people's attention, so starting with a story can be a great way to lure your readers into the information you want to impart."

Show

"Let me show you what I mean. Here's how your classmate Reuben starts his article on sibling rivalry."

> *No air was blowing in Adam's face as he warmed the bench during the soccer championship game. His brother, Joey, ran up and down the soccer field with sweat running down his face with the crowd cheering him on.*
>
> *"Why aren't I the one running around there instead of sitting out," Adam thought to himself.*
>
> *It was just then when Joey dribbled around the defender and scored the winning goal in the game.*
>
> *"YEA!!! NICE SHOT JOEY!!! AWESOME!!! GO GO GO GO!!!" yelled the crowd while his teammates lifted him up.*
>
> *A feeling boiled up inside of Adam when everyone cheered for Joey. "Why am I not there having everyone acknowledge that I'm great?" Adam felt neglected and angry.*
>
> *Jealousy, sadness, envy can drive siblings into dangerous fights.*

"Do you see how Reuben's story directly connects with what he teaches his readers—how it's a snapshot of sibling rivalry? Do you also see how right away, we're pulled into his piece because he lures us into the world of the story?

Like when Adam thinks, *Why aren't I the one running around there instead of sitting out,* I immediately want to know more about what happens with Adam and Joey, or with anyone like them; I also want to learn what people can do when we encounter this kind of difficulty, and so I keep reading."

Active Involvement

Tell

"I know you won't all begin with a story, and that is fine; there are a lot of good ways to begin nonnarrative pieces. But for a moment, I want you to imagine how your introduction would go if you did begin with a story that introduces readers to your topic."

Coach

To coach students through their thinking, I said some of the following.

- "If your piece is about an issue, something bad or difficult in the world, your story might show conflict around that issue."
- "If your piece is about a person, place, or object, your story might show what that person, place, or object does."
- "Once you have a possible story, think about how you're going to write it so it lures your readers inside the piece. Your first sentence might be an action, something someone says, or it might describe the setting."

Following the strategy lesson, Patricia wrote the introduction for her article shown in Figure 13–3. The beginning of Patricia's piece reads more like a story than an article. Except were it a story, we would find out what happens to the narrator, and instead, Patricia uses her story as a jumping-off place to introduce facts. She still lets her readers know what to expect when we read her article: information on attention deficit disorder (ADD), what it is, how it affects people in general, and more specifically, how it affects young people. But now, Patricia does much more than introduce her topic. She also effectively pulls us into her piece by pulling us into the details of someone's life, someone for whom we feel compassion, perhaps with whom we empathize. I know that when I read this, I want to find out more about this child and how ADD affects him; in turn, I want to find out more about ADD itself, and so I keep reading Patricia's piece.

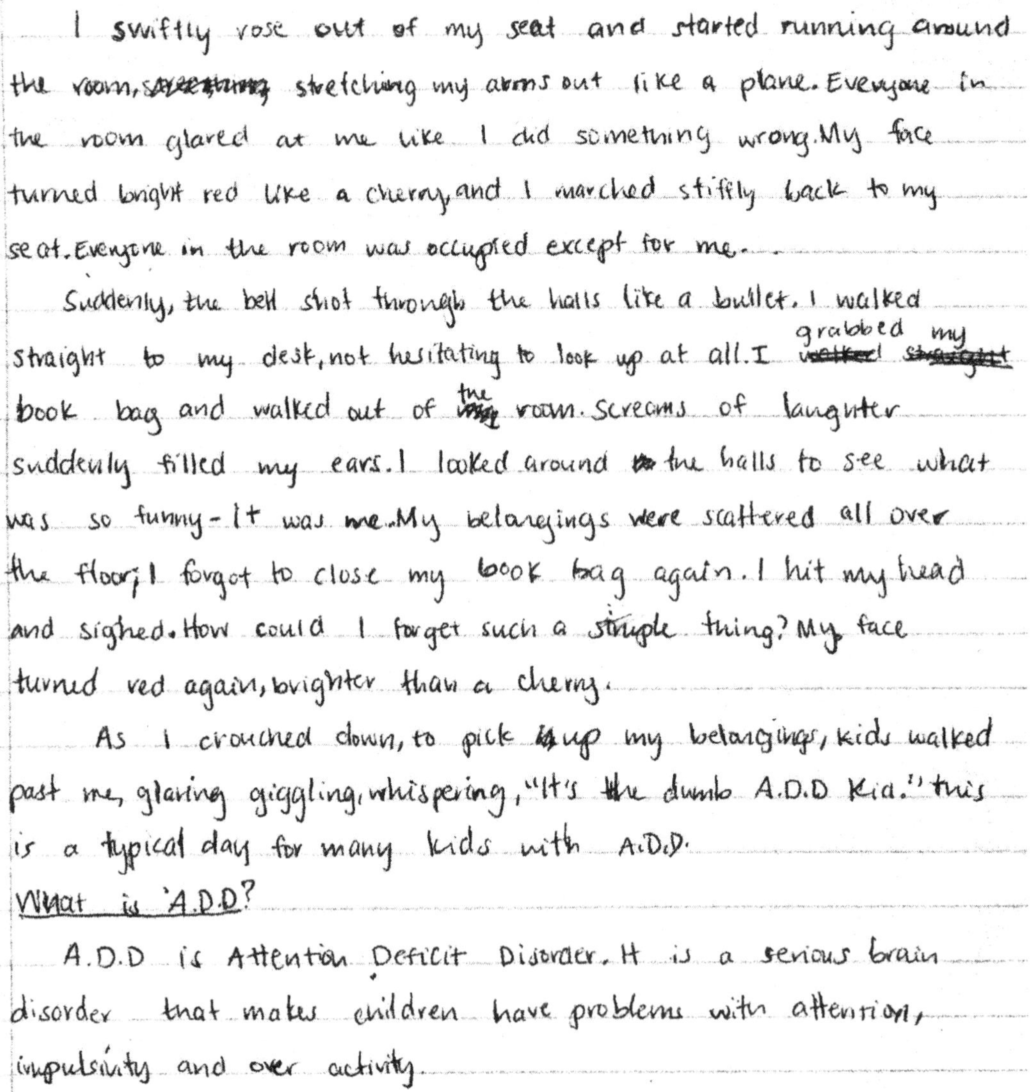

I swiftly rose out of my seat and started running around the room, stretching my arms out like a plane. Everyone in the room glared at me like I did something wrong. My face turned bright red like a cherry, and I marched stiffly back to my seat. Everyone in the room was occupied except for me...

Suddenly, the bell shot through the halls like a bullet. I walked straight to my desk, not hesitating to look up at all. I grabbed my book bag and walked out of the room. Screams of laughter suddenly filled my ears. I looked around the halls to see what was so funny - It was me. My belongings were scattered all over the floor; I forgot to close my book bag again. I hit my head and sighed. How could I forget such a simple thing? My face turned red again, brighter than a cherry.

As I crouched down, to pick up my belongings, kids walked past me, glaring giggling, whispering, "It's the dumb A.D.D Kid." this is a typical day for many kids with A.D.D.

What is A.D.D?

A.D.D is Attention Deficit Disorder. It is a serious brain disorder that makes children have problems with attention, impulsivity and over activity.

Figure 13–3 *Patricia's introduction: using a story*

* * *

As writers, the pen is our voice. We put words on the page when we have something to say. So of course, we want people, our readers, to perk their ears and listen. But unless we pique their interest early on in what is to come, our words will fall on deaf ears. This means that once we teach students how to gather and craft powerful information, we need to teach them how to introduce that information in ways that will call readers to attention and lure them into the hearts of their pieces.

CHAPTER 14

Crafting Conclusions

I am proud that I am known among friends and family for giving heartfelt gifts. Very often I handcraft them. Always I choose them with a particular person in mind. And always, I include a card to tie everything together, to sum up my feelings, my intentions, and the origin of what lies inside the wrapping paper. Each year, my husband makes loving fun of me on Christmas morning because I individually wrap every stocking stuffer, even the miniature candies, and tape a little note to the top ("a tiny tradition" or "something sweet for my sweetheart").

Conclusions are similar to introductions in that both should convey the author's purpose for writing—her thoughts and feelings and objectives; in fact, several of the strategies for writing introductions also work for writing conclusions, and vice versa, such as using a story, a provocative question, a quote. Still, what is so special about the conclusion is that it provides a final opportunity to convey our purpose for writing, much like my cards convey my purpose for giving. Conclusions are our last chance to say whatever it is we want our readers to know, and our last chance to say it memorably.

When we do not take advantage of this opportunity, our ideas either spill out into nowhere as a row of books spills onto the floor when a bookend is missing, or they fall flat like a helium balloon sinks to the floor after a day or two of life. If you come to the end of a student's piece and find that you are somehow still searching for the end, or still searching for a reason to hold onto the information in their pieces, it may be because he has not yet learned to craft powerful conclusions. In turn, you might teach the following strategies.

Relay New Thinking: *One way writers conclude our nonnarrative pieces is with new thinking we want our readers to consider based on the information in the text.*

Any piece of information, with a little bit of digging, leads to new information. Many nonnarrative writers use this knowledge to structure their entire pieces; they compose journeys of thought, texts in which they begin in one place and carry their readers from idea to idea, each one connected like a string of multicolored Christmas lights: different and yet tied together somehow. But even when we do not structure a piece as a journey, we can use the concept to compose a powerful conclusion. We can say to our readers: This is what I know or what I think, and now that I have shared it with you, here is something else to consider before you go.

Teaching

Tell

When I conferred with third-grader Tal, I said, "When we get to the end of a nonnarrative piece, writers often ask ourselves, What does all this information make me think? What new thought do I have that I want to leave with my readers? We do this so our readers walk away still thinking about what they just read; it makes it so they can't stop thinking about our piece."

Show

"Let me show you how this student ends his piece with new thinking. His whole essay is about how hard it is that his father isn't around very much, and he gives three reasons why: because he doesn't get a man's perspective on things, because his mother gets stressed out, and because he misses his dad. When he gets to his conclusion, he briefly revisits these ideas, but then he includes new thinking; this is what he writes:

> *It's hard having a father who isn't around very much because I rarely get a man's perspective on things, my mom gets stressed out a lot, and because I just miss knowing my dad. Even though it's hard, I know I'm luckier than a lot of my friends who don't know their fathers at all or don't like their fathers at all. Unlike some of my friends, when I really want to know or ask something, I can call up my dad or wait until the next time I see him, and when I do see him, we always have a good time*

together. But when I have kids, I plan to be around a lot more so they don't have to feel what I feel.

"Do you see how this writer only has one sentence (his first one) on the ideas in the rest of his piece, and then he has several sentences of new thinking? And do you see how the new thinking connects with and builds on his ideas? For example, he doesn't write that it actually isn't that hard, after all, having a father who isn't around; instead, he writes that even though it's hard, he's still luckier than some kids. By ending with something new to consider, he sends his readers away still thinking about and engaged with his piece."

Active Engagement

Tell

"I want you to try this. When you publish your piece, you might decide to end in a different way, which is absolutely fine; but for now, practice what I taught by writing a conclusion that includes new thinking." Though not always necessary, I often find it helpful for students to return to their notebooks at this point to develop their ideas; in this instance, I said to Tal, "Open your writer's notebook and freewrite by asking yourself, What does all this stuff make me think now? When you've uncovered some new thinking, use it to rewrite your conclusion."

Coach

To support students with this work, I say things like:

- "How do the things you write about impact you or others?"
- "What might someone else think about the information in your piece?"
- "Write, *This makes me think . . . which makes me think . . .*"
- "Finish the sentence: *I realize that . . .*"

Before our conference, Tal ended her essay as shown in Figure 14–1. Tal's initial conclusion fulfills the bottom-line requirements of a conclusion: it revisits the ideas in her piece in a final effort to impart her thinking to her readers. But her conclusion is neither memorable nor engaging. After our

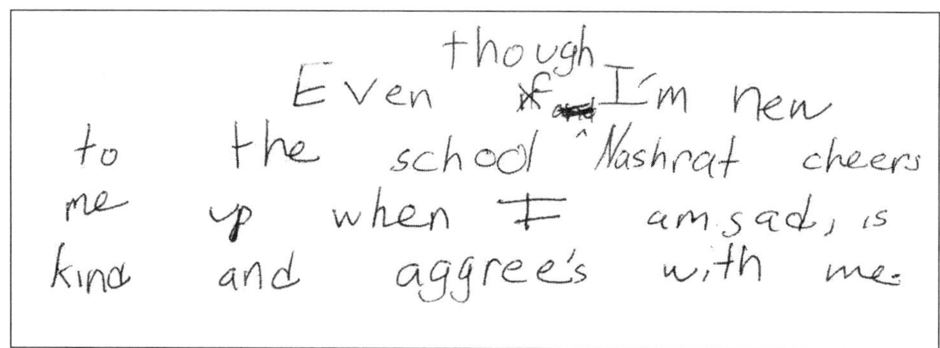

Even though I'm new to the school Nashrat cheers me up when I am sad, is kind and aggree's with me.

Figure 14–1 *Tal's initial conclusion*

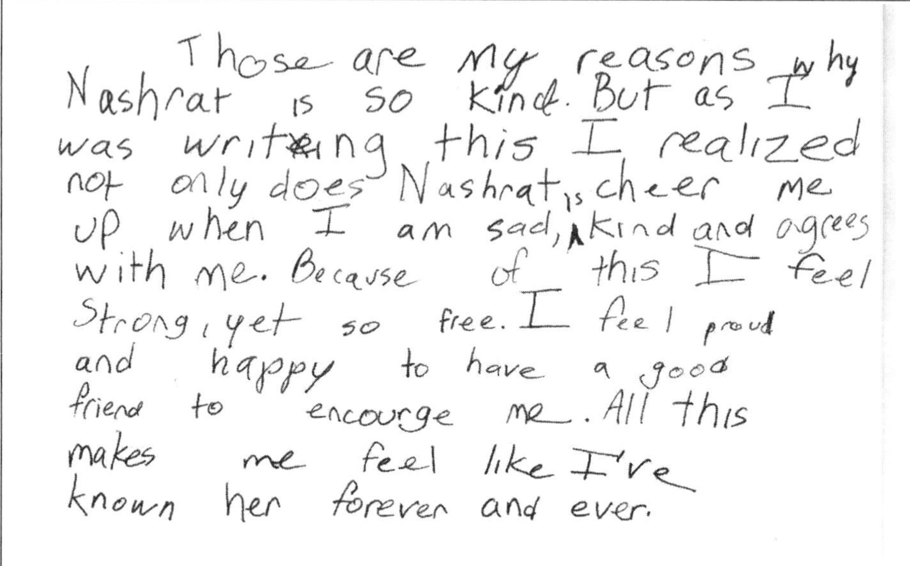

Those are my reasons why Nashrat is so kind. But as I was writing this I realized not only does Nashrat cheer me up when I am sad, is kind and agrees with me. Because of this I feel Strong, yet so free. I feel proud and happy to have a good friend to encourge me. All this makes me feel like I've known her forever and ever.

Figure 14–2 *Tal's revised conclusion: relaying new thinking*

conference, Tal finished her entry and then used it to revise her conclusion as shown in Figure 14–2.

Teaching students to consider their new thinking is a powerful strategy for concluding a piece, not only because it teaches them to send their readers away with something new to consider, but because it challenges students to once again deepen their own thinking. Tal, for example, realizes that her friendship with Nashrat is important not simply because she is a good friend; not simply because she cheers her up, is kind and agrees with her. Much more intriguing is Tal's realization that her friendship with Nashrat makes her feel strong and proud, and because of this, Tal feels like she has known her forever.

Plead for Action: *One way writers conclude our nonnarrative pieces is with a plea for action based on the information in the text.*

In their book, *For a Better World: Reading and Writing for Social Action* (2001), Randy and Katherine Bomer teach us how to get our students invested in social causes and how to use writing to promote those causes; for example, they show us how we might teach students to write speeches and letters meant to ignite action, how to create petitions and posters to instigate change.

Even when our students' overarching purpose when writing nonnarrative is to inform rather than to incite, we can learn from Katherine and Randy. We can teach our students that one way to make the information in their pieces more powerful is to tell readers in the conclusion how they might make use of what they have just learned—to tell them how they might turn knowledge and thought into action.

Teaching

Tell

When I pulled a small group of seventh graders for a strategy lesson, I said, "One way to conclude your pieces is with a plea for action; it's like saying to your readers, Now that you know all this information, here is what you can do about the matter at hand. Especially when we write about topics that incite strong emotions or that open our readers' eyes to an injustice of some kind, we want to give them tools with which to address the issue and make a difference in the world."

Show

"Let me show you what I mean. I'm writing a piece on how what we eat is harming us, causing things like cancer and obesity and diabetes. I include a lot of information on things like the effects of the amount of sugar we consume and how we grow our fruits and vegetables with pesticides that hurt us and destroy the land. Let me think for a minute about how I might end with a plea for action. Right now, I'm thinking, What do I do about these things? Well, one thing is I really try to buy only organic food. And I don't order meat in restaurants unless I know it was raised humanely and without hormones. I'm also thinking about the things I don't do but feel like I should, like spreading what I know to other people. For example, I could start a program that educates students in schools about nutrition. Or I could join an organization that fights against using chemicals and hormones in and on our food.

"That's a lot of information; let me try and put at least some of that in my conclusion. Hmm . . . I'm not sure how to get started. Maybe I could start with a general statement about needing to make a difference; of course it needs to connect with the content in my piece: *We need to do all we can to change the way we raise our food and the way we eat.* I think that works.

"Now I could put in some of those specific things we can do: *Start buying organic. Even though it's more expensive, it could save your life and that of the planet. Don't eat meat in restaurants unless you know it is hormone-free. And look for ways to get involved. Join an organization that educates people about what to eat and why. Campaign for healthier farming conditions.* I like that I've given so many different things people can do, both big and small. Now I just need to conclude my plea. Maybe I could revisit the information in my piece by briefly saying why it's so important to do these things; something like: *If we don't make a change, our bodies, our animals, and our environment will continue to suffer.*

"Do you see how I give very concrete advice about what my readers can do to make a difference? Did you notice how I came up with what to say by asking myself some questions like, What do I do? What do I wish I did? What could other people do? By giving my readers tools for change, my piece becomes a much more powerful tool for change, as well.

Active Engagement

Tell

"I want each of you to try this now with your pieces. As always, you can write and choose whatever kind of ending you'd like; but for now, try writing a conclusion that includes a plea for action, something your readers can do now that they know what they know, so your pieces have the potential to make even more of a difference in the world."

Coach

To support students in the group, I said things like:

- "Why did you write this piece? What would you like people to do to address your concerns?"
- "What might improve the issues you raise in your piece? You could suggest to your readers that they do some of those things."
- "What do people in the world do in response to the issue at hand, or in similar situations? Could your readers do any of those things, too?"

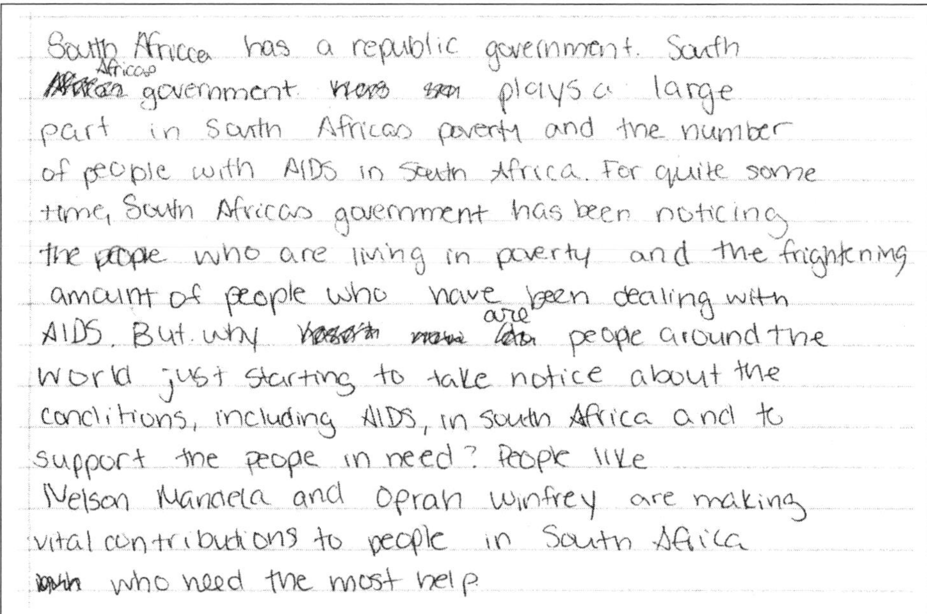
South Africa has a republic government. South
Africas government plays a large
part in South Africas poverty and the number
of people with AIDS in South Africa. For quite some
time, South Africas government has been noticing
the people who are living in poverty and the frightening
amount of people who have been dealing with
AIDS. But why are peope around the
world just starting to take notice about the
conditions, including AIDS, in South Africa and to
support the peope in need? People like
Nelson Mandela and Oprah Winfrey are making
vital contributions to people in South Africa
who need the most help.

Figure 14–3 *Emily's initial conclusion*

In her article on AIDS in South Africa, Emily gathered and relayed information on who has AIDS in South Africa and why the numbers are so high and rising. In her initial draft, she ended with the paragraph shown in Figure 14–3.

Emily's conclusion does not quite feel like a conclusion to me, mostly because of the last sentence where she introduces a new and narrow fact. That Mandela and Oprah contribute money to South Africans in need does not reflect the bigger information in Emily's piece, and so it seems to be an opening for more to come, something about the relevance of this fact in connection with the rest of the piece, rather than a conclusion of what has already come.

After the strategy lesson, Emily tried a different conclusion as shown in Figure 14–4. Emily's conclusion now feels like a conclusion because she connects what Oprah and Mandela are doing to help fight AIDS with a plea for her readers to help, as well. Emily could strengthen her plea, and thus her conclusion, by visiting those websites herself in order to learn more specific things people can do. But in the meantime, she clearly understands the strategy and thus has more tools as a writer for ending her pieces well.

What is so powerful about teaching students to conclude with a plea for action is that it teaches them that writing has power, and that they, in turn, have power as writers to change the world.

Quote Another Source: *One way writers conclude our pieces is by including and responding to an outside quote that connects with the information in our piece.*

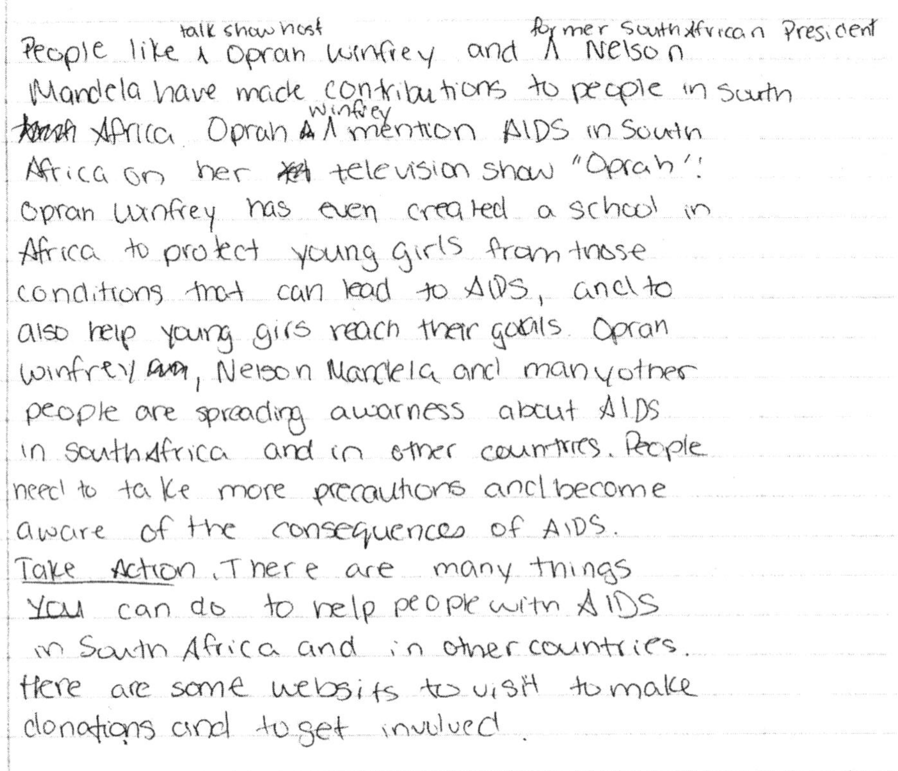
People like talk show host Oprah Winfrey and former South African President Nelson
Mandela have made contributions to people in South
Africa. Oprah Winfrey mention AIDS in South
Africa on her television show "Oprah"!
Oprah Winfrey has even created a school in
Africa to protect young girls from those
conditions that can lead to AIDS, and to
also help young girls reach their goals. Oprah
Winfrey, Nelson Mandela and many other
people are spreading awarness about AIDS
in South Africa and in other countries. People
need to take more precautions and become
aware of the consequences of AIDS.
Take Action. There are many things
You can do to help people with AIDS
in South Africa and in other countries.
Here are some websits to visit to make
donations and to get invulved.

Figure 14–4 *Emily's revised conclusion: pleading for action*

We teach writers that one way to gather information is to quote outside sources because we know that weaving other voices through a piece gives our information and our perspective validity. Before we send our readers away, we want to assure them of our knowledge and when applicable, convince them of our claims, which is why we often end with a quote, as well.

Teaching

Tell

When I conferred with fifth-grader Emma who was finishing an essay on the inhumane treatment of crocodiles and alligators, I said, "Writers sometimes end our nonnarrative pieces with a quote from an outside source that connects with the overall information in our piece. Using a quote can validate the information in our piece because it sends readers away knowing that other people think the way we do, and so perhaps they should think this way, too."

Show

"Let me show you an example. In this article, 'Can Kids Stop Kids from Smoking?' the author writes about different things young people are doing, such as running antismoking advertisements and visiting elementary schools to teach kids about the dangers of smoking. Look at her last paragraph; she ends her article with a quote: *'Tobacco companies try to tell kids it's cool to smoke,' says Leonardo Casas, 16, of REBEL. 'We frame the message so that kids can see it's cooler not to.'*

"Do you see how her quote connects with and almost summarizes the overall information in the article? In all the preceding paragraphs, the author includes information on the dangers of smoking and on young people trying to get that message across. Her end quote, which says smoking is not cool, is like a confirmation of everything she writes. This means that when we finish her article, we have yet another person's voice ringing in our ears saying what she wants us to know, which makes it more likely that we'll believe and hold onto the information in her piece."

Active Engagement

Tell

"I want you to try this now. You will need to look over your research notes and you might even do some more research, because you want to find a quote that connects with the overall information in your piece."

Coach

To help guide Emma's work, I said things like:

- "What is the big thing you want your readers to know? Where might you find someone else who thinks or knows these same things?"
- "Let's look at one of the texts you used for your research: Reread it and underline any parts that seem to summarize your main points. Then consider whether any of those parts would make a good quote."
- "When you find your quote, you might ask yourself, What do I want my readers to know or think about this? You could use that answer to write a response to the quote."

See Figure 14–5 for Emma's conclusion. Emma's quote is not only provocative; it speaks directly to the ideas in her piece. Using it to conclude her essay drives home her point with authority and with emotion, making it very difficult for her readers to walk away unchanged by the information she conveys.

* * *

When we write nonnarrative, our driving purpose is to inform our readers. Whether we are writing expository, procedural, or informational texts, we want our readers to walk away knowing something very specific about us, about a place or about an object, about the world. But in order to effectively impart our thinking, we must leave a lasting impression. Otherwise, our readers will soon replace the information we present with more engaging wisdom or guidance or news. Just as the fireworks on the Fourth of July always end with a grand explosion of noise and color, the conclusion of a nonnarrative piece should end with a grand explosion of thought.

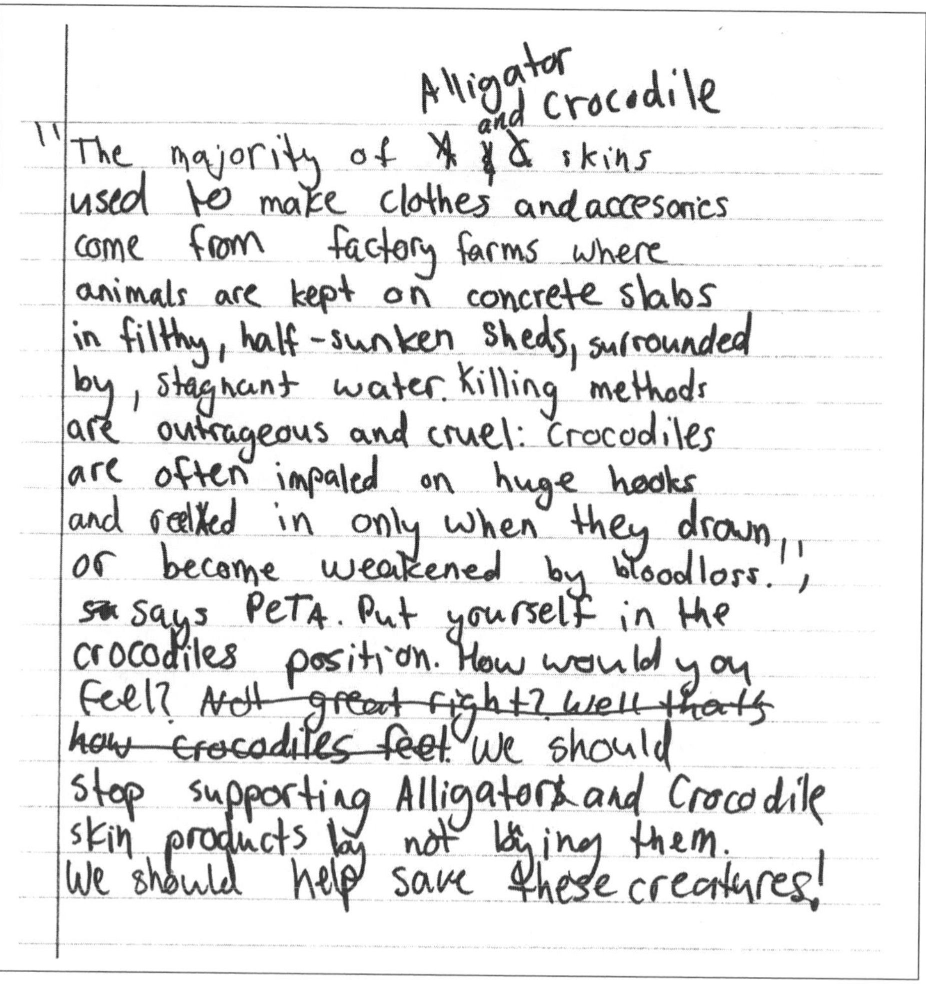

Alligator and Crocodile

"The majority of A & C skins used to make clothes and accesories come from factory farms where animals are kept on concrete slabs in filthy, half-sunken sheds, surrounded by, stagnant water. Killing methods are outrageous and cruel: Crocodiles are often impaled on huge hooks and reeled in only when they drown, or become weakened by bloodloss.", says PETA. Put yourself in the crocodiles position. How would you feel? ~~Not great right? Well that's how crocodiles feel.~~ We should stop supporting Alligators and Crocodile skin products by not buying them. We should help save these creatures!

Figure 14–5 *Emma's conclusion: quoting an outside source*

INTRODUCTION: CONVENTIONS

A common misperception is that teaching conventions is not a valued part of writing workshop. Perhaps this misunderstanding arises from the fact that many of us who believe in writing workshop believe we should get students writing and *then* we should teach them how to write better. Whether the "better" refers to lifting the quality of a lead or lifting the quality of the spelling, I do strongly believe that students should engage with writing—that students should actually *write*—before we weigh them down with rules.

I think of my son, fifteen months old now and trying so hard to feed himself with a spoon. Not only do I have to wrap my hand around his to help him scoop from the bowl; most bites, even once we get them on the spoon, fall midair before making it to his mouth. Were I to say, "Harrison, *no,* this is how you hold the spoon," or "*No,* food goes on the plate or in your mouth, not on the floor or on your shirt" every time he failed to follow the general rules for eating, he might never learn to eat on his own; and even if he did, he would very likely develop some real issues about eating.

Once Harrison does manage to independently fill his spoon and feed himself, I will surely teach him better ways to eat. Eventually, I will teach him more effective ways to hold silverware and how to make less of a mess, just as I will teach him how to chew with his mouth closed and wipe his face with a napkin. But first, he needs to explore, muck around, have fun, get comfortable.

And so do our writers. *Especially* our writers who most typically struggle with conventions. So often, our most resistant or most struggling writers are the ones who forget their end punctuation and their paragraphs. And so often, I see teachers focusing on convention work with these students in every conference and every strategy lesson because "They really need it!" What better way to turn a child off from writing forever.

Once students are actually writing—once they know how to find and get on the page topics that matter to them—I generally suggest to teachers that they teach conventions through direct instruction about every sixth to tenth minilesson, and when needed, about about every third to fifth conference or strategy lesson. By direct instruction, I mean explicitly naming and showing students a rule as it already exists in the world; I mean teaching the kinds of strategies I outline in the following chapters.

In addition to explicitly teaching convention rules, many teachers continue to support the "mucking around." Writers and educators like Janet Angelillo, Mary Ehrenworth, and Vicki Vinton have taught me the power of teaching conventions through inquiry; by asking students to explore what they notice about commas, about verb tense or sentence structure, students can discover for themselves rules of print. In doing so, they get a better sense that rules are not arbitrary but exist for reasons.

Whether teaching through direct instruction or through inquiry, we clearly want our students to learn to write with proper conventions; doing so is imperative if they are going to do well. But let us first help our students discover the power of writing so we do not inadvertently teach them that writing is about finding the right spelling or the right place to use a period. Instead, we want to teach them that writing is about exploring the world and our place in it; it is about finding our voices and expressing them. And we want to teach our students that writers consider conventions not to blindly follow someone else's rules but to craft their own voices in the most meaningful and powerful ways possible so they will be heard with understanding and with respect.

CHAPTER 15

Using Periods

As teachers, we have to get good at transitioning students from one activity to the next. We need to learn tools for gathering everyone's attention, steps for giving closure to one part of the day and getting everyone ready for what is to come. Without these tools, confusion and even chaos ensue, causing one block of time to bleed into the next as teacher and student alike try to make sense of what is happening and of what should be happening.

As writers, we have to get good at using periods for similar reasons: without them, confusion and chaos ensue. Of course, learning takes time (which is why most new teachers seek help with management). For this reason, I expect teachers in kindergarten and first and second grade classrooms will do minilessons during the year on using periods; I expect the majority of very young writers will need support in this area. But even in the upper grades where, in most cases, a majority of students have internalized proper use of periods, there is almost always one writer, if not a small handful of them, who needs additional support in this area; even in fourth- and sixth- and eighth-grade classrooms, most teachers find a need to teach the use of periods inside of conferences or strategy lessons.

If you have students who still do not use periods consistently or appropriately, you will first want to assess the particular issue at hand for each writer: Is she forgetting to use periods altogether? Is she overusing periods and creating ineffective fragments? Is she using periods when she edits her work but not when she composes? Depending on your assessment, you might teach to individuals, to small groups of writers who share similar needs, or in some cases to your whole class, one or more of the following strategies.

Say Complete Thoughts: *One way writers decide when to use periods is by saying a complete thought in our heads and writing it down with a period at the end, then repeating the process.*

For many of our writers, they struggle to use periods, or to use them correctly, because they do not yet know how to identify a sentence versus a fragment. Although it is tempting to teach this difference, it is much more complicated than it may seem. I have seen many try to teach their students about sentences through parts of speech. "Every sentence has a subject and verb," teachers sometimes say. But students often struggle with this, as well. After all, some sentences certainly do not seem to have a subject and a verb; many students will have a hard time understanding, for example, that the sentence, "Stop!" has an inferred subject. And then we have to explain how something like "She ran to the" is not actually a sentence even though yes, it contains a subject and a verb.

I have found that even when students struggle to understand the definition of a sentence and identify one in writing, they almost always understand when something does or does not make sense in conversation. I often ask students, "If I walked up to you and said, 'She ran to the!' would that make sense to you?" Almost never has a young writer responded with a "Yes."

Teaching

Tell

Knowing this, I say "One way to figure out where to use periods is to say a complete thought in your head, then write it down with a period at the end and repeat the process. This way, you're sure to have your readers stop and think (which is what periods do) at places that make sense."

Show

"Watch me as I use this strategy to write about the fire drill we had last week. I want to write about how the alarm went off and we all jumped in our seats because we were so surprised to hear the noise, but as soon as we realized what was happening, we hurried into line. I'm going to write my first thought in my head. Let me think, what was the very first thing that happened? The fire alarm went off and for a second everyone was totally silent and then there was a lot of talking and whispering as everyone—

"Wait! That is a *lot* of different thoughts! Let me back up, try again, but much slower this time because I really just want to think of the very first thing that happened. So what happened first? Well . . . The fire alarm went off. OK! That certainly makes sense to me; if someone said that to me, I would know what they were talking about. So let me write that down with a period at the end. What was the next thing that happened? We jumped up. That makes sense to everyone, right? Let me write that down with a period at the end."

Active Engagement

Tell

"Let's try it together now. What is the very next thing that happened when we had the fire drill? Get the whole thought in your head and check that it would make sense if someone ran up and said the thought to you.

"I want you all to try this now in your own writing. Whatever you're working on right now, I want you to say your next complete thought in your head—something that makes sense to you—and then write it down with a period at the end. Then repeat the process with your next thought and your next."

Coach

To coach students, I ask some of the following questions. I am sure to question sentences that make sense as well as those that do not because I want students to rely on themselves instead of on me to uncover errors.

- "Read your first sentence out loud. Does it make sense? Keep reading each sentence out loud and listen to whether it makes sense on its own."
- "If I ran up to you and said [a sentence the student wrote], would you understand what I meant?"

Before I send students back to their seats, I let them know that saying each thought in their heads before they write it down is temporary. I want them to understand that soon, they won't need to use this strategy because using periods will come easily and naturally, at which point they can write *as* instead of *after* they compose thoughts in their heads.

Combine Fragments: *One way writers decide when to use periods is by checking for and fixing fragments. To do this, we read each sentence separately* *and ask ourselves, "Does this make sense on its own?" When something does not make sense, we often edit our work by combining the fragment with what comes before or after it.*

When I work with writers who are just learning to use periods, I expect that for many of them, the pendulum will swing from one extreme to the other before it settles in the middle. In other words, I am not surprised when I see no periods before a lesson and then after a lesson, I see periods at the end of every line or used seemingly haphazardly every few words. In fact, I celebrate. "Wow!" I'll exclaim. "You have learned so much about periods! You have learned that writers use periods almost every single time we write. Congratulations!" Then, of course, I want to build on my compliment and teach them to use periods better.

Teaching

Tell

"One way writers figure out when to use periods is by rereading our writing aloud, looking at every series of words held by a period and asking ourselves, Does this make sense on its own? If not, we often combine it with the sentence that comes before or after; remember, writers use periods to let our readers know they have come to the end of a thought and should stop to take in that thought before moving on to the next, and we certainly do not want our readers to stop and think about things that don't make sense!"

Show

Because we are teaching students to reread their writing in this kind of lesson or conference, it is important to have a piece of text that mirrors the kind of writing they are doing so we can model rereading. We might write something like this: *The fire drill rang. Everyone jumped up from their seats and. Looked around. The teacher told the class to. Get in line. She reminded everyone to be quiet.*

"Let me show you how I reread something I wrote to check my periods. I'm going to read each sentence I've created and ask myself whether it makes sense. If it doesn't, I'm going to see whether it would make sense to combine it with the sentence that comes before or after.

"*The fire drill rang.* That makes perfect sense to me. If one of you ran up to me and said that, I would understand exactly what you were saying. So at least for now, I'm going to keep that period just where it is. Next sentence:

Everyone jumped up from their seats and. . . . And what? If someone said that to me, I'd be waiting for something more; so no, my period doesn't work there. Let me see whether it would be better if I combined this sentence with the sentence before: *The fire drill rang and everyone jumped up from their seats and. . . .* And what?! No, it still doesn't work. How about if I combine it with the following sentence: *Everyone jumped up from their seats and looked around.* Yes! That makes sense! So I'm going to combine these two sentences by crossing out this middle period and making my *L* lowercase."

Active Engagement

Tell

"Now it's your turn to try." In a minilesson, where I know I will have some students whose writing does not contain fragments, I have them practice on the second half of the text I composed. Students could either edit my writing on the chart paper by discussing their thoughts with a partner, or I could copy and distribute a piece of text for them to edit in writing, either with a partner or on their own. In a conference or strategy lesson, where I know every participant creates fragments and therefore has their own writing with which they can practice the strategy, I usually have them apply my teaching to their own work.

Coach

Regardless of the situation, when difficulty arises, I say things like:

- "Read a little to me, starting from right here. I want you to take a full breath at every period and ask yourself, Does what I just read make sense?"
- "Listen while I read some of your writing aloud. I'm going to stop at every period and your job is to raise your hand when you hear something that does not make sense."
- "You still have [two] sentences that do not make sense; reread this page again and see if you can find them."

Break Apart On-and-On Sentences: *One way writers know how to use periods is by finding our sentences that go on and on with an* and, or, but, so *or* then *and seeing whether it would make sense to replace any of those words with a period.*

If creating sentence fragments rests on one side of the pendulum, creating on-and-on sentences rests on the other side. But when our students fall on the fragment side of the pendulum, we can usually teach them to "hear" their fragments; we can usually teach them to use their knowledge of oral language to recognize when a period does not make sense.

When our students fall on the on-and-on side of the pendulum, it is usually more difficult for them to hear their incorrect use of periods; perhaps because on-and-on sentences still make sense, or perhaps because they sometimes sound the way we speak, students often struggle to recognize when they are using too few periods. Easy to recognize, however, is their use of *and, or, but, so,* and *then*—words that often combine independent clauses. We can therefore teach writers to notice when they use these words and to consider whether they could instead use a period in any of these instances. In a single sitting, as shown in this section, I usually teach students to notice one to three of these words. I introduce the others in follow-up teaching.

The first time I work with students who tend to write on-and-on sentences, I teach this as an editing strategy. During follow-up work, I teach students how to reconsider their on-and-on sentences as they compose text. I begin this teaching by reminding them of what they already know: "You already know that when you reread your pieces, you can find and fix your on-and-on sentences by noticing words like *and, so* and *then* and considering whether it would make sense to replace any of these words with a period. But writers don't spend their whole lives writing on-and-on sentences and then fixing them up during the editing stage. Instead, they learn to write without on-and-on sentences from the very start." As always, once I create a context for my teaching, I introduce my teaching point.

Teaching

Tell

"Whenever you write, you can avoid on-and-on sentences by considering *before* you put your thought on paper whether you could use a period to begin a new sentence instead of using words like *and, so,* and *then* to keep a sentence going. This way, you can make sure as you write that you are giving your readers a chance to breath and think; otherwise, your readers will have a very difficult time taking in what you have to say to them."

Show

"Let me show you what that looks like. I'm going to write a story about our fire drill, and I want you to notice how I think about periods as I write: *The fire drill rang*—and. . . . Now let me think: do I want to use an *and* there to write, *and we all jumped?* Or do I want to use a period and write, *The fire drill rang.* Period. *We all jumped?* You know, I want to use a period instead of an *and* because I feel like it slows down the story a little; it helps my readers to really hear the fire drill, and then to stop and really see us jumping up. *The fire drill rang. We all jumped. Some kids got really quiet*—so. . . . Again, I need to think about whether I want to use a period. I was going to write, *so they could hear the teacher.* If I used a period instead, it would be, *Some kids got really quiet. They could hear the teacher.* Actually, this time I like it better without the period because it shows my readers that the reason the kids were quiet was because they wanted to hear what the teacher had to say. It's really one thought, so I want it to be one sentence. *Some kids got really quiet so they could hear the teacher*—and then. . . . I was going to write, *and then the teacher told everyone to put down their books and get in line.* But instead, I'm going to use a period because otherwise my sentence is going to go on and on. *The teacher told everyone to put down their books*—and . . . Hmm. Should, *get in line* be its own sentence? No, that doesn't make sense. I need to keep my *and* here: *The teacher told everyone to put down their books and get in line.*

"Do you all see how I'm thinking about words like *and, so,* and *then* as I write; do you see how I stop before I write one of those words and think about whether I want to use a period instead? Do you notice that sometimes I do want to use one of those words instead of a period, either because the sentence makes more sense that way or because I want to keep thoughts that go together in the same sentence?"

Active Engagement

Tell

"Now I want you to try. You can either finish an entry or start a new one. Either way, I'm going to give you a couple minutes to write several lines in your notebook. Remember, as you're writing, stop yourself before you write an *and, so,* or *then,* and think about whether it would make sense and sound just as good to use a period instead."

Coach

To help students, I might say:

- "I see a lot of on-and-on sentences, which tells me you aren't stopping yourself *before* you write an [*and, but, or, so,* or *then*]. Slow yourself down by putting your pencil down and saying each thought in your head before you actually write it. That way you can listen for those words and sometimes use a period instead."
- "What's the next thing you plan to write. Say the sentence to me and listen to whether it has an [*and, but, or, so,* or *then*]. Can you replace one of those words with a period and make a new sentence?"

Listen for Fragments and On-and-On Sentences: *One way writers know when to use periods is by reading our work out loud, stopping at every period and anywhere else we want our readers to breathe and think. For every stop, writers consider whether we want to remove a period, add a period, or leave a period as it is.*

Like any punctuation, we use periods to direct our readers, to let them know how we want them to read our work. So it makes sense and is important to teach our students to practice reading their writing as a way to reflect on their use of periods. However, I have greater success teaching students to listen for under- or overuse of periods when the teaching comes after one or more of the other teaching points in this chapter. Whereas the other strategies in this chapter offer very specific and concrete guidance, this strategy asks students to integrate all their knowledge as readers and writers about periods and sentence structure. Easier to say one complete thought in our heads and write it down with a period; easier to find an *and* and ask, Can I replace this with a period? than to read our work out loud and listen for the overall sound and pace of our writing.

Again, I would begin this minilesson, conference, strategy lesson, or teaching share by reminding students of what I have already taught and what they already know on this topic; of course, this will vary from student to class. Depending on the teaching that has come before, I might say something like, "A few weeks ago, we talked about periods, about how writers often consider whether they can replace words like *and, but, or, so,* and *then* with a period to give their readers a chance to breathe and think. I know you've been working on using periods in ways that really help your readers take in the information on the page, so today I want to teach you something else you can do."

Teaching

Tell

"We use periods to let our readers know we want them to stop and think. One way to check your use of periods is by reading your work out loud, making sure to really stop at every single period and to not stop anywhere there isn't a period. As you do this, you want to consider whether you do, in fact, want your readers to stop in each of those places, and whether there are places you don't ask your readers to stop but would like to."

Show

To demonstrate this strategy, I again want to create a text that mirrors what my students are doing. Because I ask students to integrate a range of knowledge about periods, I am sure to include fragments and on-and-on sentences, as well as sentences that feel appropriate just as they are. I might write something as follows:

> *The fire drill rang and everyone jumped up. From their seats. The ringing continued for what felt like a long time. Everyone looked around and then the teacher told the class to get in line and kids were talking but the teacher reminded everyone to be quiet so most of the kids stopped talking or some started whispering. The whole class walked out of the room and toward the front door. Once the class was outside everyone just waited. Until the principal said it was okay to go back to class.*

As I model my teaching point, and as I support students to use the strategy, I highlight the importance of holding on to our audience as we write; in other words, I show how I keep thinking about what would help my readers, and I ask my students to consider the same about their readers. "Do I really want my readers to stop here? Perhaps I want them to have all this information at once, and then stop to think about what it means," I might say. Or similarly, "Whew! I think I'm asking my readers to read way too much, way too quickly in this part. I don't give them a chance to breathe at all as I throw more and more information at them! I better find a place to give them a little break." I want my students to understand that using periods is less about the simple fact of creating sentences and more about the bigger purpose of directing our readers—of letting them know when to speed up or slow down their reading, when to linger or stop or gasp for breath.

Active Engagement

Tell

"Here's another page of my story," I say in a minilesson or teaching share; or in a conference or strategy lesson, I more likely say, "Turn to the last page you wrote." Then I say, "I want you to reread this out loud, making sure to really stop at every single period and to not stop anywhere there isn't a period. As you do this, consider whether you do, in fact, want your readers to stop in each of those places, and whether there are places you don't ask your readers to stop but would like them to."

Coach

To support students with on-and-on sentences, I say things like:

- "Is there an *and, but, or, so,* or *then* you could replace with a period?"
- "Reread this part again and for each sentence, see if you can get to the end without taking a breath . . . You were reading really fast there, trying to get to the end so you could breathe! Sometimes it's fine to have sentences that long, but often, it's a sign that your readers could use a little breathing and thinking break. Reread it again and see whether you could add a period somewhere to give your readers a chance to make sense of what you write."

To support students with fragments, I say things like:

- "Let's read some of these sentences out loud; for each one, we're going to ask whether it makes sense." When a student notices something that doesn't make sense, I say, "How could you make it make sense? Could you combine it with the sentence that comes before or after?"
- "Look up from the paper and tell me what you are [or what you think the writer is] trying to say here. Say it in a complete thought. Now look back at the paper and fix the sentence so it reads the same way you just said it."

* * *

We all know the saying, "Rules are meant to be broken." How true this is when it comes to written conventions, and in this case, when it comes to using periods. As a rule, one uses periods at the end of a sentence, and as a rule, a sentence is a complete, independent thought that contains a subject and a verb. But knowing this, I often use periods to create fragments. To emphasize. To slow things down. Similarly, I often create sentences that go on and on and on when I want my readers to move quickly from one thought to the next and to keep going and going without taking a breath.

I would not know how to do these things, however, if I did not know and understand how to use periods; if I did not know the rules, I would not understand how to break them in purposeful ways. As always, purpose is the key. So as always, let us not forget to teach our students *why* writers use periods. Let us not forget to teach them that, above all, writers use periods to create meaning and rhythm for our readers.

CHAPTER 16

Using Correct Spelling

I once heard my colleague Mary Chiarella talk with a group of educators about the tail she grew as a new teacher. "I always had three, four, five students following me around the classroom," she explained. "They would tug on the back of my shirt, call after me, 'Mary! Mary!' It took me awhile to learn that the more I answered questions as they arose, the more dependent my students became. And the more dependent they were, the less I got done and the less they got done."

There are certain predictable questions students ask us again and again for as long as we allow them to be dependent on us, one of which is "How do I spell ___?" If we let it happen, hands will shoot into the air every few minutes for the duration of writers' workshop to ask that question alone. Every year, I strongly urge teachers to stop answering the question. If we really want our students to be able to write independently for extended periods of time, we need to teach them to hold their questions for later and to keep writing even when they encounter difficulty. After all, we want them to be able to function as writers when we are not around; when they are at home, or in college, or at work, we want them to be able to keep writing even when things get hard.

Another issue, of course, is when writers struggle to spell but never think to ask for help. Although we might applaud them for doing the best they can and for writing away despite their difficulty, we also want to teach them ways to address their difficulty. So either way—if you have students who quietly or loudly struggle with spelling—you might teach the following strategies.

Jot Possible Spellings in Margins: *One way writers spell words correctly is by trying different spellings in the margins and using the one that looks best.*

I believe wholeheartedly that we should teach students to be readers and writers in the world, not simply readers and writers in the classroom, and so I aim to teach real-life strategies and habits, the kinds of things readers and writers really do. These days, many of us use spell check when we come to a word we are not quite sure how to spell. But when I am writing with paper and pen and I want to write a word I do not know how to spell, the first thing I do is jot in the margins.

Teaching

Tell

"One thing writers do to help us spell tricky words is quickly jot the word two or three different ways in the margins of our paper and then use the one that looks right to us. This is an excellent strategy to use when you're in the midst of writing and don't want to interrupt the flow of getting your ideas down on the page. Even when we are not sure how to spell a word, we often have ideas about different ways the word might go; and very often, when we're looking at different spellings, we can recognize when something looks wrong, or right, or at least more right than another spelling."

Show

"I did this yesterday when I was writing on the subway. I came to a word that always trips me up. *Beautiful.* I can never remember how to spell that word! I copied the page I was writing so you could see exactly what I did. I was writing about my son, and see here, I started to write, *He seems to get more beautiful every day.* But when I came to *beautiful,* I got stuck as I often do with this word. I always seem to get confused about where the *a* and *e* go, and about whether there is more than one *u* in there or not. So see here . . . I very quickly jotted the word a few times in the margin. *Beatiful. Beutiful. Beautiful.* The third spelling looked right to me, so that's the one I used as I kept writing."

Active Engagement

Tell

"I want you try this now. I'm going to name a few words that you all know and often use when you write, but that are also tricky for many of you to spell. When I say the word, I want you to jot it two or three times on your paper and circle the one that looks best to you. You're not erasing; you're quickly jotting a few different possibilities."

Coach

The words I use of course depend totally on the students before me and what is in their zone of spelling development. As I explain to students, I choose words for the active engagement that the majority of students use often and can *almost* spell correctly. I might say, "Ready? Spell *usually.*" To coach students, I say things like:

- "If you aren't quite sure how to spell the word, or if you think what you wrote looks like it could be wrong, quickly try a few other spellings."
- "Remember, the point is to quickly jot the word two or three different ways so you can keep getting your thoughts down on the page. I'm going to give you twenty more seconds . . . ten . . . five. . . ."

I continue the active engagement by saying, "If you haven't yet, circle the spelling that looks best to you. Eyes up here for a minute. I'm going to spell the word correctly so you can see whether you circled the right one.

"I'm going to give you another word now. *February.* Again, if you aren't quite sure, or if it doesn't look right the first way you spell it, try a couple different ways. Circle the one that looks best." Again, I support them by saying things like:

- "Say the word again and quickly jot all the letters you hear. Now look at the word and get ready to spell it again, differently this time."
- "Think about what might look right and quickly jot that down."
- "Which part of the word are you unsure about? Try spelling just that part differently, either by rearranging the order of the letters or by trying new letters."

In less than a minute, I say, "OK, eyes up here so I can show you how to spell the word."

Another way to involve participants in this lesson is to ask them to bring with them their own writing and to practice the strategy as an editing tool. "It's time for you to try the strategy," I say to the writers before me. "I want you to quickly reread some of your writing looking for a word you are not quite sure you spelled correctly. As soon as you come to a word like that, I want you to spell it two or three different ways in the margin and then use the spelling that looks best to you. Once you do it in one place, you can look for another word you aren't sure about and try the strategy again."

Use Known Words to Spell Unknown Words: *One way writers figure out how to spell words is by using a word we know how to spell to help us write a word we do not know how to spell.*

When our students are reading and they come to a word they do not know how to read, one thing we teach them is to look inside the word for familiar words or parts of words. The hope is that if they can read *shut,* they can figure out how to read *shuttle;* that if they can read *for,* they can figure out how to read *afford.*

When we have students who struggle to spell when they write, we can connect for them this work they do as readers with the work they need to do as writers. "When you read, you have things you do to figure out tricky words, one of which is to look for words you know inside the words you don't know. You can do something very similar when you write."

Teaching

Tell

"Writers often figure out how to write words they don't know how to spell by using words they do know how to spell to help them. Because words often follow spelling patterns of some kind, we can try this strategy whenever we come to a tricky word."

Show

"Let me show you what I mean. Last night, I started this entry; so far, I have, *I was so late, I ran down the street as fast as a*—and then I stopped, because I wanted to write, *shuttle,* but I have no idea how to spell that word. Let me see if this strategy will help me. What words do I know that could help me? Let me think of words that sound like *shuttle: puddle* and *huddle* sound like *shuttle,* but I don't know how to spell those words, either!" (If a student trying this *did* know how to spell puddle or huddle, I would not be concerned if she used her knowledge to spell *shuttle* as *shuddle;* the point of this strategy is not to get students to spell every word perfectly, but to get them to spell in thoughtful ways and with more independence.)

"I can try something else; let me think of words that are part of the word *shuttle. Sh* . . . That's not a word. *Shut*—oh, that's a word! And I think I know how to spell that. Let me write *shut* in the margins of my story. OK, so if that's *shut,* then what would *shuttle* be? Shut-tul, shut-tul," I say, sounding out the word. "It sounds like *tul* on the end, so let me write that and see if it looks right. *Shuttul.*" Again, knowing that your aim is not to teach students how to write each word perfectly, you might spell the word slightly incorrectly in your story. Or, if your students are generally stronger spellers who recognize when things do not look right, you might say, "You know, that doesn't quite look right. I wonder what else might make that *tul* sound. Hmm . . . I know from other words, like *people,* for example, that sometimes there is a silent *e* after the *l* instead of there being a vowel before the *l.* Let me see if that looks better: *shuttle.* That looks right to me! Now I can keep writing my story!

"Did you all see how when I got stuck, I thought of words I know how to spell and used them to help me? First I tried thinking of rhyming words, and sometimes that works. But because I didn't know how to spell those rhyming words, I thought of smaller words inside my bigger word.

"And then did you notice how I also checked to see if the word looked right? Did you see how I again thought of words I know (*people* in this case) to help me figure out how to make it look right?"

Active Engagement

Tell

"I want you to try what I just did. Let's pretend you're all writing a story and you want to use but don't know how to spell the words I'm about to give you. I want you to use words you know to help you spell these words you may not know."

Coach

As always, the words you ask your students to spell will depend totally on the students before you and their particular strengths and needs as spellers. Depending on your assessment, you might ask students to try the strategy by saying, "You know how to spell *art.* Write that word down. Now I want you to use that word to help you spell *article.* What sounds—what letters—come before *art?* Which come after *art?*

"Everyone has *article?* Look up here quickly; I'm going to spell *article* so you can check your spelling and see how close you got. OK, now I want you to use *art* to help you spell *sparkle.*" You might give your students three or four words to spell, words that are within their zone of development but that you anticipate a majority do not easily know how to spell.

As always, when teaching this strategy in a conference or strategy lesson, you may have already identified words with which the writer or writers struggle—words that led you to teach this particular strategy. In this case, you might ask them to practice the strategy in their own writing.

As I coach students, I keep stressing, "Do the best you can," to push them toward independence. I also use the steps I highlighted during the teaching as strategies for support. For example, I might say:

- "What are some words that sound like the word you want to spell? Do you know how to spell any of those words, or parts of any of those words?"
- "Say the word you want to spell out loud and listen for smaller words inside of it. Try spelling that smaller word; do the best you can if you're not sure. Now, what sounds come before or after that smaller word that make the word you want to write?"

Seek Spelling in Familiar Places: *One way writers spell is by considering where we have seen a word spelled correctly, and if possible to do so quickly, we return to check the spelling.*

In upper grade classrooms where a majority of students struggle with spelling, teachers and students build a word wall: a wall of frequently used words (*because, people, every*) that are commonly misspelled by the majority of those students. Words are organized alphabetically on the wall and added weekly as new words and spellings are introduced to the class. The expectation is that any word on the wall is spelled correctly every time writers write. In classrooms that do not contain word walls, words still obviously line the walls and shelves on charts, in books, in student writing. As such, we can teach students to use their environments as a resource for spelling.

Teaching

Tell

"I want to teach you that if you come to a word you don't know how to spell, but that you know you've seen nearby, whether on a chart or the word wall or anywhere else easy to reach, you can go there to check the spelling.

"You only want to use this strategy when you know the spelling you plan to copy is correct, and when you know you can find the word quickly because you do not want to waste valuable writing time searching high and low for a spelling."

Show

"Let me give you an example of when this strategy worked well for me. Last night, I was writing at my desk when I came to a word I didn't know how to spell; it's actually a word I use all the time—*everyone*—but I can never remember whether it is one or two words. But I had just seen the word! I knew it was on the first page of the picture book I read to my son before he went to bed, and the book was sitting on the couch nearby. So I quickly got up, opened to the first page, and checked my spelling against the spelling in the book. I knew the word would be spelled correctly because of where it was—in this case, a published text—and it was so quick and easy to find, it probably took me about thirty seconds.

"What I did not do was spend ten minutes running around my house, looking for an example of *everyone.* I also did not look in places where the word might be spelled incorrectly; for example, I did not look in my six-year-old niece's story."

Active Engagement

Tell

"I want you to try this now. Open to a blank page in your notebooks. I'm going to give you a few words, one word at a time, that I know a lot of you use when you write. Because this strategy is only good to use when you can do it quickly, I'm going to give you thirty seconds to try and find and write each word."

Coach

"If you can't find a word, don't worry, just listen and look for the next one I give you. Ready? *People.*" As always, the words I give depend on the students before me; I try to name words that the majority of students before me use but do not consistently spell correctly. To support them as they work, I think out loud about different possible locations.

- "Hmm, where might that word be? Do we have a chart about [people]?"
- "Could it be on the word wall?"
- "Might it be in the title of one of the texts we've been reading?"

After about thirty seconds, I continue the active engagement, saying, "OK, if you found the word, write it quickly. Can someone point to where they found the word? OK, here comes the next word: *Characters* . . . I know I've seen that word recently."

Most students will love practicing this strategy as it will feel like an exciting treasure hunt. I wrap up once they have practiced finding and copying two to three words.

Use a Dictionary: *One way writers spell correctly is by looking up words in a dictionary.*

I use the other strategies in this chapter when I am in the midst of writing. When I'm not sure how to spell a word, I'll quickly jot in the margins or use words I know to help me come up with a close if not perfect spelling. But there are times when "close" is not good enough. There are times when it is more important for me to spell a word correctly than it is for me to keep getting down my thoughts. During times like these, I usually turn to a dictionary.

Teaching

Tell

"When we aren't sure how to spell a word and it is in a piece of writing that is about to go public in some way, we want to do everything we can to find the right spelling, even if it takes a little more time. One thing we can always do is look for the word in a dictionary, where we know the word will be spelled correctly."

Show

"For example, the other day I was writing a letter to my boss and I wanted to sign it, *Sincerely, Jenny,* but I wasn't sure how to spell *sincerely.* I did some of the things I usually do when I'm not sure about a word, things you all know to do, but I still wasn't sure I spelled the word correctly.

First, I tried to use a word I know to help me, but the spelling didn't look right. Then I jotted the word in the margins, but after three or four tries, I still wasn't sure if any of them were correct. Oftentimes, I simply pick the best option and keep on writing because I'm more concerned with getting my thoughts down than with getting down the absolutely perfect spelling. But this time, because it was a letter to my boss, I felt nervous about doing that; I didn't want to send my boss something with misspelled words. So, to guarantee I had the correct spelling, I looked up the word in the dictionary.

"I'm going to re-create for you what I did; watch how I look up *sincerely* in the dictionary. First, I need to get to the right section; because the word starts with an *s,* I'm going to flip to where all the *s* words are.

"Now I need to look at the next letter in my word—*i.* So let me flip to where the *si* words are. Ooh, you know what I notice? Look at this: at the top of each page, it lists the first and the last word on the page; like right here, it says, *sign* and *silt,* which means *sign* is the first word on the page and *silt* is the last. Let me think, *sincerely* . . . *sin* . . . that's after both of those words; *sin* comes after *sil.* Let me turn the page. Ooh! At the top of this page, it says *silt* and *sine.* Hmm. I don't know what comes after the *n* in *sincerely*, it could be a *c* or an *s.* I guess I have to look in both of those places. Let me start with *c* because it comes first. If it's a *c,* it will be on this page, somewhere between *silt* and *sine.* I'm just going to run my finger down these pages and see whether there's a word that looks like *sincerely.* If I get to *d* words without finding it, I'll flip to the *s-i-n-s* words and look there. . . .

"Wait! I found it! *S-i-n-c-e-r-e-l-y!* Now I can copy it down exactly as it's spelled in the dictionary!

"Did you all notice how I found my word?

- First, I used the first letter to find the right section in the dictionary.
- Then I used the second letter to get closer alphabetically.
- When I was close, I used the top of the dictionary page, where it lists the first and last words on the page, to see whether my word was on that page or a later page.
- When I was no longer sure what letter came next, because the whole problem is I didn't know how to spell the word, I just ran my finger down the page, looking for a word that looked like the word.
- When I finally found my word, I carefully copied the exact spelling."

Active Engagement

Tell

"Now you get to try this. I'm going to give you one or two words, and I want you to spell them correctly on your paper by looking them up in the dictionaries I passed out."

Coach

"Let's start with *extraordinary,* I might say, if I know most of the writers will know what that word means but will not know how to spell it. "What letter does that start with?" I ask. "Yes, an *e*. See if you can find the right spelling."

As students work, I support them by naming the steps, with wait time in between each one, that I highlight above in the teaching.

* * *

If we are going to teach our students to write in purposeful ways, then we need to make our teaching as purposeful as possible, which means always asking ourselves, and always sharing with our students, when and why writers might use a given skill and strategy. To answer this question, we need to consider not only writers in general, but the specific writer before us, and the specific situation before them.

Writers in general, for example, often jot words in the margin rather than jumping up to grab a dictionary when collecting and exploring ideas that are not yet meant for public reading. On the other hand, an individual writer who happens to be a strong speller but struggles with a short list of words may decide, even when in the very early stages of a piece, to use a dictionary when she wants to settle her uncertainty and begin to practice and internalize a word's correct spelling.

Writers in general will use a dictionary when editing work for publication. But an individual writer who struggles with spelling might have too many spelling questions and not enough time to look up every single word in a dictionary; this writer might be better off relying on an expert speller rather than a dictionary for final corrections.

As with any skill, whether teaching spelling in a minilesson, conference, strategy lesson, or teaching share, we not only want to assess the very general need ("these writers struggle with spelling"), we also want to consider the context ("these writers are getting ready to publish"), and we want to assess the particulars ("these writers tend to spend a very long time trying to spell every single word correctly") in order to pick the most appropriate strategy to teach.

CHAPTER 17

Punctuating Dialogue

Punctuating dialogue sometimes feels like building a house. Less dangerous, perhaps, when things go wrong, and yet, so utterly complicated it is hard to imagine how one ever gets it right! The placement of each comma, quote, capital letter, like the placement of each beam and nail, is dependent on everything that comes before and after. Any decision about punctuating dialogue can feel overwhelming. With so many rules to learn, most of us learned them in stages, which means, of course, that we should teach them in stages, too.

Most teachers from second grade and up are faced with the need to teach and reteach at least some of the convention rules surrounding dialogue. As with any skill, when you notice students do not follow the general convention rules surrounding dialogue, first assess what, exactly, they fail to do. Then you might teach one or more of the following strategies.

Place Quotation Marks Around Spoken Words: *One way writers punctuate dialogue is by putting quotation marks before the first and after the last word a character says to show readers that someone is speaking.*

As with any skill, but certainly with one as complicated as punctuating dialogue, we need to be thoughtful about where to begin our teaching, and we need to be thoughtful about how much to teach at once. For example, when I work with someone who does not yet follow any of the rules, I do not introduce them to the whole list, nor do I begin with when and where to use commas. Instead, I start at what feels like the beginning—with the concept that writers show their readers when someone is speaking.

Teaching

Tell

"Writers usually show when someone is speaking by putting quotation marks in front of the first and after the last word a character says. This way, readers know it is time to listen to what a character has to say and to read the words in the character's voice."

Show

"Let me show you what I mean. I want to write a story about the day my parent's separated. I remember calling my dad on the phone and begging him to come home. As I write, watch how I use quotation marks to show that my characters are talking and to show what they're saying: *I dialed my dad's new number. As soon as I heard his voice, a loud sob poured out of me. Please come home, Daddy, I cried.*

"Wait," I say as I stop writing. "I'm saying something out loud there, but my readers might not realize that if I don't use quotation marks. I really want them to know that I'm talking to my dad, so I better reread a little to figure out exactly when I start speaking. OK, I say, 'Please come home, Daddy.' Since *please* is the first word I say, I'm going to put quotation marks in front of that word and then at the end of my sentence after *cried.* Wait! I don't say 'I cried,' so those words shouldn't be in quotes. The last word I say is *Daddy,* so I need to put my quotation marks after that word. OK, let me reread, make sure it looks right, and then I'll keep going: *As soon as I heard his voice, a loud sob poured out of me. "Please come home, Daddy," I cried.*

"That looks right and makes sense. Now my readers will know to listen to what I say to my dad, and they will know to read those words in the voice of a crying little girl, both of which will help them to better understand and enter into the world of my story. Next I want to write what my dad said back to me. I know I need to put quotes at the very beginning of what he said: "*Oh, Pumpkin, I'm so sorry*—and that's all he said at first, so I'm going to put quotes after the *sorry: "Oh, Pumpkin, I'm so sorry," my dad said.* My readers will now know to read those words in the voice of a sorry father speaking to his crying daughter."

Because this is a first lesson on punctuating dialogue, I use other correct punctuation, such as the question mark and comma inside the quotes, but I do not highlight these moves for the writers. Instead, I say, "Do you see how I'm thinking about what my characters are saying, and putting all those words, but only those words, inside quotation marks? For example, I don't put things like *she said* inside of quotation marks. Do you see how using quotation marks helps my readers make better sense of what is happening in my story because it lets them know when someone is speaking and exactly what they're saying?"

Active Engagement

Tell

"I want you to try this now; I want you to help me figure out how to punctuate the rest of this conversation between my father and me by noticing what we say to one another and putting quotation marks around those words," I say before giving students a photocopy of my next several sentences with unpunctuated dialogue:

> *Can't you just come home, now? I begged. Please!*
> *My dad took a deep breath. I wish I could, he said quietly.*
> *So then come home! I tried to stop crying but couldn't. I really miss you, I said.*
> *I miss you, too, Sweetheart. I really do.*

"Let me read this to you first; then, with your partner, I want you to add in the quotation marks. Remember, you need to put quotes before the first word and after the last word a character says so readers can keep track of what everyone is saying."

Coach

When students encounter difficulty, I say things like:

- "Is your character saying *he said?*"
- "Put your left finger in front of the first word your character says and your right finger after the last word; your quotation marks go where your fingers are—around everything your character is saying."

Capitalize the Beginning of Dialogue: *One thing writers do when punctuating dialogue, is capitalize the first spoken word to show it is the beginning of what a character is saying.*

Once writers consistently use quotation marks to identify what characters say, I generally teach them one new rule at a time. As always, I connect what I plan to teach with what they already know so they have a context for their learning. "You already know that writers begin every sentence with a capital letter so readers know it's the start of something," I say.

Teaching

Tell

"Writers also capitalize the first word of what a character is saying, even when it isn't the very beginning of the sentence, because it shows that it *is* the beginning of the character's sentence."

Show

"For example, look at this sentence: *I called my father and begged, "Can't you just come home, now?"* Even though *I* is the first word in the sentence, can't is the first word in the narrator's sentence, and so it needs to be capitalized. Otherwise, readers would think *can't you just come home now* was part of a longer sentence from the narrator.

"Let me show you another example: *"Sweetheart," my dad said, "if I could be there with you, I would."* Do you see how I capitalize *sweetheart* because it's the beginning of my dad's sentence, and I do not capitalize *if* because it's the middle of his sentence?

"So again, just like we capitalize the beginning of a sentence so readers know it's the beginning of a thought, we similarly need to capitalize the beginning of our characters' sentences so our reader's know it's the beginning of *their* thoughts."

Active Engagement

Tell

"I want you to try this now. I'm going to show you the next part of my story; none of the words that my characters say are capitalized. With your partner, discuss which words I need to capitalize and why."

> *I didn't understand. I asked, "why don't you come home, then?"*
>
> *"pumpkin," my dad started, " this is about your mother and me. it has nothing to do with you." He took a breath and kept going. "no matter what, I will always be here for you."*

"but dad," I pushed, even though I knew what he meant. "can't you be here for me now? all I want is for you to come home."

My dad held back his own tears and said, "baby, I know you do. but even though I'm not there, I'm still here for you."

Coach

When writers encounter difficulty, I say things like:

- "Where's the beginning of this character's sentence; where is the beginning of what the character says?"
- "Don't read what I've written, but say the whole first sentence this character says." (So, for example, in my first sentence, I want students to say, "Why don't you come home, then?") Point to where that sentence begins. How do you show it's the beginning of a sentence? Now point to where that sentence ends? Everything in between is the middle of her sentence, so none of those words need to be capitalized (unless, of course, there is another reason to capitalize something, like someone's name)."

Use Commas and End Punctuation: *One way writers punctuate dialogue is by placing a comma after the* he said *or* she said *when it comes before the spoken words and by placing punctuation that ends the dialogue inside the quotation marks. When the spoken words come first, they are followed by a comma, exclamation point, or question mark inside the quotation marks, and the* said *is followed by a period.*

Once we have laid the foundation with our writers, taught them when to use quotation marks and what to capitalize, things really begin to get complicated! Suddenly, every rule seems to have exceptions, or nuances, at least. So, for example, we cannot simply say, "Punctuation goes inside the quotes" or "A comma always separates what is being said from the person saying it." When our more experienced writers fail to punctuate dialogue correctly, it is usually because they have not yet internalized the finer distinctions.

"What I want to teach you today is complicated," I might say. "Most of you know what is most important about punctuating dialogue; you know that writers show when someone is speaking by putting quotation marks around what is being said. And many of you know other rules, as well, like that writers use commas to separate *he said* or *she said* from what is being said and that punctuation often goes inside the quotation marks. But if you're like me, you struggle to keep all these rules straight in your heads;

maybe you forget to use a comma or a question mark, or maybe you place it in a slightly incorrect place."

Teaching

Tell

"Today I want to teach you some of the more complicated and very specific rules about punctuating dialogue. I want to teach you:

- When the *he said* or *she said* comes before the spoken words, a comma is used after the *said,* and the punctuation that ends the dialogue is *inside* the quotation marks.
- When the spoken words come first, they are followed by a comma, exclamation point, or question mark *inside* the quotation marks, and the *said* is followed by a period."

Show

"I've written those rules on chart paper, followed by an example so you can see what I mean."

- When the *he said* or *she said* comes before the spoken words, a comma, is used after the *said,* and the punctuation that ends the dialogue is *inside* the quotation marks.

  She said, "I don't want to play with you today!"
  He said, "That's okay with me."

- When the spoken words come first, they are followed by a comma, exclamation point, or question mark *inside* the quotations, and the *said* is followed by a period."

  "I don't want to play with you today!" she said.
  "That's okay with me," he said.

"It helps me to think about baby ducks following around their mom; can you get that image in your heads? The mom is always first in line and those little ducks go everywhere their mom goes. With dialogue, the commas and end punctuation are like those little ducks: they attach themselves to and follow the mom wherever she goes.

"For example, do you see how, in the first example, the *she said* and *he said* come first, just like the mama duck is always first in line, and so the comma follows it around? In other words, the comma attaches itself to the *she said* and goes *outside* the quotation marks. On the other hand, still looking at the first example, do you see how the punctuation that ends the entire sentence is *inside* the dialogue? That's because now, the dialogue comes before the punctuation and is like the mama duck first in line, so the punctuation attaches itself to those spoken words.

"It's very similar in the second example. Do you see how when the dialogue comes first, the punctuation—whether a comma, question mark, or exclamation mark—attaches itself to that dialogue and goes *inside* the quotation marks?"

Active Engagement

Tell

"I want you to try this now. Before the lesson, I gave each partnership a piece of paper with three sentences on it. Together, I want you to practice punctuating the dialogue following these rules," I say, pointing to the chart I just shared. "Remember to think about that mother duck; remember that commas and end punctuation attach themselves to whatever comes before them, which means that when what comes before is dialogue, the punctuation goes inside the quotation marks."

I might give students the following sentences to edit:

Why don't you want to play with me he asked.

She said because I am very tired today.

Maybe we can play tomorrow he said.

Notice how I am sure to include examples of dialogue that comes before and after who is speaking. And I include examples of dialogue that needs to be punctuated with a comma as well as with a question mark or an exclamation point.

Coach

As students work, I coach them by saying things like:

- "How are you going to separate what is being said from who is saying it so your readers know those are two different parts of the sentence?"

- "What comes first here: who is speaking or what is being said? Remember the punctuation attaches itself to whatever comes just before it, so is the punctuation going to go inside the quotation marks with what is being said, or outside with who is saying it?"

Refer to Other Authors: *Because there are so many rules for punctuating dialogue, writers sometimes punctuate dialogue by turning to a published story to study, and we copy how that author punctuated dialogue.*

Teaching students to reference a page in their independent reading books is perhaps my favorite way to teach writers how to punctuate their dialogue. The strategy is appropriate for any writers, whether just learning to use quotation marks, or beginning to internalize all the nuances of punctuating dialogue. I often use this strategy myself; there are so many things to remember about what to capitalize and where to place the punctuation that even when I think I finally know all the rules, a new situation seems to arise. Luckily, because almost any story contains dialogue, we can turn to the authors whose books line our shelves for guidance.

Teaching

Tell

"Whenever you are not quite sure of one or more of the many rules about punctuating dialogue, you can get help from almost any of the story writers on your shelf. Because published texts have all been edited by a conventions expert, you can open to a page with dialogue (in most stories, it won't take you long to find one), and study and then copy what the writer does."

Show

"Watch me as I try that. Here's a conversation in one part of the piece I wrote; I started to punctuate the dialogue, but there are a couple things I wasn't sure about. For example, over here," I say, pointing to a part of my story, "I didn't know whether my question mark should go inside or outside the quotes. And over here, I didn't know whether I should capitalize this word.

"I grabbed our read-aloud text and when I opened it, I only had to flip one or two pages before I found a conversation between characters. Here's an overhead of that page. Just watch how I study and then copy how this author does the things I want to do in my own writing."

As I move back and forth between the published excerpt and my own writing, I think out loud for my students, naming for them what I notice and highlighting how I use that to punctuate my own writing. I say things like, "In my writing, my question mark comes at the end of something the character asks. Let me see what this writer does when one of her characters asks a question. . . . Hmm, I actually don't see any questions, but I *do* see an exclamation point right here when the character yells, and it's *inside* the quotes. I bet the same rule applies when it's a question, so I'm going to put my question mark inside the quotes, too.

"OK, now my next question is whether I should capitalize this word or not. I know writers capitalize the beginning of a character's sentence, but because I split that sentence up by writing, *'What,' Wendy asked, 'do you think you're doing?'* I'm not sure whether I need to capitalize the *d*. Let me look for a place where this author does something similar; if she doesn't on this page, I can see if she does on the next page, which I also copied. . . . Wait, right here she has *she said* in the middle of a sentence! And look, she doesn't use a capital when the character starts talking again. I guess that makes sense, because it isn't the beginning of the character's sentence. Now I know I can make my *d* lowercase."

"Do you see how I first figured out what my questions are, and then I looked in a published story for a similar example? Do you notice how the example doesn't have to be identical as long as I know the rule will be the same; so, for example, even though my character was asking a question and the character in the published text was yelling something, I figured the rule about where to put question marks and exclamation points is the same. I also figured that if I write, *she said,* and a published writer writes, *David said,* the punctuation should be the same."

Active Engagement

Tell

"Now I want you to try. Here's the rest of the conversation in my story. As you can see, there are several other places where I wasn't sure how to punctuate things, when to begin new paragraphs, what to capitalize. I've underlined four places where I need help. First, for each thing I underlined, I want you and your partner to study what this published author did in a similar situation; then, I want you to discuss and get ready to tell me what I should do."

Coach

As students work, I say things like:

- "Point to a sentence in this published text where the author starts with [dialogue or *she* or *he said*] just like you do. Now start at the beginning of the author's sentence and name every piece of punctuation she uses. Each time you name something, look to your sentence and make sure you haven't missed or misplaced anything."
- "What exactly are you trying to figure out right now; what is happening in this sentence that is confusing you? Now skim the page of this published story to find a place where the author does what you want to do, and copy her punctuation."

* * *

For me, one of the difficult things about punctuating dialogue (aside from all the rules) is that the reasons for doing one thing versus another is not always immediately clear to me. With periods, for example, I know to use them when I want my readers to stop and think—when I want them to digest a complete thought before moving on to the next thought. But punctuating dialogue feels more like rote memorization, at least once I get into the more complicated rules. When I push myself, I can come up with a reason why the comma sometimes goes inside and sometimes goes outside the quotation marks (because it attaches itself to whatever comes first), but the reason does not feel organic. It feels more like a trick for remembering.

Knowing this, I am especially patient with my students as they begin to learn the rules for punctuating dialogue. Again, I start with what feels like the most logical and hence the easiest to learn—that writers signal that someone is speaking by putting those words inside quotation marks. And then, once I assess what, exactly, is causing difficulty for my students, I try to break each rule down into its simplest form while also giving them time to notice and explore and try for themselves to punctuate dialogue for a range of circumstances.

CHAPTER 18

Using Paragraphs

I hate clutter. Everything in my living and working environments has a place, and I find it very difficult to focus on anything when things are out of their place. As teachers, many of us move through our days at such a frenetic pace that it is often difficult to keep our physical environments in order. When I had my own classroom, I might drop my conference notes on a shelf as I herded students from writing workshop to the lunchroom; on my way back to the classroom, I might shove notes from a lunchtime workshop in another corner and within the hour, bury them with announcements from the office. My classroom always felt somewhat in disarray by the end of the school day.

But no matter how exhausted I was, no matter how many student papers I had to read or lessons I had to plan, I could never sit down to work, nor bring myself to go home, without first putting everything back in place. Because for me, clutter and mess are inevitable distractions. I simply cannot focus when my living or working environments are in disorder.

Though not everyone suffers from what my husband refers to as my "clutter neurosis," most of us do appreciate a sense of order in the texts we read. We appreciate when authors arrange their thoughts and scenes in ways that allow us to focus on and hence make sense of information on the page. And paragraphs are an important tool authors use to organize their writing for the readers who come to visit.

If, when you read your students' pieces, you feel like you are trying to navigate your way through my classroom at the end of the day—if you feel unsure where to find the beginning of a scene or the origin of an idea just as I was unsure where to find my conference notes or my favorite pen—it may be because your students do not understand how to use paragraphs to organize their writing. In turn, you might teach any of the following strategies.

Signal a Shift in Topic or Idea: *One reason writers use paragraphs is to let readers know when we are about to shift the topic or idea.*

Paragraphs are probably most commonly talked about as a way to signal to readers that a new topic or idea is being introduced in the text. But really, this is how nonnarrative writers use paragraphs. In an article or speech, an essay or letter, we usually begin a new paragraph to signal to our readers that we are shifting, or honing, our focus toward new thinking or facts.

Teaching

Tell

"Writers use paragraphs to help readers organize and keep track of different information, especially changes in information. For example, writers usually begin a new paragraph when we shift to a new topic or idea."

Show

"Let me show you what I mean. Here are a few paragraphs from a student's piece. I'm going to read this to you, and I want you to notice how every time Adrien shifts to a new topic, he starts a new paragraph. I also want you to notice that as his reader, every time he starts a new paragraph, I get ready to focus on something slightly different."

> ***What Is Obesity?***
>
> *"What exactly is obesity?" you ask. Obesity is what doctors call having too much body fat. It is also a risk factor for other diseases which include:*
>
> **heart disease*
> **joint problems*
> **liver disease*
> **skin disease*

"Do you see how that first paragraph gives a brief overview of obesity and its effects? Because Adrien is about to start a new paragraph, I'm already getting my mind ready to shift focus. Here's the first sentence of his next paragraph: *Then there are those who ask, Why, exactly, are people obese?* OK, so now, instead of thinking about the effects of obesity, I'm thinking about the causes. Let me see if that's right.

> *Then there are those of you who ask, "Why exactly are people obese?" There are multiple answers to this question. The most known cause of obesity is probably consumption of too many calories. When somebody takes in more calories than are burned, the extra calories are stored as fat. The average amount of calories a twelve-year old should take in is 2,200. People who are obese have most likely been taking in more calories than needed for years.*

"I was right, this whole paragraph is about causes, but even more specifically, it is about calorie consumption as a cause. Now I see another new paragraph, so I'm again getting ready to learn something slightly different.

> *As unusual as it seems, genetics also plays a large role in weight gain. Studies have proven that certain genes are important contributors toward the progress of obesity.*

"OK, I'm going to stop there, because we can see that yes, even though this paragraph is still about causes, now it's about genetics instead of calories, so I did need to shift my focus again.

"Do you see that Adrien uses paragraphs to organize his information, which helps me make sense of and keep track of things as I read? Every time I saw a new paragraph, I knew I had to get ready to shift my focus, which made it easier for me to internalize the information.

"Do you see how sometimes he uses a new paragraph when the topic change is more drastic, like when he puts effects of obesity in one paragraph and causes in another? But do you also see how sometimes the shift is more subtle, like when he puts one cause of obesity in one paragraph and another cause in the next? He probably wouldn't have made separate paragraphs if he only had one sentence to say on each cause because his readers wouldn't be overwhelmed by too much different information at once. But because Adrien has several sentences, grouping them in paragraphs again makes it easier for us readers to sort through and make sense of the information."

Active Engagement

Tell

"I want you to try this now." In a conference or strategy lesson, I ask students to reread their own writing and add in paragraphs. During whole class teaching, I flip to a new overhead or piece of chart paper on which text is written without any paragraphs, or I write a series of sentences on individual strips of paper. "I want you to decide where to start a new paragraph by finding where a new topic or idea begins."

Coach

When students encounter difficulty, I say things like:

- "Go back to the beginning (or to the beginning of the last paragraph). What is this first sentence about? Now read the next sentence. Is that on the same topic or idea? Read sentence by sentence until you notice a shift in information."

  When students struggle to identify the main idea, I say:

- "I'm going to read this first sentence and then say it back in my own words to name what it's mostly about. Now I want you to read the next sentence and say it back in your own words. Are those two sentences on the same topic, or on a slightly different topic?"

Signal a New Speaker: *One reason writers use paragraphs is to show readers someone new is speaking.*

Just as we often call students to line one table at a time, we usually call new speakers to a conversation one paragraph at a time. As readers, we know it is sometimes confusing to keep track of who is speaking, especially, though not only, when there are no dialogue tags (no *he said* or *she said*) to help us follow the back-and-forth in a conversation. Accordingly, if we think about paragraphs as an organizational tool, it makes perfect sense to use them as a way to help readers keep track of who is talking.

When we teach this strategy, we might make explicit the connection between reading and writing as a way to emphasize the reason for using paragraphs in this way. "Last night I was reading my book when I came to this part where some of my characters were having a conversation," we might say. "Back and forth and round and round they went to the point where I got totally confused! I had to reread to figure out who was saying what."

Teaching

Tell

"Writers usually start a new paragraph every time someone new speaks to help readers keep track of who is saying what."

Show

"Let me show you what I mean," I say before showing an enlarged copy of an excerpt from a familiar text. "These paragraphs are much shorter than most paragraphs, but look, that's because the author starts a new one every time someone new speaks. So in this first paragraph, it's the narrator talking; we know that because it says, *I said.* Then look, it says, *my mom said,* so we know the mom is talking; but we also know it's someone new talking because the author started a new paragraph.

"In these following paragraphs, the author doesn't even write *I said* or *my mother said* anymore; and yet, we can keep track of who is saying what because of the paragraphs. If those paragraphs weren't there, it would look like this," I say before showing an enlarged copy of the same text written in one, long paragraph. "If I had to read it like this, listen to how confusing it would be," I say as I read aloud part of the text written without paragraphs. "Yikes, it's so much harder, even impossible sometimes, to keep track of who is saying what!

"Do you see how important it is to help our readers make sense of things by starting a new paragraph every time someone new talks?"

Active Engagement

Tell

"Here's another page from the book, written without paragraphs," I might say during a minilesson or teaching share. During a conference or strategy lesson, when I know everyone's writing reflects a need for the strategy, I might say, "I want you to flip to a page in your notebook where people are having a conversation—where there is more than one person talking.

"Read over this conversation, and help your readers keep track of who is saying what by starting a new paragraph whenever someone new speaks. You can write a ¶ in front of the word that should be the start of a new paragraph. Of course, when you're writing instead of editing something, you don't need to write the ¶; you can simply start a new paragraph by indenting on the next line, just like this author does."

Coach

To support students, I say things like:

- "Point to the first time someone speaks. Who's talking here? Who talks next? Point to where that person starts talking and use a paragraph to show that someone new is speaking."

- "Point to the first time someone speaks. Now run your finger beneath each word as you read aloud, and as soon as someone else starts to talk, use a paragraph to show the change in speaker."

I do not worry, in a lesson like this, that students will sometimes use paragraphs imperfectly. For example, when a new character's action comes before his or her words, students new to the rule often begin a new paragraph with those words instead of the action. Once students understand the concept of using paragraphs to signal changes in the speaker, we can teach a follow-up lesson in which we teach them the nuances of this rule.

Signal Scene Changes: *One way writers use paragraphs is to show changes in time or place.*

Just as nonnarrative text naturally lends itself to using paragraphs as a way to signal a new topic or idea, narrative text naturally lends itself to using paragraphs to signal changes in time or place. I again introduce this strategy by connecting it to the work students do as readers. "You know how sometimes, when you're reading, your characters are suddenly somewhere totally different and you have no idea how they got there? Like maybe they were on the playground and then they're suddenly in the kitchen; or they were at school, and suddenly it's the weekend, but you missed how they got to that new time or place?"

Teaching

Tell

"Writers often start a new paragraph when there is a change in time or place because it helps our readers keep track of what is happening in the story."

Show

"Let me show you what I mean. I'm going to start an entry about when I was teased at school, and I want you to notice how I use paragraphs as I write to let my readers know when my characters have moved to a different time or place." When I write, I am careful to write a simple story that allows me to focus on the strategy at hand; for example, I do not write with dialogue or inner thinking as I often would with a story because I do not want to distract students with other reasons for using paragraphs.

"Let's see, I think I'll start my story when I wake up and don't want to go to school. I know that whenever I write, I always need to start with a paragraph, so I'm going to indent my first sentence."

> *As soon as I woke up, I realized it was a school day, so I rolled over and hid under my pillow. I really didn't want to face another day of teasing. But my mom came and told me I had to get up and get ready. When we pulled in front of my school, I—*

"Wait, I started my story at home, and now the narrator is in front of the school. That's a change in time and place, but I didn't use a paragraph to let my readers know that. They might get confused about what's happening; they might not realize my characters aren't at home anymore, so I better go back and add a paragraph. Once I've already written something, I can use this symbol," I say, adding the paragraph symbol to my piece. "This time, I'm going to pay closer attention as I write to when I change the time or place of my story."

> *As soon as I woke up, I realized it was a school day, so I rolled over and hid under my pillow. I really didn't want to face another day of teasing. But my mom came and told me I had to get up and get ready. ¶ When we pulled in front of my school, I begged my mom to take me to work with her. I even tried to tell her I wasn't feeling well, but she knew I was fine. Physically at least. She kissed my head, said she loved me, and watched me leave the car and walk into the building.*

"Hmm . . . right now I'm wondering whether I should have started a new paragraph there because walking into the building is a little bit later than being in the car, and it's also a different place. But you know, I think it's OK all in the same paragraph because I actually show the narrator moving from one place to the next, so my readers shouldn't get confused. It's not like earlier in the story when the characters pull in front of the school and are suddenly somewhere else without me showing how they got there.

"But the next thing I want to write is what happens when I get into the classroom. That's a different place than the front of the school building, and I don't want to show my character actually walking down the hall and up the stairs and into her class; I just want her to *be* in her class, so I know I need to start a new paragraph."

> *When I got to my classroom, all the girls turned and stared at me. Then they turned back to each other, pretending I wasn't even there.*

"Now I want to write about what happens later that day. That's another time, so I need to start a new paragraph again."

When I got to my classroom, all the girls turned and stared at me. Then they turned back to each other, pretending I wasn't even there.
Later that day, they were still ignoring me.

"OK, I'll finish my entry later, but do you all see what I'm doing? Do you see how I start a new paragraph whenever the character jumps to a new time or place, but not when I actually show the character moving to a new time or place? Do you see how I start a new paragraph by indenting on the next line, but when I forget to start a new paragraph, I can still use this symbol to show there should be a paragraph; and if I rewrite my story, I'll know to make a paragraph when I see that sign. Do you also see how certain phrases, like *When I got . . .* and *Later that day . . .* are clues that time or place is changing—clues that I should start a new paragraph?"

Active Engagement

Tell

"Now it's your turn to try. I actually have the next part of the story written out; each sentence is on a different strip of paper, and each sentence is numbered in order from one to fourteen. I'm going to read all these sentences to you, and then I want you and your partner to discuss which sentences (which numbers) should be the start of a new paragraph; remember, look for places where the narrator jumps to a new time or place."

1. *Maybe it was better to be ignored than outright teased.*
2. *But I still wanted to go home.*
3. *During recess, it was the same thing.*
4. *After I walked from my classroom to the yard with my head down, I found a bench and sat on it all alone.*
5. *I watched all the other girls in my class playing in groups.*
6. *Some girls played hopscotch together.*
7. *Some played tag.*
8. *The ones who were supposed to be my friends played kickball.*
9. *I didn't play anything at all.*
10. *By the end of the day, I felt more alone than ever.*

11. *I hadn't spoken to anyone all day long.*
12. *I looked at the clock for the millionth time, counting the minutes until I could go home.*
13. *When my mom finally came to pick me up, I burst into tears.*
14. *I told her I never wanted to go to school again.*

Coach

When students encounter difficulty, I coach them by saying things like:

- "Look for phrases that signal a change in time or place; remember in the first part of my story, it was things like, *Later that day* . . . and *When I got to. . . .*"
- "Where is the narrator in this first sentence? When do you think this is happening? Now read the next sentence. Is the narrator in the same time or place?"
- "Do you see the character moving to this new time or place, or does she jump there—suddenly appear there from one sentence to the next?"

* * *

As a writer, I use paragraphs when I feel something changing in the way I think or feel. As a reader, I use paragraphs to get ready for similar change. Paragraphs are like a flashing yellow light, saying, "OK, something is about to happen here; you need to shift gears in preparation for this change on the horizon!" Shifting gears when I read allows me to better navigate information on the page; it helps me to better understand the literal (perhaps they get me ready to learn about causes of obesity, now, instead of effects); and it helps me to not miss the inferential (for example, that time has just passed or that a character is on the edge of change). Teaching our students to use paragraphs means teaching them how to organize their thinking and how to help their readers make meaning from their words.

CHAPTER 19

Editing

A common misunderstanding among teachers is that teaching conventions is the same as teaching editing. Some teachers wait until students are getting ready to publish to teach them how to use end punctuation or correct spelling. These *are* things we might teach during the editing stage. However, we also want to teach conventions while students are collecting and drafting and revising. And, across the year, we should also teach other skills during the editing stage. For one, writers do not simply check conventions during the editing stage; we also check for meaning. For another, to edit well we need to know a lot more than how to use proper conventions or how to write with meaning. We also need to know about the *process* of editing; instead of only teaching our students how to fix the mistakes they find, we also need to teach them how writers find mistakes in the first place.

Of course, we cannot expect students to find mistakes if we have not taught them what is and is not a mistake; for example, we cannot expect them to check for periods if they do not know how to use periods. But once our students do know at least some basic rules about writing with meaning and about using correct conventions, we want to show them how to uncover the places where they do not apply what they know. If your students struggle to find their errors even after you have taught them certain rules, you might teach one or more of the following strategies.

Search Word by Word for Misspellings: *Writers sometimes search for spelling errors by reading our pieces* backward *word by word while moving our fingers under each one. When we find a mistake, we correct it if we can, or circle it if we need to come back to it later with help.*

For many of us, it is easier to find mistakes in other people's writing than in our own, in part because when we read and reread something time and again, the abnormal begins to look normal. This tendency is often exacerbated when we reread too quickly as many of our student writers are prone to do. Teaching our students to reread their pieces backward while moving their fingers under each word is really about teaching them to slow down enough to see each word; it is about teaching them to catch the abnormalities rather than unknowingly whiz past them.

Teaching

Tell

"Writers sometimes check for spelling errors by reading our pieces *backward,* word by word, while moving our fingers under each one. We do this because when we read normally, our brains naturally correct for meaning, which means we often miss errors. Reading backward can help us check for spelling, instead. When we find a spelling mistake, we correct it if we can, or circle it if we need to come back to it later with help."

Show

"Watch me as I start to edit my draft by checking for spelling. Here are the last two paragraphs of my piece." In the text I use to demonstrate my teaching point, I misspell a range of words so I can model how I fix misspelled words by drawing from the repertoire of strategies I have taught the class. For example, if there is a class word wall, I misspell high-frequency words that could be found there; depending on what I have taught, I also include more complicated words that would require most students to seek outside help, either from a dictionary or an expert speller. In these ways, I can model fixing words on the spot as well as circling words to fix once I seek assistance. My teaching text may look as follows, depending on the spelling needs of the students before me:

> *Kassy knew her mom wuz rite. She knew she didn't really want to be freands with anyone who treeted her like Wendy did, and so she knew she shoold stop trying to be her frend at all. But it was still hard. It was skarey to think about going to sckool toomarow and staying as far away as she coold from Wendy becuz then she reely woold be alown. Of course, she wuz alown most days, anyway. And at leest this way, she woold be alown becuz of her own chuseing.*

> *Kassy wipt her tears with the bakk of her hand. "I can't whayt to grow up," she sayed. Then she coureled up as small as she coold and rested her head on her mam's lap.*

"I'm going to start at the end and read backward, searching for words that don't look right to me," I say. "*Lap. Mam's.* 'Mam's?' I meant to write *mom.* That's an easy one to fix because I know how to spell that word; let me just write an *o* there instead of an *a. Her. On. Head. Her. Rested. And. Coold.* 'Coold?' I don't know what that means, or what I was trying to write there. I better go to the beginning of the sentence and read forward to figure out what that word is supposed to be: *Then she curled up as small as she coold.* Could! Hmm . . . I'm not sure how to spell that word, but I think it's on the word wall. Let me check under the *c* words. There it is! *C-o-u-l-d.* Let me fix that and keep reading: *She. As. Small. As. Up. Cureled.* Wait, I'm not sure know how to spell *curled,* but that doesn't look right to me. I don't think it's on the word wall, either. Let me just circle it for now and I'll come back to it later. *She. Then. Say-ed.* 'Say-ed.' I think I was trying to write *said.* I always get confused with that word. I know it's all over the book I'm reading right now because usually when someone speaks the author writes, *he said* or *she said.* I have the book right here, so I can copy the spelling really quickly from any page with dialogue. Yes, see, there it is! *S-a-i-d.*

"Do you all see how I'm reading backward and slowly so I can really see words that don't look right to me? Do you see how sometimes, I have to stop and read forward, thinking about the meaning of a sentence so I can figure out what it was I was trying to spell? And do you see how, when I find a misspelled word, I use everything I know about spelling words correctly to fix it up: I use the word wall, I use other sources, I use what I know about a word. And if I can't fix it on the spot, do you see how I circle the word so I remember to correct it later, either by asking someone to help me, or looking it up in the dictionary?"

Active Engagement

Tell

"Now it's your turn to try." When I teach this strategy in a conference or strategy lesson, I know everyone present needs immediate support applying the strategy, and so I usually ask students to practice what I have taught in their own writing. In a minilesson, to ensure that everyone can practice the strategy even if they have successfully edited their spelling, I pass around a photocopy of my teaching text and say, "I want you to help me edit more of my story by reading backwards word by word, from where I left off. When you find a word that isn't spelled right, spell it correctly if you can; otherwise, circle it so you know you need to fix it later. In two minutes, we'll go over the misspelled words together."

Coach

As students work, I support them by saying things like:

- "If you aren't sure what a word says, it's probably misspelled. Read forward from the beginning of the sentence to figure out what it means, and then try to fix the spelling."
- "Remember your strategies for spelling: [check the word wall for common words; think about whether you've seen the word in the room somewhere; use words you know to help you with words you don't know how to spell.]"
- "Look for words that are misspelled more than once; make sure you copy the correct spelling every time the word is used."

Listen for What Does Not Sound Right: *Writers often check for meaning by* slowly *reading our pieces out loud and listening for parts that do not sound quite right.*

Just as it is often easier to find convention mistakes in other people's writing, it is often easier to find in other people's writing places that do not quite make sense. When we reread our own work, we often read it the way we *meant* to write it rather than the way we *actually* wrote it, which means we sometimes miss places that do not sound right. For the same reason writers sometimes read our pieces slowly while moving our fingers under each word, we also sometimes read our pieces out loud: to focus our attention in a way that will allow us to catch mistakes.

Teaching

Tell

"Writers often check for meaning by slowly reading our pieces out loud and listening for parts that do not sound quite right. Slowly reading out loud makes it more likely that we will hear mistakes; when we read in our heads, or when we read quickly, we often read things the way we *meant* to write them, instead of the way we *actually* wrote them."

Show

"Let me show you what I mean by editing part of my story. I read this last night and everything made sense to me, but I read it in my head, so I want to make sure I didn't miss anything."

> *Kassy knew her mom right. She knew she didn't not really want be friends with anyone. who treated her like Wendy did, and so she knew she should should stop trying to be her friend at all. But it was still hard it was scary to about think going to school tomorrow and staying as far away as she could from Wendy because then she really would be alone. Of course, she was alone. most days, anyway. At least this way, she would be alone because of her own choosing.*

"*Kassy knew her mom was right. She knew she didn't really want to be*— Wait. I know I'm reading out loud, but I realize I'm reading at a normal pace when I should be reading slowly. If I don't slow down, I still might read things the way I meant to write them, so let me go back and read again: *Kassy knew her mom right.* Oh, that doesn't make sense. I need to add in the *was. She knew she didn't not really want*—Uh?! Let me try that again: *She knew she didn't not really want*—What I *meant* to write was, *She knew she didn't really want* . . . oh, I see, I switched the words around here; let me fix that. *She knew she didn't really want to be friends with anyone. Who treated her like Wendy did*—wait, that isn't what I meant to write, and it doesn't quite make sense. Those sentences need to go together, so let me take out the period. *She knew she didn't really want to be friends with anyone who treated her like Wendy, and so she knew she should should*—Ooops, I need to cross out one of those *shoulds. She knew she should stop trying to be her friend at all. But it was still hard it was scary to about think going to school tomorrow and staying as far away as she could from Wendy because then she really would be alone.* Whoa. That was a really long sentence; I couldn't even say it all without taking a breath, so let me go back and find a place where I can use a period to give my readers a thinking break: *But it was still hard it was scary*—That could be two sentences: *But it was still hard. It was scary. . .*

"Do you notice how I read slowly so I actually catch parts that don't make sense, and quietly so I don't bother other writers? Do you see how I pay attention to words that are missing or in the wrong places, but also to my punctuation because things like periods affect whether or not things make sense? Do you also see how, once I correct something, I go back to the beginning of the sentence and keep reading from there to make sure the whole sentence sounds right?"

Active Engagement

Tell

"That's what I want each of you to do right now. I want you to quietly, slowly, and carefully, start reading your pieces out loud, listening for the parts that don't sound right. And I want you to start fixing those places when you find them."

Coach

As writers work, I listen to them read, I notice their corrections, and to support them I might say:

- "Read again, but this time, point and read word by word to slow yourself down."
- "When you get to the end, read everything again to make sure you didn't miss anything."
- "Really read your punctuation to make sure it creates the right meaning."

Use a Checklist: *One way writers edit our pieces is by using a checklist of things we know to do to guide us.*

Most of us carry editing checklists in our brains; because we have internalized basic convention skills, we automatically look for things like periods, capitals, correct spelling, and so on before we make our writing public. But for many of our students who have not yet internalized these skills, a written checklist can serve as an important guide to their editing, a reminder of things to look for as they reread their work.

There are two important things to consider when teaching students to use editing checklists. First, we should not include anything on a checklist that students have not yet learned through explicit teaching. This not only means that different grades and different classes will have different checklists, but that checklists will change over the course of a school year. For example, a third grade classroom filled with students who in September struggle to use periods and capitals will get lessons during the first month of school on when and how to use periods and capitals; when it comes time to edit their work, "periods" and "capitals" will likely be the only things on their editing checklist. On the other hand, a third grade classroom filled with students who not only use periods and capitals correctly but also exclamation points and question marks may instead learn during the first month of school about using paragraphs; in turn, their first editing checklist will include "end punctuation" and "paragraphs." In both scenarios, as the year progresses and as the teacher gives more convention minilessons, the editing checklist will grow so that where there were a couple items on the list in September, there may be a dozen or more items on the list by May or June.

Also keep in mind that students can have, and often should have, personal editing checklists. Whatever convention skills we teach in a minilesson should be added to the class list, but most of us also teach conventions in conferences and strategy lessons. Whether providing extra support or extension-teaching, we can have students add to personal editing checklists the convention skills we teach them outside of minilessons.

The second critical point about teaching our students to use editing checklists is that we are *not* teaching (or reteaching) every skill on the list. Instead, we are teaching how to use a list to direct their editing.

Teaching

Tell

"Writers sometimes use an editing checklist to help us fix our mistakes because it reminds us of all the things we need to check before publishing a piece."

Show

"Watch me as I use this list to help me remember everything I need to check before I publish my writing. Right now I have three things on my list: periods, capitals, and spelling. I don't think I can check for all those things at once, but periods and capitals go together, so first I'm going to reread my writing looking for all the places I should have a period and a capital; then I'll reread my writing again to check for any misspelled words. Here's the beginning part of my draft."

> *Kassy knew her mom wuz rite she knew she didn't really want to be Freands with anyone who treated her like Wendy did so she knew she shoold stop. trying to be her frend at all. but it was still hard. It was scary.*

"OK, periods and capitals, that's what I'm paying close attention to: *Kassy knew her mom was right she knew. . . .* Wait, that was the end of my thought, I definitely need a period there. Let me reread with one in: *Kassy knew her mom was right.* Period, and then I need to capitalize the beginning of the next sentence. OK, periods and capitals; let me keep reading: *She knew she didn't really want to be Friends*—Wait, *friends* shouldn't be capitalized because it's the middle of the sentence and it isn't anyone or anything's name. *She knew she didn't really want to be friends with anyone who treated her like Wendy did so she knew she should stop. Trying to be her friend at all but*—Uh? That makes no sense. Let me read that again: *She knew she didn't really want to be friends with anyone who treated her like Wendy did so she knew she should stop. Trying*—OK, I need to take that period out and put these sentences together because this second sentence doesn't make sense on its own: *She knew she didn't really want to be friends with anyone who treated her like Wendy did so she knew she should stop trying to be her friend at all. But*—I need to capitalize that: *But it was still hard. It was scary.*

"OK, I think my periods and capitals are good now. I'm going to put a check next to periods and another next to capitals to show that I corrected both of those things. Now, what else do I need to do? Spelling! Right. So I'm going to reread my writing again, and this time I'm going to look carefully for any misspelled words."

"Did you all see what I'm doing? Did you see how I'm using my editing checklist as a reminder of everything I need to check before I publish my piece? Did you notice how I don't try to look for everything all at once because I know my brain can't think about so many things at the same time? So I made a little plan for myself (that I would start with periods and capitals because they go together), and then I moved on to the next thing on my list. And did you see how I checked things off as I corrected them so I can keep track of what I've done and what I still need to do?"

Active Engagement

Tell

"Now it's your turn to try. I want you to use the checklist to help me edit the next part of my piece," we might say in a minilesson. In a conference or strategy lesson, we might also ask students to use the class checklist or, we might ask them to use their own, individualized checklist to edit their writing. But again, what is important in either situation is that we are not teaching students how to use periods or how to spell unknown words; instead, we are teaching them how to use a written list of things they already know how to do to guide their editing.

Coach

As students work, I say things like:

- "Remember to think about which things on the list you can check at the same time, like I checked for periods and capitals together."
- "Reread this part again; you missed [two] mistakes."
- "Point to each word as you read to slow yourself down."

Find an Editor: *One way writers edit our pieces is by asking someone else to read our work and check for any missed mistakes.*

Because it is often easier to find mistakes in other people's writing but also because it is always helpful to have another perspective, most of us ask someone else to read our writing when we want to make it the very best it can be. We can teach students to ask a writing partner to read their work before publication and to use everything they have learned about conventions when reading one another's work.

Once we do a lesson like this, we can expect students all year long to seek out their own editors before publishing a piece of writing. Some teachers hold students accountable for this by telling writers to have their editor(s) sign the bottom of their drafts. Doing so also holds writing partners accountable for taking their roles as editors seriously; signing their name emphasizes the notion that they have an important job to do when editing someone's work, and lets them know that they, too, are responsible for the state of their partners' writing.

It is important that as we teach students to seek out editors, we also teach that the author always has final decision over the choices he makes. The editor's job is to read with a new eye, to find missed mistakes and offer suggestions. The writer's job is to listen and consider, and to make changes that feel right to her.

Teaching

Tell

"Before making our writing public, we almost always ask at least one other person to read it and check for missed mistakes. By the time we're ready to publish, we've usually reread our writing so many times that we often don't notice our mistakes, and so a second pair of eyes can help us catch what we've missed. When you're ready to have someone edit your work, you could ask a writing partner, sibling, principal, or parent, anyone at all, as long as you ask at least one person you trust to do a good job."

Show

Modeling the teaching point is somewhat different in this lesson; traditionally, I show an example of a strategy, but it does not make much sense to ask students to watch as I hand over my writing for someone else to read. Instead, I might say to students, "I want to share with you some examples of writers who asked someone else to read their work and check for missed mistakes. Yesterday, Caroline used her writing partner for this exact reason. She had read and reread her own piece several times, corrected all the mistakes she found, but wanted to be really sure her writing was ready to go out into the world. So during workshop she asked Naomi, her writing partner, to be her editor because she knows Naomi is really good at spelling and punctuation. 'Would you read this for me and make sure I didn't miss any mistakes?' Caroline asked Naomi. And guess what, Naomi found two errors that Caroline had missed—a misspelled word and a period that should have been a question mark.

"John did something slightly different. He also wanted someone to read over his work, but he and his writing partner know they both struggle with spelling, so John knew that in addition to giving his piece to his writing partner, he needed to find someone who could help him with his spelling. He also asked Naomi for help because he knows she is a very strong speller.

"And do you know what Stephanie, John's writing partner, did? Again, because both she and John struggle with spelling, Stephanie knew she wanted someone in addition to John to edit her piece. Stephanie took her piece home and asked her older brother to help her with her spelling. Now she is confident that her writing really is ready for publication."

Active Engagement

Tell

When I teach this strategy, I do not ask students to practice editing someone else's work; the point of the lesson is less about actual editing and more about finding someone else to check your writing. In order to get students to practice my teaching point, I might say, "OK, writers, now I want you to try what I am teaching you. Can you take a moment to think about at least two people you know who are good at using correct punctuation, spelling, and grammar when they write?"

Coach

As writers think, I say things like:

- "Think about your main concerns, the things that are hard for you when it comes to spelling and punctuation. Now think of people who are good at these things."
- "Remember, you can think about people inside and outside of school as long as they are people who are available and who you trust can help you edit your work."

* * *

Although we want to teach our students to do their very best to edit their writing, we also want to teach them that editing is not a solitary process. We want to teach them that every author of all the books that line the shelves at school, in libraries, and in their homes, had an editor, had someone to find the mistakes the author never knew were there. In turn, as we teach editing across the year, we want to do two things: We want to teach our students how to take all their accumulated knowledge about conventions and find the places in their own writing where they forgot to apply one of these rules. And, we want to teach them how to be the best peer editors they can be; we want to teach our students that when they act as an editor, there is an author depending on them to help get their work ready to line hallways and refrigerators and shelves.

This means that when we teach students how to edit, we are not simply teaching them how to edit *their* writing; we are teaching them how to edit *anyone's* writing. And of course, the more editing practice they have—the more they edit one another's pieces—the better they will get at not only finding the mistakes in their own work, but at avoiding the mistakes in the first place.

WORKS CITED AND OTHER PROFESSIONAL PUBLICATIONS

Anderson, Carl, 2000. *How's It Going? A Practical Guide to Conferring with Student Writers.* Portsmouth, NH: Heinemann.

———. 2005. *Assessing Writers.* Portsmouth, NH: Heinemann.

Angelillo, Janet. 2002. *A Fresh Approach to Teaching Punctuation.* New York: Scholastic.

Atwell, Nancie. 1998. *In the Middle.* Portsmouth, NH: Heinemann.

———. 2002. *Lessons That Change Writers.* Portsmouth, NH: Heinemann.

Bomer, Katherine. 2005. *Writing a Life: Teaching Memoir.* Portsmouth, NH: Heinemann.

Bomer, Randy. 1995. *Time for Meaning: Crafting Literate Lives in Middle and High School.* Portsmouth, NH: Heinemann.

Bomer, Randy, and Katherine Bomer. 2001. *For a Better World: Reading and Writing for Social Action.* Portsmouth, NH: Heinemann.

Calkins, Lucy. 1986. *The Art of Teaching Writing.* Portsmouth, NH: Heinemann.

———. 2003. *Units of Study for Primary Writing: A Yearlong Curriculum.* The Teachers College Reading and Writing Project. Portsmouth, NH: Heinemann.

———. 2005. *Big Lessons from Small Writers.* DVD. Portsmouth, NH: Heinemann.

Calkins, Lucy, Amanda Hartman, and Zoë White. 2005. *Conferring with Primary Writers.* CD-ROM. Portsmouth, NH: Heinemann.

———. 2005. *One to One: The Art of Conferring with Young Writers.* Portsmouth, NH: Heinemann.

Calkins, Lucy, and M. Colleen Cruz. 2006. *Writing Fiction: Big Dreams, Tall Ambitions.* In *Units of Study* by Lucy Calkins. Portsmouth, NH: Heinemann.

Calkins, Lucy, M. Colleen Cruz, Marjorie Martinelli, Mary Chiarella, Ted Kesler, Cory Gillette, and Medea McEvoy. 2006. *Units of Study for Teaching Writing, Grades 3–5.* Portsmouth, NH: Heinemann.

Calkins, Lucy, and Cory Gillette. 2006. *Breathing Life Into Essays.* In *Units of Study* by Lucy Calkins. Portsmouth, NH: Heinemann.

Ehrenworth, Mary, and Vicki Vinton. 2005. *The Power of Grammar: Unconventional Approaches to the Conventions of Language.* Portsmouth, NH: Heinemann.

Fletcher, Ralph. 1993. *What a Writer Needs.* Portsmouth. NH: Heinemann.

Fletcher, Ralph, and JoAnn Portalupi. 1998. *Craft Lessons: Teaching Writing K–8.* York, ME: Stenhouse.

———. 2001. *Non-Fiction Craft Lessons.* Portland. ME: Stenhouse.

———. 2001. *Writing Workshop: The Essential Guide.* Portsmouth, NH: Heinemann.

Graves, Donald H. 1994. *A Fresh Look at Writing.* Portsmouth, NH: Heinemann.

Harvey, Stephanie. 1998. *Nonfiction Matters.* York, ME: Stenhouse.

Harwayne, Shelley. 2003. *Learning to Confer.* Video. Portsmouth, NH: Heinemann.

Heard, Georgia. 2002. *The Revision Toolbox.* Portsmouth, NH: Heinemann.

Mermelstein, Leah. 2007. *Don't Forget to Share: The Crucial Last Step in the Writing Workshop.* Portsmouth, NH: Heinemann.

Murray, Donald M. 1968. *A Writer Teaches Writing.* Boston: Houghton Mifflin.

———. 1996. *Crafting a Life in Essay, Story, Poem.* Portsmouth, NH: Heinemann.

———. 2005. *Write to Learn.* Boston: Thomson Wadsworth.

Ray, Katie Wood. 2001. *The Writing Workshop: Working Through the Hard Parts (And They're All Hard Parts).* Urbana, IL: National Council of Teachers of English.

———. 2002. *What You Know by Heart: How to Develop Curriculum for Your Writing Workshop*. Portsmouth, NH: Heinemann.

Zinnser, William. 2001. *On Writing Well*. New York: Harper Collins.

Children's Literature Cited

Brinkloe, Julie. 1985. *Fireflies!* New York: Aladdin Paperbacks.

dePaola, Tomie. 1979. *Oliver Button Is a Sissy*. Orlando, FL: Voyager Books.

Gordon, David George. October 1999. "Scavenger Hunt." *National Geographic World*: 26–28.

Myers, Christopher. 2000. *Wings*. New York: Scholastic.

Partridge, Elizabeth. 2003. *Whistling*. New York. Greenwillow Books.

Purdom, Candace. August 1994. "So a Big, Bad Bully Is Coming After You. . . ." *Chicago Tribune Kidnews*: 1.

Silverstein, Shel. 1964. *The Giving Tree*. New York: Harper & Row.

Upadhyay, Ritu. February 2001. "Can Kids Stop Kids from Smoking?" *Time for Kids*. 6 (18): 1.

Zolotow, Charlotte. 1966. *Big Sister and Little Sister*. New York: HarperTrophy.

INDEX